WeightWatchers®

Everyone Loves

Chicken

Over 200 Delicious Family-Friendly Meal Ideas

A Word About Weight Watchers

Since 1963, Weight Watchers has grown from a handful of members to millions of enrollments annually. Today Weight Watchers is recognized as the leading name in safe and sensible weight control. Weight Watchers members are a diverse group, from youths to senior citizens, attending meetings virtually around the globe. Weight-loss and weight-management results vary by individual, but we recommend that you attend Weight Watchers meetings, follow the Weight Watchers food plan, and participate in regular physical activity. For the Weight Watchers meeting nearest you, call **800-651-6000**. Also, visit us at our Web site, **WeightWatchers.com**, or look for *Weight Watchers* Magazine at your newsstand or in your meeting room.

CORE PLAN RECIPE   SPICY   NO COOK   ONE POT   20 MINUTES OR LESS

Skewered Sesame Meatballs
with Sweet-Sour Sauce, page 27

WEIGHT WATCHERS PUBLISHING GROUP

CREATIVE AND EDITORIAL DIRECTOR	**NANCY GAGLIARDI**
ART DIRECTOR	**ED MELNITSKY**
PRODUCTION MANAGER	**ALAN BIEDERMAN**
ASSOCIATE ART DIRECTOR	**JENNIFER BOWLES**
OFFICE MANAGER AND PUBLISHING ASSISTANT	**JENNY LABOY-BRACE**
FOOD EDITOR	**EILEEN RUNYAN**
FOOD CONSULTANT	**CAROL PRAGER**
RECIPE DEVELOPERS	**DAVID BONOM** **MAUREEN LUCHEJKO** **DEBORAH MINTCHEFF** **CAROL PRAGER** **MARK SCARBROUGH** **BRUCE WEINSTEIN**
NUTRITION CONSULTANT	**U. BEATE KRINKE**
PHOTOGRAPHER	**ALAN RICHARDSON**
FOOD STYLIST	**MICHAEL PEDERSON**
PROP STYLIST	**CATHY COOK**
DESIGN/PRODUCTION	**LYNDA D'AMICO**

ON THE FRONT COVER, CLOCKWISE, FROM BOTTOM LEFT:
Tandoori-Style Chicken Salad, page 63
Barbecued Chicken and Tangy Coleslaw Sandwich, page 39
Wild Mushroom and Goat Cheese-Stuffed Chicken Breasts, page 140
Cranberry-Braised Cornish Hens, page 225
Spicy Oven-Fried Chicken, page 296
Asian Chicken and Noodle Bowl, page 99
Turkey Fajita with Nectarine Salsa, page 171
Easy Turkey Lasagna, page 220
Curried Chicken and Mango Wraps, page 44

ON THE BACK COVER FROM LEFT:
Chile-Rubbed Chicken with Fresh Pineapple Salsa, page 261
Chicken Cakes with Tomato Jam, page 13

About Our Recipes

We make every effort to ensure that you will have success with our recipes. For best results and for nutritional accuracy, please keep the following guidelines in mind:

• Recipes in this book have been developed for Weight Watchers members who are following either the **Core Plan** or the **Flex Plan** on the **TurnAround**™ program. All **Core Plan** recipes are marked with our **Core Plan** recipe icon ☑. We include *POINTS*® values so you can use any of the recipes if you are following the **Flex Plan** on the program. *POINTS* values are assigned based on calories, fat (grams), and fiber (grams) provided for a serving size of a recipe.

• All recipes feature approximate nutritional information; our recipes are analyzed for Calories (Cal), Total Fat (Fat), Saturated Fat (Sat Fat), Trans Fat (Trans Fat), Cholesterol (Chol), Sodium (Sod), Carbohydrates (Carb), Dietary Fiber (Fib), Protein (Prot), and Calcium (Calc).

• Nutritional information for recipes that include meat, poultry, and fish are based on cooked skinless boneless portions (unless otherwise stated), with the fat trimmed.

• We recommend that you buy lean meat and poultry, then trim it of all visible fat before cooking. When poultry is cooked with the skin on, we suggest removing the skin before eating.

• Before serving, divide foods—including any vegetables, sauce, or accompaniments—into portions of equal size according to the designated number of servings per recipe.

• Any substitutions made to the ingredients will alter the "Per serving" nutritional information and may affect the **Core Plan** recipe status or the *POINTS* value.

• It is implied that all fresh fruits, vegetables, and greens in recipes should be rinsed before using.

Mediterranean Lemon Chicken with
Artichokes and Orzo, page 146

Contents

Appetizers
and
Lite Bites

CHAPTER ONE

Pretzel-Coated Chicken Bites
with Mustard-Chipotle Sauce

Crunchy and tasty pretzels make a great coating for chicken pieces. When chopping pretzels in a food processor, watch carefully to avoid over processing: You want the pretzels to be in little pieces, not crumbs. Chipotle pepper sauce (a new product made by the same company that produces Tabasco) has a deliciously smoky, but not overly hot, flavor.

1. Preheat the oven to 400°F. Spray a shallow baking pan with nonstick spray.

2. Pulse the pretzels in a food processor just until finely chopped, not ground (or crush with a meat mallet or rolling pin). Transfer to a zip-close plastic bag.

3. To make the mustard sauce, combine the mayonnaise, mustard, pepper sauce, vinegar, and pepper in a small bowl.

4. Put the chicken in a medium bowl and toss with 2 tablespoons of the mustard sauce until evenly coated. Add the chicken to the pretzels and seal the bag. Shake bag until chicken is evenly coated with pretzels.

5. Place the chicken in the baking pan in one layer. Spray the chicken lightly with nonstick spray. Bake until golden on the outside and cooked through, about 15 minutes. Pile the chicken on a plate and serve with the remaining mustard sauce.

PER SERVING (3 chicken bites with 2 teaspoons sauce): 95 Cal, 2 g Fat, 1 g Sat Fat, 0 g Trans Fat, 26 mg Chol, 219 mg Sod, 7 g Carb, 0 g Fib, 10 g Prot, 8 mg Calc. *POINTS* value: *2*.

tip The sauce can be made up to a day ahead and the chicken chunks can be coated up to several hours ahead. Both should be stored in the refrigerator until baking time. The sauce is also delicious with steamed green beans and baked potatoes.

MAKES 8 SERVINGS

- 2 ounces (1 cup) **low-fat unsalted mini pretzels**

- ⅓ cup **fat-free mayonnaise**

- 2 tablespoons **whole-grain Dijon mustard**

- 2 teaspoons **chipotle pepper sauce**

- 1 teaspoon **red-wine vinegar**

- ¼ teaspoon freshly **ground pepper**

- ¾ pound **skinless boneless chicken breasts**, cut into 24 chunks

Chicken Skewers with Spicy Peanut Dipping Sauce

When the weather permits, it's good to grill these kebabs rather than broil them—it will take about the same amount of time for the chicken to cook through. For extra flavor, sprinkle about a cup of soaked hickory-wood or apple-wood chips over the charcoal just before cooking the chicken. If using a gas grill, put the chips in a foil package with some holes poked in, and place on top of the lava coals. To prevent the wooden skewers from burning under the broiler, we soak them in water for at least 30 minutes before using.

1. Place the chicken between pieces of plastic wrap and pound to an even thickness. Cut the breasts lengthwise, on the diagonal, into 16 (1-inch-wide) strips. Combine the chicken, yogurt, curry powder, salt, and pepper in a large bowl; toss to coat. Cover and refrigerate at least 30 minutes or up to several hours.

2. Meanwhile, soak 16 (6–8-inch) wooden skewers in water for at least 30 minutes.

3. To make the dipping sauce, whisk together the peanut butter, hot water, vinegar, soy sauce, oil, garlic, and hot pepper sauce in a small bowl until blended and smooth. Taste the sauce and season with additional pepper sauce, if desired. Transfer the sauce to a serving dish; cover and set aside.

4. Spray the broiler rack with nonstick spray; preheat the broiler.

5. Thread 1 chicken strip onto each skewer in a snake-like fashion. Cover the ends of the skewers with foil to prevent them from charring. Arrange the skewers on the broiler rack. Broil 5 inches from the heat, turning once, until the chicken is browned on the outside and cooked through, about 6 minutes. Pile the skewers onto a plate and serve the sauce alongside.

PER SERVING (2 skewers with 1 tablespoon sauce): 117 Cal, 6 g Fat, 1 g Sat Fat, 0 g Trans Fat, 26 mg Chol, 288 mg Sod, 3 g Carb, 1 g Fib, 12 g Prot, 41 mg Calc. *POINTS* value: 3.

MAKES 8 SERVINGS

- 3 (¼-pound) **skinless boneless chicken breast** halves
- ½ cup **plain fat-free yogurt**
- 1½ teaspoons **curry powder**, preferably Madras
- ½ teaspoon **salt**
- ⅛ teaspoon freshly **ground pepper**
- ¼ cup **smooth peanut butter**
- ¼ cup hot **water**
- 1½ teaspoons **red-wine vinegar**
- 1 tablespoon **reduced-sodium soy sauce**
- 1 teaspoon **Asian (dark) sesame oil**
- 1 small **garlic clove**, minced
- ¼ teaspoon **hot pepper sauce**, or to taste

Chicken Cakes with Tomato Jam

Chicken Cakes with Tomato Jam

Panko bread crumbs—made from Japanese bread that is slowly dried, then shredded into flakes—give foods a deliciously different flavor because they retain their crispness even after cooking. They are found in Asian markets and in the international aisle of some large supermarkets. You can substitute regular dry bread crumbs if you can't find the panko variety.

1. Lightly spray a jelly-roll pan with nonstick spray.

2. Put the chicken into a food processor and pulse until finely chopped. Transfer to a medium bowl. Add the egg whites, mayonnaise, mustard, and pepper; mix until well blended.

3. Put the bread crumbs on a plate. Shape level measuring tablespoons of the chicken mixture into 1½-inch cakes, coat with the bread crumbs, and place in the jelly-roll pan. Refrigerate for at least 30 minutes or up to several hours.

4. Preheat the oven to 425°F.

5. To make the tomato jam, heat the oil in a medium saucepan over medium heat. Add the onion and ginger; cook, stirring, until softened, about 5 minutes. Stir in the tomatoes, sugar, and cayenne; bring to a boil. Reduce the heat and simmer, stirring occasionally, until the tomato mixture thickens, about 15 minutes. Remove from the heat.

6. Meanwhile, lightly spray the chicken cakes with nonstick spray. Bake for 10 minutes. Turn the cakes over and spray with nonstick spray. Bake until golden and heated through, about 10 minutes longer. Arrange the chicken cakes on a platter and top each with about 1 teaspoon of the tomato jam. Serve at once.

PER SERVING (2 chicken cakes): 60 Cal, 2 g Fat, 0 g Sat Fat, 0 g Trans Fat, 17 mg Chol, 93 mg Sod, 3 g Carb, 0 g Fib, 7 g Prot, 13 mg Calc. *POINTS* value: *1*.

MAKES 16 SERVINGS

- 1 pound **skinless boneless chicken breasts**, cooked and coarsely shredded
- 2 **egg whites**, lightly beaten
- 2 tablespoons **fat-free mayonnaise**
- 2 teaspoons **Dijon mustard**
- ¼ teaspoon **freshly ground pepper**
- 6 tablespoons panko **bread crumbs**
- 2 teaspoons **olive oil**
- ¼ cup finely chopped **onion**
- 1 tablespoon finely chopped peeled **fresh ginger**
- 1 (14½-ounce) **can diced tomatoes**, drained
- 1 teaspoon **sugar**
- Pinch **cayenne**

✔ Grilled Chicken Strips with Turkish Yogurt Sauce

This very flavorful yogurt sauce also makes a great dipping sauce for raw vegetables. If you don't have time to drain the yogurt, you can substitute authentic plain, fat-free Greek yogurt, available in specialty-food stores. You'll need about a cup. Somewhat more expensive, it is very thick and flavorful.

1. Line a sieve with a double thickness of cheesecloth or two sheets of damp paper towels and set over a bowl. Spoon the yogurt into the sieve and set aside in the refrigerator for about 2 hours. Discard the drained liquid and put the yogurt into the bowl. Add the scallions, 1 tablespoon of the lemon juice, the garlic, jalapeño pepper, the ⅛ teaspoon salt, and ⅛ teaspoon of the pepper. Stir to mix well. Transfer to a serving bowl and refrigerate until ready to serve.

2. Meanwhile, soak 16 (6–8-inch) wooden skewers in water for at least 30 minutes.

3. Spray the grill or broiler rack with nonstick spray; prepare the grill or preheat the broiler.

4. Put the chicken strips into a medium bowl; sprinkle with the remaining 1 tablespoon lemon juice, ¼ teaspoon salt, and ⅛ teaspoon pepper; toss to mix well. Thread 1 chicken strip onto each skewer in a snake-like fashion. Cover the ends of the skewers with foil to prevent them from charring.

5. Place the skewers on the grill or broiler rack and grill or broil about 4 inches from the heat until cooked through, about 3 minutes on each side. Pile the skewered chicken onto a small platter; drizzle the oil over yogurt sauce. Serve the sauce with the chicken.

PER SERVING (2 skewers with 2–3 tablespoons sauce): 110 Cal, 2 g Fat, 1 g Sat Fat, 0 g Trans Fat, 35 mg Chol, 190 mg Sod, 6 g Carb, 0 g Fib, 16 g Prot, 134 mg Calc. *POINTS* value: *2*.

MAKES 8 SERVINGS

- 2 cups plain **fat-free yogurt**

- 3 **scallions**, finely chopped

- 2 tablespoons **fresh lemon juice**

- 1 small **garlic clove**, minced

- ½–1 **jalapeño pepper**, seeded and minced (wear gloves to prevent irritation)

- ⅛+¼ teaspoon **salt**

- ¼ teaspoon freshly **ground pepper**

- 1 pound **skinless boneless chicken breast** halves, cut crosswise into 16 strips

- ½ teaspoon **olive oil**

Chicken Yakitori with Bell Pepper and Scallion

In Japanese, Yakitori means "chicken that is seared with heat." Often the chicken is not seasoned before being cooked. Instead, it is presented with a pleasing variety of highly seasoned sauces set out in small decorative bowls. This version of yakitori is glaze-grilled: It is coated with a slightly sweet soy sauce and miso mixture, which gives it a lavish sheen. Miso is a fermented soybean paste which can be found in Asian stores and health-food stores.

1. To make the marinade, peel and finely grate the ginger. Put the ginger into a piece of cheesecloth and squeeze it to extract as much ginger juice as possible into a medium bowl. Add the mirin, soy sauce, miso, and sugar to the ginger juice, stirring until well mixed. Add the chicken and toss to coat. Cover and refrigerate for at least 30 minutes or up to several hours.

2. Meanwhile, soak 24 (6–8-inch) wooden skewers in water for at least 30 minutes.

3. Spray the broiler rack with nonstick spray; preheat the broiler.

4. Thread 1 piece of chicken, bell pepper, and scallion onto each skewer. Place the skewers on the broiler rack. Broil about 4 inches from the heat, turning the skewers once or twice, until the chicken is browned on the outside and cooked through, about 10 minutes.

PER SERVING (2 skewers): 87 Cal, 3 g Fat, 1 g Sat Fat, 0 g Trans Fat, 24 mg Chol, 217 mg Sod, 5 g Carb, 1 g Fib, 9 g Prot, 19 mg Calc. *POINTS* value: *2*.

MAKES 12 SERVINGS

- 1 (4-inch) piece **fresh ginger**

- ¼ cup **mirin (rice wine) or dry sherry**

- 2 tablespoons **reduced-sodium soy sauce**

- 2 tablespoons **white or yellow miso**

- 2 tablespoons packed **brown sugar**

- 1 pound **skinless boneless chicken thighs**, cut into 24 chunks

- 1 large **red or green bell pepper**, seeded and cut into 24 pieces

- 5 **scallions** (white and light green portion only), cut into 24 pieces

Spinach and Chicken Triangles

The combination of spinach, feta cheese, onion, and seasonings encased in phyllo pastry is a Greek favorite known as *spanakopita*. In the Mediterranean, it is popular street food sold in various shapes and sizes. Our Americanized version adds chicken. To ensure that the filling is the right texture, be sure to squeeze all of the moisture out of the spinach. If you are fond of fresh mint, it makes a great addition to the filling.

1. Heat the oil in a large nonstick skillet over medium heat. Add the onion and cook, stirring frequently, until golden, about 7 minutes.

2. Combine the onion, spinach, chicken, feta cheese, dill, egg white, salt, and pepper in a medium bowl until well mixed.

3. Preheat the oven to 375°F. Spray 2 jelly-roll pans or baking sheets with nonstick spray.

4. Place 1 phyllo sheet on a work surface. Cover the remaining sheets of phyllo with plastic wrap to keep them from drying out as you work. Lightly spray the phyllo sheet with nonstick spray. Cut it lengthwise into 4 strips. Put a rounded teaspoon of the spinach mixture in one corner of each phyllo strip and fold the phyllo diagonally over the filling to form a triangle. Continue to fold the phyllo (as if folding a flag) to the end of the strip. Place the phyllo triangles, seam-side down, in a jelly-roll pan. Cover with a damp paper towel to prevent the phyllo from drying out. Repeat with the remaining phyllo and filling to make a total of 56 triangles.

5. Bake the triangles until the phyllo is puffed and golden, about 15 minutes. Serve hot, warm, or at room temperature.

PER SERVING (4 pieces): 117 Cal, 2 g Fat, 1 g Sat Fat, 0 g Trans Fat, 10 mg Chol, 189 mg Sod, 17 g Carb, 1 g Fib, 6 g Prot, 44 mg Calc. *POINTS* value: *2*.

MAKES 14 SERVINGS

- 2 teaspoons **olive oil**

- 1 large **onion**, chopped

- 1 (10-ounce) package **frozen chopped spinach**, thawed and squeezed dry

- 1 cup finely chopped **cooked chicken breast**

- ⅓ cup finely crumbled **reduced-fat feta cheese**

- ¼ cup chopped **fresh dill**

- 1 **egg white**

- ¼ teaspoon **salt**

- ⅛ teaspoon **freshly ground pepper**

- 14 (12 x 17-inch) sheets **phyllo dough**, thawed according to package directions if frozen

Spinach and Chicken Triangles

Herbed Chicken Salad on Warm Corn Cakes

We like to use stone-ground cornmeal for these corn cakes because you get a slight crunch from the germ and hull in the meal, which also makes it more nutritious. Stone-ground cornmeal is available in health-food stores and many supermarkets. It keeps best in the refrigerator. You can also use the more exotic blue cornmeal, made from blue corn.

1. To make the chicken salad, combine the chicken, cilantro, mayonnaise, scallion, jalapeño pepper, lime juice, ¼ teaspoon of the salt, and the ground pepper in a medium bowl until well mixed. Cover and refrigerate at least 1 hour or up to overnight.

2. To make the corn cakes, combine the flour, cornmeal, baking powder, and the remaining ¼ teaspoon salt in a medium bowl. Combine the milk, egg whites, and oil in a small bowl. Add milk mixture to flour mixture; stir just until blended.

3. Spray a large nonstick skillet or griddle with nonstick spray and set over medium-high heat. Drop the cornmeal batter, by scant measuring tablespoons, into the skillet, about 2 inches apart. Cook just until bubbles begin to appear around the edges, about 1½ minutes. Flip corn cakes and cook until golden on bottom, about 1 minute longer. Transfer to a shallow baking pan and cover loosely with foil. Repeat with the remaining batter, making a total of 28 corn cakes.

4. To serve, spoon about 1 tablespoon of the chicken salad onto each warm cake, garnish each with a cilantro leaf, and arrange on a platter.

PER SERVING (2 pieces): 86 Cal, 2 g Fat, 0 g Sat Fat, 0 g Trans Fat, 17 mg Chol, 174 mg Sod, 8 g Carb, 1 g Fib, 8 g Prot, 39 mg Calc. *POINTS* value: *2*.

tip The corn cakes can be cooked 2 to 3 hours ahead, then warmed in a 200°F oven for about 10 minutes. For the best flavor, let the chicken salad stand at room temperature for about 20 minutes before serving.

MAKES 14 SERVINGS

- 2 cups chopped **cooked chicken breast**
- ¼ cup chopped **fresh cilantro**
- 3 tablespoons **fat-free mayonnaise or sour cream**
- 1 **scallion**, finely chopped
- ½–1 **jalapeño pepper**, seeded and minced (wear gloves to prevent irritation)
- 1 tablespoon **fresh lime juice**
- ½ teaspoon **salt**
- ⅛ teaspoon **freshly ground pepper**
- ½ cup **all-purpose flour**
- ½ cup **yellow cornmeal**, preferably stone-ground
- 1 teaspoon **baking powder**
- ⅔ cup **fat-free milk**
- 2 **egg whites**
- 1 tablespoon **canola oil**
- **Cilantro leaves**, for garnish

Cajun-Style Chicken Dip

This full-flavored dip can also be made with cooked shrimp, crabmeat, or chopped cooked turkey breast instead of chicken. Serve the dip with baby-cut carrots, broccoli florets, or zucchini strips. Or, serve with baked potato chips—an ounce, about 12, per serving will increase the *POINTS* value by 2.

Combine the sour cream, cream cheese, lemon juice, cumin, salt, pepper, hot pepper sauce, and cayenne in a medium bowl until well blended. Add the chicken, onion, and dill; stir until blended. Transfer the dip to a serving bowl. Serve at once or cover and refrigerate for up to several hours.

PER SERVING (2 tablespoons): 41 Cal, 1 g Fat, 0 g Sat Fat, 0 g Trans Fat, 15 mg Chol, 119 mg Sod, 2 g Carb, 0 g Fib, 6 g Prot, 33 mg Calc. *POINTS* value: *1*.

tip Here's a great way to serve this dip as finger food: Cut off the tops of large cherry tomatoes and scoop out the insides with a melon baller. Then, use the melon baller to stuff the tomatoes with the dip. Line a platter with greens or banana leaves (to prevent slippage) and arrange the tomatoes on top.

MAKES 8 SERVINGS

⅓ cup **fat-free sour cream**

2 tablespoons **fat-free cream cheese**

1 tablespoon **fresh lemon juice**

¼ teaspoon **ground cumin**

¼ teaspoon **salt**

¼ teaspoon **freshly ground pepper**

¼ teaspoon **hot pepper sauce**

⅛ teaspoon **cayenne**

1 cup finely chopped **cooked chicken breast**

2 tablespoons minced **onion**

1 tablespoon chopped **fresh dill**

Chicken Tea Sandwiches

Chicken Tea Sandwiches

Fresh tarragon and lemon add delightful flavor to these little tea sandwiches. You can prepare the sandwiches early in the day and store them, covered with lightly dampened paper towels, then with plastic wrap, in the refrigerator for up to 8 hours. Let the sandwiches sit at room temperature for about 30 minutes before serving.

1. Combine the chicken, mayonnaise, scallions, tarragon, lemon zest, lemon juice, salt, and pepper in a medium bowl until well mixed.

2. Place the slices of dark bread on a work surface. Top each slice with 2 cucumber slices. Spread $\frac{1}{4}$ cup of the chicken salad over the cucumber on each slice of bread, spreading it all the way to the edge. Top each with a slice of the white bread. Cut each sandwich on the diagonal to form 4 sandwich triangles, making a total of 24 triangles.

PER SERVING (2 sandwich triangles): 85 Cal, 2 g Fat, 0 g Sat Fat, 0 g Trans Fat, 19 mg Chol, 242 mg Sod, 9 g Carb, 1 g Fib, 8 g Prot, 22 mg Calc. *POINTS* value: *2*.

MAKES 12 SERVINGS

- 2 cups finely chopped **cooked chicken breast**

- 3 tablespoons **fat-free mayonnaise**

- 2 **scallions**, finely chopped

- 1 tablespoon chopped **fresh tarragon**

- Grated **zest of 1 lemon**

- 1 tablespoon **fresh lemon juice**

- $\frac{1}{2}$ teaspoon **salt**

- $\frac{1}{8}$ teaspoon **freshly ground pepper**

- 6 ($3\frac{1}{2}$-inch-square) thin slices **dark bread**, crusts removed

- 12 ($3\frac{1}{2}$-inch-long) very thin slices **seedless cucumber**

- 6 ($3\frac{1}{2}$-inch-square) thin slices **white bread**, crusts removed

Endive Spears with Chicken Salad and Red Grapefruit

This somewhat unusual combination of ingredients is as pleasing to the eye as it is to the palate. Prepare this dish when tasty ruby red grapefruit is in season. When choosing grapefruit, pick it up and feel its weight. Choose grapefruit that is relatively heavy for its size so you can expect lots of flavorful juice. Also, take a good look and make sure that the skin is firm all over, without any wrinkling at the stem end, which would indicate fruit past its prime.

1. Cut off the base of each endive; separate the endive into spears. Set aside the 16 largest spears. Finely chop enough of the remaining endive to equal ⅓ cup. Peel and section the grapefruit. Cut 8 of the grapefruit sections crosswise in half. Reserve any remaining grapefruit sections for another use.

2. Combine the chopped endive, the chicken, 2 tablespoons of the chives, the oil, vinegar, salt, and pepper in a medium bowl.

3. Place a grapefruit section at the wide end of each endive spear. Place a 1-tablespoon mound of the chicken mixture next to each grapefruit section. Sprinkle with the remaining 1 tablespoon chives. Arrange the stuffed endive spears on a platter.

PER SERVING (2 stuffed endive spears): 54 Cal, 2 g Fat, 0 g Sat Fat, 0 g Trans Fat, 14 mg Chol, 167 mg Sod, 4 g Carb, 1 g Fib, 6 g Prot, 22 mg Calc. *POINTS* value: *1*.

MAKES 8 SERVINGS

- 2 large heads **Belgian endive**
- 1 **red grapefruit**
- 1 cup finely chopped **roasted chicken breast**
- 3 tablespoons chopped **fresh chives**
- 2 teaspoons **basil-flavored olive oil**
- 2 teaspoons **champagne vinegar or white-wine vinegar**
- ½ teaspoon **salt**
- ⅛ teaspoon **freshly ground pepper**

Endive Spears with Chicken Salad and Red Grapefruit

Roasted Tomato and Chicken–Topped Parmesan Crisps

Roasting tomatoes intensifies their flavor and brings out their natural sweetness, whether you use fresh tomatoes from a local farmers' market during the height of summer or tomatoes from the supermarket in the dead of winter. These tomatoes are also great tossed with pasta, served over grilled fish, or mixed with cooked zucchini or eggplant. Make a double batch and store them in a covered container in the refrigerator for up to 5 days.

1. Preheat the oven to 375°F. Spray a shallow baking pan with nonstick spray and line a baking sheet with parchment paper or foil.

2. Arrange the tomatoes, cut-side up, in the baking pan. Brush with the oil and sprinkle with the salt and pepper. Roast until the tomatoes are tender and the skins wrinkle, about 1 hour. Remove from the oven and let cool.

3. Meanwhile, stir together the Parmesan cheese and flour in a small bowl. Drop the cheese mixture by tablespoons onto the lined baking sheet about 2 inches apart, making a total of 16 mounds. Spread each mound of cheese to form 2-inch rounds. Bake until golden, 8–10 minutes. Let the crisps cool about 2 minutes. Using a wide spatula, transfer the cheese crisps to a rack to cool completely.

4. To serve, place the Parmesan crisps on a platter. Place a piece of chicken on each crisp, top with a tomato half, then sprinkle with the basil.

PER SERVING (1 piece): 52 Cal, 3 g Fat, 1 g Sat Fat, 0 g Trans Fat, 11 mg Chol, 207 mg Sod, 2 g Carb, 0 g Fib, 5 g Prot, 87 mg Calc. *POINTS* value: *1*.

tip The crisps can be made up to 3 days ahead. Store between sheets of wax paper in an airtight container at room temperature. For additional flavor, you can sprinkle the tomatoes (before roasting) with some dried oregano or thyme or top with a sprinkling of chopped fresh basil.

MAKES 16 SERVINGS

- 8 medium **plum tomatoes**, halved lengthwise
- 2 teaspoons **extra-virgin olive oil**
- ½ teaspoon **salt**
- ⅛ teaspoon **freshly ground pepper**
- 1 cup (4 ounces) grated **Parmesan cheese**
- 1 tablespoon **all-purpose flour**
- ¼ pound thin-sliced **deli roast chicken breast**, cut into 16 pieces
- 4 **fresh basil leaves**, thinly sliced

Chicken and Cheddar Quesadillas

These quesadillas are prepared the classic way—half of each tortilla is covered with the filling ingredients and then the unfilled half is folded over, forming a half-moon shape. Quesadillas are often fried. In this lighter version, they are lightly sprayed with nonstick spray and heated in a skillet until the tortillas are temptingly crisp.

1. Place the tortillas on a work surface; sprinkle the cheese evenly over half of each tortilla. Arrange the chicken, roasted peppers, cilantro, and scallions evenly over the cheese. Sprinkle each with a few drops of hot pepper sauce. Fold the unfilled half of each tortilla over the filling, lightly pressing down on the tortillas.

2. Heat a large nonstick skillet over medium heat. Spray the top of each quesadilla with olive-oil nonstick spray. Place 3 of the tortillas, sprayed-side down, in the skillet. Cook until crisp on the bottom, 1–2 minutes. Spray the tops of the tortillas with nonstick spray and turn them over. Cook until crisp on the second side, 1–2 minutes. Transfer the quesadillas to a cutting board and cover loosely with foil. Cook the remaining 3 quesadillas. Cut each quesadilla into 4 wedges, making a total of 24 wedges. Stack the wedges on a serving plate and serve hot or warm.

PER SERVING (2 wedges): 115 Cal, 2 g Fat, 1 g Sat Fat, 0 g Trans Fat, 10 mg Chol, 362 mg Sod, 16 g Carb, 1 g Fib, 7 g Prot, 97 mg Calc. *POINTS* value: *2*.

MAKES 12 SERVINGS ☛

- 6 (8-inch) **fat-free flour tortillas**

- 1 cup (4 ounces) **shredded reduced-fat cheddar cheese**

- ¼ pound thinly sliced **cooked chicken breast**

- ½ cup **roasted red peppers**, drained and chopped

- ½ cup loosely packed **fresh cilantro** leaves

- 2 **scallions**, thinly sliced

- **Hot pepper sauce**

**Skewered Sesame Meatballs
with Sweet-Sour Sauce**

Skewered Sesame Meatballs with Sweet-Sour Sauce

Small wooden or bamboo picks make attractive skewers on which to serve these lite bites. If you want to make the snow peas really pretty, instead of simply snipping off the stem, use small kitchen scissors to trim off the stem end by cutting the ends of the snow peas into a v-shape. Be sure to roll the turkey mixture into firm, round meatballs to help them hold their shape when skewered. The meatballs can be kept warm in a 200°F oven for about an hour after baking.

1. Preheat the oven to 375°F. Spray a jelly-roll pan with nonstick spray.

2. To make the meatballs, combine the turkey, water chestnuts, bread crumbs, egg whites, soy sauce, shallot, and ginger in a medium bowl until well blended. Shape the mixture into 36 meatballs and place in the pan. Sprinkle the meatballs with the sesame seeds, then lightly spray with nonstick spray. Bake until the meatballs are cooked through, about 20 minutes.

3. Meanwhile, bring a large saucepan of water to a boil. Add the snow peas and boil for 1 minute. Drain and rinse under cold running water to stop the cooking. Drain again.

4. Bend a snow pea in half and thread onto a wooden pick, then skewer a meatball onto the same pick. Repeat with the remaining 35 snow peas and 35 meatballs. Pile the skewers onto a platter and serve the dipping sauce alongside.

PER SERVING (3 skewers with 1 tablespoon sauce): 96 Cal, 2 g Fat, 0 g Sat Fat, 0 g Trans Fat, 25 mg Chol, 195 mg Sod, 9 g Carb, 1 g Fib, 10 g Prot, 23 mg Calc. *POINTS* value: *2*.

tip It's useful to keep fresh ginger on hand to add bold flavor to many dishes. Here's how to store fresh ginger: Peel the ginger and cut it into thin, round slices. Then put the ginger into a glass jar, cover with dry sherry, and refrigerate for up to several weeks. Or, wrap the ginger slices in small packets of foil and freeze for up to several months. There is no need to thaw the ginger before using it—simply slice, chop, or mince while frozen.

MAKES 12 SERVINGS

1 pound ground **skinless lean turkey breast**

1 (7-ounce) **can whole water chestnuts**, drained and finely chopped

¼ cup plain **dry bread crumbs**

2 **egg whites**

2 tablespoons **reduced-sodium soy sauce**

1 large **shallot**, finely chopped

1 tablespoon minced peeled **fresh ginger**

1 tablespoon **sesame seeds**

36 **snow peas** (about 3 ounces), trimmed

¾ cup **bottled sweet-and-sour dipping sauce**

 Chopped Chicken Liver Spread

Replacing some of the chicken liver with green peas adds just a bit of sweetness and lightens the texture of this delicious, old-fashioned appetizer—*and* it lowers the fat content. Serve the spread in a bowl surrounded by colorful crudités, such as carrot and celery sticks, red and yellow bell pepper strips, and juicy grape tomatoes. Melba toast is a traditional accompaniment. Up the *POINTS* value by 1 for every 6 melba toast rounds.

1. Heat the oil in a large nonstick skillet over medium heat. Add the onion and cook, stirring frequently, until translucent, about 5 minutes. Add the livers, peas, salt, sage, and pepper; cook, stirring occasionally, until the livers are cooked through, about 10 minutes. Remove the skillet from the heat and let mixture cool slightly.

2. Transfer the liver mixture to a food processor and pulse to form a rough puree. Add the hard-cooked egg whites and pulse until almost smooth. Transfer the mixture to a serving bowl.

PER SERVING (generous 2 tablespoons): 44 Cal, 2 g Fat, 0 g Sat Fat, 0 g Trans Fat, 74 mg Chol, 172 mg Sod, 3 g Carb, 1 g Fib, 4 g Prot, 8 mg Calc. *POINTS* value: *1*.

MAKES 12 SERVINGS

- 1 tablespoon **olive oil**
- 1 large **onion**, chopped
- ½ pound **chicken livers**, rinsed and patted dry
- 1 cup **frozen peas**, thawed
- ¾ teaspoon **salt**
- ½ teaspoon **dried sage**
- ¼ teaspoon freshly **ground pepper**
- Whites of 2 **hard-cooked eggs**

Turkey-Mushroom Potstickers with Dipping Sauce

These classic dumplings are a cinch to make using wonton wrappers. They can be filled and shaped ahead of time (without cooking them), then covered and refrigerated overnight or frozen for up to 3 months.

1. To make the dipping sauce, combine the lime juice, 3 tablespoons cold water, the fish sauce, sugar, half of scallion, and the crushed red pepper in a small bowl.

2. Put the cabbage into a strainer. Slowly pour the boiling water over the cabbage. When the cabbage is cool enough to handle, squeeze out the excess water. Combine the cabbage, turkey, mushrooms, egg white, cilantro, soy sauce, oil, cornstarch, ground pepper, and the remaining half scallion in a bowl until blended.

3. Line a baking sheet with parchment paper. To make the dumplings, place 10 wrappers on a work surface (keep the remaining wrappers covered with a damp paper towel so they don't dry out) and place 1 rounded measuring teaspoon of the cabbage mixture in the center of each wrapper. Lightly brush the edges of the wrappers with water. Fold the wrappers in half and press the edges together to seal. Place the dumplings on the baking sheet and cover with plastic wrap. Repeat with the remaining wrappers and filling, making a total of 50 dumplings.

4. Spray a large nonstick skillet with nonstick spray and set over medium-high heat. Arrange half of the dumplings in the skillet. Cook until golden on the bottom, about 2 minutes. Add ¼ cup cold water. Reduce the heat and steam, covered, until cooked through, about 4 minutes. Uncover and cook until the water evaporates, about 4 minutes longer. Transfer the dumplings to a baking sheet and keep warm. Repeat with the remaining dumplings and ¼ cup more cold water. Serve the dumplings with the dipping sauce.

PER SERVING (2 dumplings with 1 teaspoon dipping sauce): 66 Cal, 1 g Fat, 0 g Sat Fat, 0 g Trans Fat, 14 mg Chol, 82 mg Sod, 10 g Carb, 0 g Fib, 4 g Prot, 8 mg Calc. *POINTS* value: *1*.

MAKES 25 SERVINGS

⅓ cup **fresh lime juice**

Cold water

1 tablespoon **Asian fish sauce** (nam pla)

1 tablespoon **sugar**

1 **scallion**, finely chopped

Pinch **crushed red pepper**

1 cup finely chopped **napa or savoy cabbage**

2 cups **boiling water**

½ pound **ground skinless lean turkey breast**

6 **shiitake mushrooms**, stems discarded, caps finely chopped

1 **egg white**

2 tablespoons finely chopped **fresh cilantro**

2 tablespoons **reduced-sodium soy sauce**

2 teaspoons **Asian** (dark) **sesame oil**

1 teaspoon **cornstarch**

⅛ teaspoon freshly **ground pepper**

50 (3 to 3½-inch) **round wonton wrappers**

Sandwiches, Wraps, and Pizzas

CHAPTER TWO

Chicken, Salsa Verde, and Avocado in Ciabatta

Ciabatta means "old slipper," and that's just what this classic Italian bread looks like. It is similar to the rolls used in Mexico to make sandwiches, which they call "*tortas.*" Why not serve it as they do south-of-the-border with radishes, lime wedges, and roasted jalapeño peppers on the side?

1. Spray a nonstick ridged grill pan with nonstick spray and set over medium heat. Sprinkle the chicken with the salt and pepper. Add the chicken to the pan and cook, turning occasionally, until browned on the outside and cooked through, 12–14 minutes.

2. Meanwhile, combine the salsa and sour cream in a small bowl; set aside.

3. Slice the bread horizontally almost all the way through; spread open. Pull out some of the bread from the center, if desired. Spread the sour cream mixture on both sides of the bread. Cut each side of the bread crosswise into quarters. Arrange a piece of chicken and 3 slices of avocado on each of the bottom halves of the bread. Close the bread and serve the sandwiches at once while still warm.

PER SERVING (1 sandwich): 333 Cal, 11 g Fat, 2 g Sat Fat, 0 g Trans Fat, 51 mg Chol, 568 mg Sod, 32 g Carb, 4 g Fib, 25 g Prot, 69 mg Calc. *POINTS* value: *7*.

tip It isn't always easy to find ripe avocados. Plan ahead and set one aside on a counter for a few days to ripen.

MAKES 4 SERVINGS

- 4 (3-ounce) **skinless boneless chicken breast halves**

- ¼ teaspoon **salt**

- ⅛ teaspoon coarsely ground **black pepper**

- 2 tablespoons **salsa verde** (green salsa)

- 1 tablespoon **fat-free sour cream**

- 1 (½-pound) loaf **ciabatta bread**

- 1 **Haas avocado**, halved, pitted, peeled, and cut into 12 slices

Chicken, Salsa Verde, and
Avocado in Ciabatta

Chicken Panzanella Sandwich

Panzanella—the classic tomato and bread salad—is deconstructed here and turned into a wonderful sandwich using those same ingredients plus grilled chicken. You can toast the bread before assembling the sandwich if you like.

1. Spray a nonstick ridged grill pan with nonstick spray and set over medium heat. Sprinkle the chicken with the salt and pepper. Add the chicken to the pan and cook, turning occasionally, until browned on the outside and cooked through, 12–14 minutes.

2. Meanwhile, combine the oil, vinegar, and capers in a small bowl; set aside.

3. Rub 4 slices of the bread with the cut sides of the garlic. Brush the oil mixture on the garlic-rubbed sides of the bread. Arrange the chicken, tomato, and basil evenly on the bread. Top with the remaining 4 slices of bread then cut each sandwich in half. Serve at once or wrap in plastic wrap and refrigerate for up to 4 hours.

PER SERVING (1 sandwich): 320 Cal, 10 g Fat, 2 g Sat Fat, 0 g Trans Fat, 68 mg Chol, 507 mg Sod, 27 g Carb, 4 g Fib, 30 g Prot, 56 mg Calc. *POINTS* value: *6*.

tip If you refrigerate the sandwich, let it stand at room temperature for about 15 minutes before serving.

MAKES 4 SERVINGS

- 4 (¼-pound) **skinless boneless chicken breast halves**
- ¼ teaspoon **salt**
- ⅛ teaspoon **freshly ground pepper**
- 4 teaspoons **olive oil**, preferably extra-virgin
- 1 teaspoon **red-wine vinegar**
- 1 teaspoon **capers**, drained and chopped
- 8 slices **country-style bread**
- 1 **garlic clove**, halved
- 8 large slices **tomato**
- 8 large **fresh basil leaves**

Grilled Portobello, Chicken, and Mozzarella Heros

These warm sandwiches offer a delightful combination of textures and flavors. If you want, you can assemble them ahead of time, wrap them in foil, and refrigerate until the next day. They are delicious warmed in a 350°F oven (simply remove the foil and place on a baking sheet) until the cheese is melted and the sandwiches are hot, about 8 minutes.

1. Combine the oil, sun-dried tomatoes, salt, and pepper in a medium bowl.

2. Spray a ridged grill pan with nonstick spray and set over medium heat. Add the chicken and mushrooms and cook, turning occasionally, until the chicken is browned on the outside and cooked through and the mushrooms are tender, 12–14 minutes.

3. Transfer the chicken to a cutting board; let rest about 5 minutes. Put the mushrooms in the bowl with the sun-dried tomato mixture. Cut the chicken, on the diagonal, into slices. Add to the mushroom mixture and toss until well combined.

4. Slice the rolls horizontally almost all the way through; spread open. Pull out some of the bread from the center, if desired. Place the warm chicken mixture on the bottoms of the rolls and top evenly with the arugula and cheese. Close the rolls and cut each sandwich in half.

PER SERVING (½ sandwich): 241 Cal, 8 g Fat, 2 g Sat Fat, 0 g Trans Fat, 55 mg Chol, 388 mg Sod, 16 g Carb, 1 g Fib, 24 g Prot, 95 mg Calc. *POINTS* value: *5*.

MAKES 4 SERVINGS

1 tablespoon **olive oil**

1 tablespoon finely chopped **sun-dried tomatoes** (not oil-packed)

¼ teaspoon **salt**

¼ teaspoon **freshly ground pepper**

3 (¼-pound) **skinless boneless chicken breast** halves

2 (3-ounce) **Portobello mushroom caps,** sliced

2 **seeded hero rolls**

8 **arugula or spinach leaves**

¼ cup (1 ounce) **shredded part-skim mozzarella cheese**

Chicken with Caramelized Onion and Tomato on Rye

This comforting sandwich has a deep, sweet flavor from caramelized onion and a lovely tang from sour cream. It makes a perfect supper with a bowl of soup. Be sure to give the onion its full 10 minutes of cooking so it has time to mellow its flavor.

1. Heat the oil in a large nonstick skillet over medium heat. Add the onion, thyme, salt, and pepper. Cook, stirring frequently, until the onion turns deep golden brown, about 10 minutes. Transfer to a bowl and cover to keep warm.

2. Put the same skillet over medium heat. Add the chicken and cook, turning occasionally, until browned on the outside and cooked through, 12–14 minutes.

3. Spread 1 teaspoon of the sour cream on each slice of bread. Divide the onion between 2 of the bread slices, top with the tomato and warm chicken, then top each with a slice of the remaining bread. Cut each sandwich in half and serve while warm.

Per serving (½ sandwich): 184 Cal, 6 g Fat, 1 g Sat Fat, 0 g Trans Fat, 36 mg Chol, 356 mg Sod, 17 g Carb, 2 g Fib, 15 g Prot, 40 mg Calc. *POINTS* value: *4*.

tip Consider making a double batch of the onions; in a few days, you'll be able to make more of these sandwiches very quickly. Also, to save time you might get two nonstick skillets going at the same time—one for the onion and one for the chicken.

MAKES 4 SERVINGS

2 teaspoons **olive oil**

1 large **onion**, thinly sliced

½ teaspoon **fresh thyme leaves**

¼ teaspoon **salt**

⅛ teaspoon **freshly ground pepper**

2 (¼-pound) **skinless boneless chicken breast halves**

4 teaspoons **light sour cream**

4 slices **rye or pumpernickel bread**

4 large slices ripe **tomato**

Roasted Chicken Panini

Made famous in Milan, one of the few places in Italy where people are ever in a hurry, the panini sandwich is their quick lunch, occasionally even eaten on the run. Sometimes served hot and other times cold, sometimes pressed and sometimes not, panini are always elegant.

1. Combine the goat cheese, roasted pepper, capers, and ground pepper in a small bowl.

2. Slice the rolls horizontally almost all the way through; spread open. Pull out some of the bread from the center, if desired. Spread the cheese mixture evenly on both sides of each of the rolls. Arrange the chicken and arugula evenly on the bottom halves of the rolls. Close the rolls. Serve at once or wrap in plastic wrap and refrigerate for up to 4 hours.

PER SERVING (1 sandwich): 211 Cal, 6 g Fat, 2 g Sat Fat, 0 g Trans Fat, 50 mg Chol, 414 mg Sod, 18 g Carb, 3 g Fib, 22 g Prot, 67 mg Calc. *POINTS* value: *4.*

tip These are absolutely wonderful as is, but if you have a sandwich or panini press feel free to use it, and serve the sandwiches toasted and warm.

MAKES 4 SERVINGS

2 ounces **reduced-fat herbed goat cheese,** at room temperature

2 tablespoons finely chopped **roasted red pepper**

1 teaspoon **capers,** drained and finely chopped

Pinch **freshly ground pepper**

4 **whole-grain sandwich rolls**

1½ cups shredded **roasted chicken breast**

16 **arugula leaves**

Barbecued Chicken and
Tangy Coleslaw Sandwich

Barbecued Chicken and Tangy Coleslaw Sandwich

Now you don't have to drive miles to that great barbecue joint for this classic sandwich. It makes a speedy and satisfying supper or lunch, and because it's so quick and delicious, it may become a weekly stand-by.

1. Combine the cabbage, sour cream, vinegar, sugar, salt, and pepper in a medium bowl. Cover and refrigerate at least 10 minutes for the flavors to develop or until ready to use, up to 6 hours.

2. Meanwhile, combine the chicken and barbecue sauce in a medium nonstick saucepan and cook over medium heat, stirring occasionally, until heated through, about 4 minutes.

3. Slice the rolls horizontally almost all the way through; spread open. Pull out some of the bread from the center, if desired. Place the warm chicken mixture then the coleslaw on the bottoms of the rolls. Close the rolls, cut in half, if desired, and serve while warm.

PER SERVING (1 sandwich): 308 Cal, 5 g Fat, 1 g Sat Fat, 1 g Trans Fat, 58 mg Chol, 692 mg Sod, 37 g Carb, 2 g Fib, 27 g Prot, 102 mg Calc. *POINTS* value: *6*.

tip Pantry items you can stir into the coleslaw if you want a little extra zing: a big pinch of freshly grated lemon zest, a handful of shredded carrots, a dash of hot red pepper sauce, your favorite chopped fresh herbs, or a finely chopped scallion—all without adding to your *POINTS* value.

MAKES 4 SERVINGS

1½ cups finely shredded **green cabbage**

3 tablespoons **fat-free sour cream**

2 teaspoons **cider vinegar**

½ teaspoon **sugar**

¼ teaspoon **salt**

¼ teaspoon **freshly ground pepper**

2 cups shredded **cooked chicken breast**

⅓ cup **barbecue sauce**

4 **kaiser rolls**

Chicken Chat and Choices

Whether you choose chicken or turkey, poultry is one of America's most popular and versatile foods. It is easy to prepare, economical, and delicious to eat in many different ways, either by itself or paired with other foods such as grains, vegetables, or fruits. It can be used in appetizers, soups, salads, sandwiches, and main dishes—and some cuts of chicken take only minutes to cook.

Chicken and turkey (with skin removed) are also excellent sources of lean protein and iron. A single serving supplies over half of the recommended Daily Value of protein.

HERE ARE SOME OF THE DIFFERENT TYPES OF CHICKEN AVAILABLE

- **Whole Broiler-Fryer**
A young, tender chicken weighing 3 to 5 pounds. Most popular cuts such as cut-up pieces, quarters, legs, thighs, drumsticks, breast halves, wings, and ground chicken are packaged from these chickens.

- **Young Roaster**
A good choice for a crowd weighing 6 to 8 pounds. Best roasted whole and carved into servings.

- **Capon**
A castrated rooster that has been raised to be plump with extra white meat, weighing 8 to 10 pounds. Good for roasting

- **Cornish Game Hen**
Usually sold whole, weighing 1¼ to 2 pounds. Best roasted, grilled, or broiled, either split or whole.

- **Free-Range Chicken**
Chicken that is raised on a farm, free to roam outdoors instead of being kept in small cages. Eats only grains without hormone additives.

- **Organic Chicken**
Chicken that is only given feed grown without pesticides or fertilizers. They are not exposed to antibiotics or hormones.

Open-Face Greek Chicken Sandwich

Here are the ingredients of the always-welcome classic Greek salad but with chicken and a low-fat cucumber-and-yogurt dressing, similar to the Greek tzatziki sauce. We like to use grape tomatoes, an oval-shaped cherry tomato. They are always vine-ripened, so great tomato flavor is assured.

1. Combine the yogurt, cucumber, dill, salt, and pepper in a small bowl. Cover and refrigerate at least 10 minutes for the flavors to develop, or until ready to use, up to several hours.

2. Spread each pita bread with about 2 tablespoons of the cucumber mixture. Top with the chicken, tomatoes, lettuce, and cheese. Drizzle with the remaining cucumber mixture, cut each sandwich in half, and serve at once.

PER SERVING (½ sandwich): 252 Cal, 7 g Fat, 3 g Sat Fat, 0 g Trans Fat, 56 mg Chol, 560 mg Sod, 26 g Carb, 3 g Fib, 22 g Prot, 151 mg Calc. *POINTS* value: *5.*

tip Shredded romaine makes a great crunchy addition to sandwiches. You can prepare it ahead: Wash and dry the romaine leaves, shred, and store in a paper towel-lined plastic bag. The paper towels will absorb moisture that accumulates, keeping the lettuce fresh and crunchy for about 2 days.

MAKES 4 SERVINGS

¾ cup **plain low-fat yogurt**

¼ cup finely chopped **cucumber**

1 tablespoon chopped **fresh dill**

¼ teaspoon **salt**

⅛ teaspoon **freshly ground pepper**

2 (7-inch) **pocketless whole-wheat pita breads**

1½ cups chopped **cooked chicken**

12 **grape tomatoes,** halved

¾ cup finely shredded **romaine lettuce**

¼ cup (1 ounce) crumbled **reduced-fat feta cheese**

Chicken and White Bean Salad in Pita Pockets

This is a great high-protein, bold-flavored combination of chicken and beans that can be put together quickly. The ingredients are similar to those found in the classic tuna and white bean salad. If you prefer, you can substitute minced shallots, chopped chives, or chopped scallions for the onion.

1. Combine the chicken, beans, onion, parsley, oil, lemon zest, lemon juice, salt, and pepper in a medium bowl.

2. Cut each pita bread crosswise in half to form 2 pockets. Spoon the chicken mixture evenly into the pita pockets, then add the tomato and watercress.

PER SERVING (½ pocket): 230 Cal, 7 g Fat, 1 g Sat Fat, 0 g Trans Fat, 45 mg Chol, 344 mg Sod, 23 g Carb, 4 g Fib, 20 g Prot, 45 mg Calc. *POINTS* value: *4*.

tip You might like to double the chicken mixture and set aside half to serve over salad greens another day. It will keep for up to 2 days in the refrigerator.

MAKES 4 SERVINGS

1½ cups finely shredded **cooked chicken**

½ cup rinsed and drained **canned small white beans**

¼ cup finely chopped **red onion**

¼ cup chopped **flat-leaf parsley**

2 teaspoons **olive oil**, preferably extra-virgin

¾ teaspoon grated **lemon zest**

1 tablespoon **fresh lemon juice**

¼ teaspoon **salt**

⅛ teaspoon **freshly ground pepper**

2 (6-inch) **whole-wheat pita breads**

4 **tomato** slices

8 **watercress sprigs**, tough stems discarded

Hoisin Chicken and Scallion Wraps

Hoisin sauce is a great condiment—it adds a ton of flavor and a wonderful sweetness. Buy a good-quality brand for truly authentic Asian taste and texture. It is available in many supermarkets and Asian markets. Hoisin sauce keeps almost indefinitely in the refrigerator.

1. Combine the chicken, hoisin sauce, scallions, and pepper in a medium bowl, tossing until mixed well.

2. Toast the tortillas in a dry large nonstick skillet over medium heat, about 1 minute on each side.

3. Divide the chicken mixture evenly onto the tortillas, top with the watercress, and roll up. Cut the rolls in half on a slight diagonal.

PER SERVING (1 wrap): 230 Cal, 5 g Fat, 1 g Sat Fat, 0 g Trans Fat, 57 mg Chol, 425 mg Sod, 22 g Carb, 4 g Fib, 25 g Prot, 38 mg Calc. *POINTS* value: *4*.

tip If you'd like to serve the wraps warm, heat the chicken, hoisin sauce, and scallions in a saucepan over medium heat until heated through. This is also terrific with shredded cooked pork or duck.

MAKES 4 SERVINGS

2 cups shredded **cooked chicken breast**

3 tablespoons **hoisin sauce**

2 **scallions**, finely sliced

⅛ teaspoon **freshly ground pepper**

4 (8-inch) **spinach or whole-wheat tortillas**

8 **watercress sprigs**, tough stems discarded

Curried Chicken and Mango Wraps

Mango is sweet, but not in a sugary-sweet way. It has a complex flavor and aroma, and it goes particularly well with curry—think curried chicken with mango chutney. There are huge differences in the curry powders available, so be sure to taste and see if you'd prefer to add a little more. Use a lettuce with vibrant green color, such as romaine or arugula.

1. Cut the chicken into ⅜-inch-wide slices on a slight diagonal.

2. Heat the oil in a large nonstick skillet over medium heat. Add the onion and cook, stirring occasionally, until softened, about 4 minutes. Add the curry powder and coriander; cook, stirring constantly, until fragrant, about 1 minute. Increase the heat to medium-high; add the chicken, salt, and pepper. Cook, stirring occasionally, until the chicken is cooked through and most of the liquid evaporates, about 7 minutes. Remove the pan from the heat, stir in the mango, and let stand about 10 minutes to cool.

3. Spoon half of the chicken filling onto each lavash, top with the lettuce, and roll up. Cut each roll in half on a slight diagonal.

PER SERVING (½ wrap): 277 Cal, 6 g Fat, 1 g Sat Fat, 0 g Trans Fat, 42 mg Chol, 694 mg Sod, 36 g Carb, 3 g Fib, 19 g Prot, 65 mg Calc. *POINTS* value: *5*.

tip It's easy to roll a wrap. Just place the filling in the center of the wrap, fold and overlap the sides towards the center, fold the bottom towards the top, and roll.

MAKES 4 SERVINGS

¾ pound **skinless boneless chicken breast halves**

1 teaspoon **canola oil**

1 **red onion**, thinly sliced

1 teaspoon **curry powder**

½ teaspoon **ground coriander**

½ teaspoon **salt**

¼ teaspoon **freshly ground pepper**

1 ripe **mango**, peeled and cut into ½-inch pieces

2 (about 12 x 18-inch) pieces lavash or 2 (10-inch, burrito-size) **fat-free flour tortillas**

½ cup finely shredded **romaine lettuce**

Curried Chicken and
Mango Wraps

Chicken, Cilantro, and Cucumber Wraps

You can make the chicken filling for these wraps up to a day ahead and refrigerate, covered. Then just before serving, toast the tortillas, and fill and roll the wraps—all in a matter of minutes.

1. Combine the chicken, cucumber, mayonnaise, cilantro, ginger, oil, salt, and pepper in a medium bowl; toss until well mixed.

2. Toast the tortillas in a dry large nonstick skillet over medium heat, about 1 minute on each side.

3. Divide the chicken filling evenly onto the tortillas and roll up. Cut the rolls in half on a slight diagonal.

PER SERVING (1 wrap): 239 Cal, 6 g Fat, 1 g Sat Fat, 0 g Trans Fat, 57 mg Chol, 517 mg Sod, 21 g Carb, 3 g Fib, 24 g Prot, 23 mg Calc. *POINTS* value: *5*.

tip Cilantro stems are very flavorful and can be finely chopped along with the leaves.

MAKES 4 SERVINGS

2 cups shredded **cooked chicken breast**

½ cup finely chopped **cucumber**

¼ cup **low-fat mayonnaise**

¼ cup chopped **fresh cilantro**

1 teaspoon minced peeled **fresh ginger**

1 teaspoon **Asian (dark) sesame oil**

¼ teaspoon **salt**

⅛ teaspoon **freshly ground pepper**

4 (8-inch) **tomato or whole-wheat flour tortillas**

Almost Pizza Margherita

Pizza Margherita is *the* classic pizza. According to history, the first pizza Margherita was created in 1889. Queen Margherita was visiting the city of Naples and expressed an interest in pizza, a food she had never tried. The owner of a local pizzeria showed his respect for the Queen by creating a pizza that contained the colors of the Italian flag—red, white, and green. This new pizza created an immediate sensation and has been enjoyed ever since. Here, we've added some chicken, which only makes it better.

1. Preheat the oven to 450°F. Split each pizza crust horizontally to make a total of 4 rounds. Place on 2 large baking sheets.

2. Combine the tomatoes, chicken, salt, and pepper in a bowl. Top the crusts with the tomato mixture and sprinkle with the cheese. Bake until the pizzas are heated through and the cheese melts, about 6 minutes. Sprinkle with the basil leaves, cut each pizza into 4 wedges, and serve at once.

PER SERVING (1 pizza): 349 Cal, 10 g Fat, 3 g Sat Fat, 0 g Trans Fat, 68 mg Chol, 576 mg Sod, 33 g Carb, 2 g Fib, 31 g Prot, 188 mg Calc. *POINTS* value: *7*.

MAKES 4 SERVINGS

- 1 (8-ounce) package individual **prebaked pizza crusts** (two 6-inch crusts)

- 1 (14½-ounce) **can no-salt-added diced tomatoes**, well drained

- 2 cups chopped **cooked chicken breast**

- ¼ teaspoon **salt**

- Pinch **freshly ground pepper**

- ⅔ cup **shredded part-skim mozzarella cheese**

- 8 **fresh basil leaves**, torn

Tex-Mex Pizza

Tex-Mex Pizza

This is not the most traditional pizza, but it is quite delicious. The Tex-Mex–flavored toppings, scattered across the top of flavorful toasted flour tortillas, may inspire you to create other great topping combinations, such as shredded cooked turkey with sautéed onions and a sprinkling of shredded cheddar cheese.

1. Preheat the oven to 450°F.

2. Heat the oil in a large nonstick skillet over medium heat. Add the chicken, bell pepper, and salt; cook, stirring frequently, until the chicken is cooked through, about 7 minutes. Transfer to a plate to cool.

3. Toast the tortillas in a dry large nonstick skillet over medium heat, about 1 minute on each side. Place the tortillas on a large baking sheet and spread evenly with the salsa; top with the chicken mixture and sprinkle with the cheese.

4. Bake until the cheese melts, about 6 minutes. Sprinkle with the cilantro, cut each pizza into 4 wedges, and serve at once.

PER SERVING (1 pizza): 286 Cal, 11 g Fat, 4 g Sat Fat, 0 g Trans Fat, 64 mg Chol, 671 mg Sod, 19 g Carb, 3 g Fib, 27 g Prot, 162 mg Calc. *POINTS* value: *6*.

tip Feel free to add a little chopped ripe avocado or a dab of guacamole just before serving this pizza ($\frac{1}{4}$ of an avocado or $\frac{1}{4}$ cup guacamole will increase the per-serving *POINTS* value by 2).

MAKES 4 SERVINGS

1 tablespoon **canola oil**

¾ pound **skinless boneless chicken breasts**, cut into ½-inch pieces

½ small **yellow bell pepper**, cut into ½-inch pieces

¼ teaspoon **salt**

4 (8-inch) **jalapeño or whole-wheat flour tortillas**

½ cup hot, medium, or mild **salsa**

⅔ cup **shredded reduced-fat Monterey Jack cheese**

1 tablespoon chopped **fresh cilantro**

Greek-Style Pita Pizza

Pocketless pita breads make very quick and easy pizza crusts, with almost infinite ways to top them. This chicken, tomato, feta cheese, and olive combination is one of our favorite toppings. Kalamata olives are very flavorful, so just a little goes a long way. If you want to save time, buy them already pitted.

1. Preheat the oven to 450°F. Place the pita breads on a large baking sheet.

2. Combine the tomatoes, chicken, onion, olives, pepper, and oregano in a bowl.

3. Spoon the chicken mixture evenly onto the pita breads, then sprinkle evenly with the cheese. Bake until the pizzas are heated through and the cheese is slightly melted, about 7 minutes. Sprinkle with the parsley, cut each pizza into 4 wedges, and serve at once.

PER SERVING (1 pizza): 400 Cal, 8 g Fat, 2 g Sat Fat, 0 g Trans Fat, 70 mg Chol, 752 mg Sod, 52 g Carb, 8 g Fib, 33 g Prot, 184 mg Calc. *POINTS* value: *8*.

tip If you happen to have fresh oregano on hand, coarsely chop a little and add it to the chicken mixture instead of using the dried oregano.

MAKES 4 SERVINGS

4 (7-inch) **pocketless whole-wheat pita breads**

2 (14½-ounce) **cans no-salt-added diced tomatoes**, well-drained

2 cups chopped **cooked chicken breast**

¼ cup finely chopped **red onion**

4 **kalamata olives**, pitted and chopped

¼ teaspoon **freshly ground pepper**

Large pinch **dried oregano**

½ cup (2 ounces) crumbled **reduced-fat feta cheese**

2 tablespoons chopped **flat-leaf parsley**

Chicken and Mushroom Bread Pizza

White truffle oil, with its amazingly heady aroma and flavor, makes this pizza very special and very elegant. The oil can be found in specialty food stores—it's a bit pricey, but you only need a little. We drizzle it over the pizza just before serving so you and your guests can enjoy its fabulous aroma.

1. Preheat the oven to 350°F.

2. Heat the olive oil in a large nonstick skillet over medium heat. Add the shallot and cook, stirring frequently, until softened, about 3 minutes. Increase the heat to medium-high. Add the mushrooms and pepper and cook, stirring frequently, until the mushrooms are very soft, 4–5 minutes. Remove the pan from the heat and stir in the chicken.

3. Pull out some of the bread from the center of the bread halves, if desired. Place the bread on a large baking sheet. Top each bread half evenly with the chicken mixture, then sprinkle evenly with the cheese. Bake until heated through, about 20 minutes. Sprinkle with the parsley and drizzle with the truffle oil. Cut each bread in half, making a total of 4 pieces and serve at once.

PER SERVING (1 piece): 329 Cal, 11 g Fat, 3 g Sat Fat, 0 g Trans Fat, 48 mg Chol, 488 mg Sod, 32 g Carb, 3 g Fib, 25 g Prot, 146 mg Calc. *POINTS* value: *7*.

tip White truffle oil is also delicious folded into mashed potatoes, stirred into a simple French vinaigrette, or drizzled over grilled mushrooms.

MAKES 4 SERVINGS

- 1 tablespoon **olive oil**
- 1 **shallot**, finely chopped
- 1 (10-ounce) package **baby bella or white mushrooms**, thinly sliced
- ⅛ teaspoon **freshly ground pepper**
- 1½ cups finely shredded **cooked chicken breast**
- 1 (8-ounce) loaf **Italian bread**, halved horizontally
- ¼ cup (1 ounce) grated **Parmesan cheese**
- 2 tablespoons chopped **flat-leaf parsley**
- 1 teaspoon **white truffle oil**

Substantial Salads

CHAPTER THREE

Grilled Chicken Salad with
Pears and Gorgonzola

Grilled Chicken Salad with Pears and Gorgonzola

Aromatic, crunchy fennel and sweet, juicy pears contrast nicely with the sharp distinctive taste of Gorgonzola cheese. For best flavor, let the cheese come to room temperature before serving. Gorgonzola is our first choice of blue cheese here, but you can substitute any good blue-vein cheese, such as Roquefort or Stilton.

1. Sprinkle the chicken with ½ teaspoon of the salt and the pepper. Spray a nonstick ridged grill pan with nonstick spray and set over medium-high heat. Add the chicken and cook until browned on the outside and cooked through, about 4 minutes on each side. Transfer the chicken to a cutting board; let rest about 5 minutes. Cut the chicken, on the diagonal, into ¼-inch-thick slices.

2. Meanwhile, to make the dressing, whisk together the vinegar, oil, honey, mustard, and the remaining ¼ teaspoon salt in a large bowl until blended. Add the chicken, salad greens, fennel, and pear; toss to coat.

3. Divide the salad among 6 plates; top evenly with the walnuts and sprinkle with the cheese. Serve at once.

PER SERVING (1⅓ cups salad, 1 tablespoon walnuts, and ½ tablespoon cheese): 220 Cal, 11 g Fat, 2 g Sat Fat, 0 g Trans Fat, 49 mg Chol, 446 mg Sod, 12 g Carb, 3 g Fib, 20 g Prot, 79 mg Calc. *POINTS* value: *5.*

tip Skip the walnuts and reduce the per-serving *POINTS* value by 1.

MAKES 6 SERVINGS

- 1 pound **skinless boneless chicken breast halves**, lightly pounded
- ¾ teaspoon **salt**
- ½ teaspoon **freshly ground pepper**
- 2 tablespoons **cider vinegar**
- 1 tablespoon **extra-virgin olive oil**
- 2 teaspoons **honey**
- 1 teaspoon **Dijon mustard**
- 4 cups **mixed salad greens**
- 1 small **fennel bulb,** trimmed and thinly sliced
- 1 ripe **Bosc pear,** cored and chopped
- 6 tablespoons coarsely chopped **toasted walnuts**
- 3 tablespoons crumbled **Gorgonzola cheese**

Bistro Chicken Salad

Similar to the classic Italian bread salad, *Panzanella,* this becomes a satisfying main-dish supper with the addition of chicken. Grape tomatoes and yellow pear tomatoes combined with strips of grilled chicken, toasted Italian bread cubes, fresh basil, and olives give the salad vibrant color |and flavor. If you can't find yellow pear tomatoes, double the cherry tomatoes or add a diced yellow bell pepper.

1. Spray a nonstick ridged grill pan with nonstick spray and set over medium-high heat. Add the chicken and cook until browned on the outside and cooked through, about 4 minutes on each side. Transfer the chicken to a cutting board; let rest about 5 minutes. Cut chicken, on a diagonal, into ¼-inch-thick slices.

2. Meanwhile, combine the bread, grape and yellow pear tomatoes, cucumber, basil, and olives in a large bowl. Drizzle with the vinegar and oil; toss well to coat. Stir in the chicken and serve at once.

PER SERVING (1¾ cups): 217 Cal, 9 g Fat, 2 g Sat Fat, 0 g Trans Fat, 34 mg Chol, 280 mg Sod, 19 g Carb, 2 g Fib, 16 g Prot, 52 mg Calc. *POINTS* value: *5*.

MAKES 4 SERVINGS

- ½ pound **skinless boneless chicken breast halves,** lightly pounded

- 3 cups **crusty Italian bread** cubes (about ¾ inch)

- 1 cup **grape or cherry tomatoes,** halved

- 1 cup **yellow pear tomatoes,** halved

- ½ **cucumber,** peeled, seeded, and diced

- 1½ cup chopped **fresh basil**

- 10 **kalamata olives,** pitted and coarsely chopped

- 3 tablespoons **red-wine vinegar**

- 4 teaspoons **extra-virgin olive oil**

Corn and Salsa Chicken Salad

Crunchy, super-sweet, fresh corn makes this southwestern chicken salad special. The corn is delicious raw, but you can use boiled or grilled corn on the cob if you like. To remove the kernels, stand the cob upright on a chopping board. Then, using a sharp knife cut the kernels down away from the cob. One ear of corn will give you about ½ cup of kernels. When fresh corn isn't available, you can use frozen.

1. To make the dressing, combine the salsa, vinegar, mustard, and 2 tablespoons of the cilantro in a medium bowl; set aside.

2. Sprinkle the chicken with the Cajun seasoning. Spray a large nonstick skillet with nonstick spray and set over medium-high heat. Add the chicken and cook until browned on the outside and cooked through, about 5 minutes on each side. Transfer the chicken to a cutting board; let rest about 5 minutes. Cut each breast, on the diagonal, into 4 or 5 slices, keeping the slices together at one end.

3. Combine the corn, tomato, avocado, scallions, and the remaining ¼ cup cilantro in a large bowl. Add the dressing and toss well to coat. Divide the salad evenly among 4 plates. Top each salad with a chicken breast with slices fanned open, then sprinkle with the chips.

PER SERVING (1½ cups salad, 1 chicken breast half, and 1 tablespoon chips): 269 Cal, 8 g Fat, 2 g Sat Fat, 0 g Trans Fat, 68 mg Chol, 646 mg Sod, 24 g Carb, 4 g Fib, 29 g Prot, 43 mg Calc. *POINTS* value: *5.*

tip To neatly crush the tortilla chips, place them in a zip-close plastic bag and lightly crush with your hand or a rolling pin.

- ½ cup prepared **salsa**
- 2 tablespoons **balsamic vinegar**
- 1 teaspoon **brown mustard**
- 2 tablespoons + ¼ cup chopped **fresh cilantro**
- 4 (¼-pound) **skinless boneless chicken breast halves**
- 1 tablespoon **Cajun seasoning**
- 2 cups **corn kernels,** fresh cut from the cob
- 1 **tomato,** chopped
- ½ **avocado,** peeled and chopped
- 4 **scallions,** finely chopped
- 8 **fat-free tortilla chips,** coarsely crushed (about ¼ cup)

Chicken Salad with Figs, Prosciutto, and Pine Nuts

This is a wonderful late summer or early autumn salad when fresh figs are in season. The honey-balsamic dressing complements both the figs and the prosciutto. For the best flavor, choose prosciutto imported from Italy such as prosciutto di Parma (sometimes called Parma ham). You can have it sliced in the deli department of the supermarket or buy it sliced in packages.

1. To make the dressing, whisk together the vinegar, oil, honey, mustard, pepper, and salt in a medium bowl until blended; set aside.

2. Spray a nonstick ridged grill pan with nonstick spray and set over medium-high heat. Add the chicken and cook until browned on the outside and cooked through, about 4 minutes on each side. Transfer the chicken to a cutting board; let rest about 5 minutes. Cut chicken, on a diagonal, into ¼-inch-thick slices.

3. Place the greens on a large serving platter. Arrange the figs around the greens. Top the greens with the chicken and prosciutto, then sprinkle with the pine nuts. Drizzle the salad with dressing and serve at once.

PER SERVING (1½ cups): 230 Cal, 9 g Fat, 2 g Sat Fat, 0 g Trans Fat, 60 mg Chol, 385 mg Sod, 14 g Carb, 4 g Fib, 24 g Prot, 70 mg Calc. *POINTS* value: *5*.

MAKES 4 SERVINGS

- 2 tablespoons **balsamic vinegar**
- 1 tablespoon **extra-virgin olive oil**
- 1 teaspoon **honey**
- 1 teaspoon **Dijon mustard**
- ¼ teaspoon **freshly ground pepper**
- ⅛ teaspoon **salt**
- ¾ pound **skinless boneless chicken breast halves**, lightly pounded
- 6 cups **mixed salad greens**
- 4 **fresh figs**, cut lengthwise into quarters
- 2 ounces thinly sliced **prosciutto**
- 1 tablespoon **toasted pine nuts**

Chicken Salad with Figs, Prosciutto, and Pine Nuts

✓ Grilled Chicken Salad with Green Goddess Dressing

This feast of a salad features grilled chicken breast atop crunchy iceberg lettuce with a creamy Green Goddess dressing. While fresh tarragon is preferred over dried for the dressing, if you don't have tarragon vinegar, simply use white-wine vinegar instead.

1. Puree the sour cream, mayonnaise, chives, tarragon, vinegar, and Worcestershire sauce in a blender.

2. Spray a grill rack with olive-oil nonstick spray; prepare the grill. Lightly spray the chicken with olive-oil nonstick spray; sprinkle with the salt and pepper.

3. Place the chicken on the grill rack and grill 4 inches from the heat, until cooked through, about 6 minutes on each side. Transfer to a cutting board.

4. Transfer 2 tablespoons of the dressing to a small bowl; set aside. Combine the salad mix and the remaining dressing in a large bowl; mix well. Divide the salad among 4 plates. Cut each chicken breast on the diagonal into ¼-inch-thick slices; arrange 1 breast half on top of each salad. Drizzle the chicken evenly with the reserved 2 tablespoons dressing.

PER SERVING (1 chicken breast half with ½ tablespoon dressing and about 1¾ cups salad): 183 Cal, 4 g Fat, 1 g Sat Fat, 0 g Trans Fat, 64 mg Chol, 540 mg Sod, 11 g Carb, 2 g Fib, 26 g Prot, 92 mg Calc. *POINTS* value: *4*.

MAKES 4 SERVINGS

½ cup **fat-free sour cream**

¼ cup **fat-free mayonnaise**

1 bunch **fresh chives,** chopped

2 tablespoons coarsely chopped **fresh tarragon**

1 tablespoon **tarragon vinegar**

1 teaspoon **Worcestershire sauce**

4 (¼-pound) **skinless boneless chicken breast halves**

½ teaspoon **salt**

¼ teaspoon **freshly ground pepper**

1 (16-ounce) bag **iceberg salad mix**

✔ Chicken, Mango, and Black Bean Salad

This salad is a wonderful blend of contrasting flavors and textures. Cool mango, chopped cilantro, and crunchy jicama help tame the heat of the fiery jalapeño and chili powder. Tender shredded chicken and black beans round out the mix. You can substitute the mango with any number of fruits— papaya, pineapple, or slices of orange or red grapefruit.

Combine the lime juice, oil, salt, and chili powder in a large bowl. Add the chicken, jicama, beans, mango, onion, cilantro, and jalapeño; mix well.

PER SERVING (1½ cups): 283 Cal, 6 g Fat, 1 g Sat Fat, 0 g Trans Fat, 60 mg Chol, 482 mg Sod, 30 g Carb, 11 g Fib, 27 g Prot, 58 mg Calc. *POINTS* value: *5.*

tip If you want to cook the chicken yourself, you'll need to use ½ pound skinless boneless chicken breasts, trimmed of all visible fat. To poach the chicken, bring 1 cup chicken broth or water to a simmer in a medium saucepan over medium heat. Add the chicken breasts and simmer, covered, until cooked through, about 10 minutes. Remove the chicken from the liquid, let cool completely, then shred or chop.

MAKES 4 SERVINGS

- 3 tablespoons **fresh lime juice**

- 2 teaspoons **olive oil**

- ½ teaspoon **salt**

- ¼ teaspoon **chili powder**

- 2 cups shredded **cooked chicken breast**

- 1 small **jicama** (about 1 pound), peeled and diced

- 1 (15½-ounce) **can black beans**, rinsed and drained

- 1 **mango**, peeled, pitted, and cut into ¾-inch chunks

- ½ cup diced **red onion**

- ⅓ cup chopped **fresh cilantro**

- 1 **jalapeño pepper**, seeded and minced (wear gloves to prevent irritation)

Tandoori-Style Chicken Salad

☑ Tandoori-Style Chicken Salad

You can prepare most of this salad the day before you plan to serve it. Simply set the chicken to marinate (step 1) and toss the cabbage and carrots with the seasonings (step 2) and refrigerate both, separately, overnight. The day of serving, cook the chicken then serve with the cabbage mixture and the extra cilantro.

1. Combine the yogurt, cumin, ginger, garlic, and ¼ teaspoon of the salt in a large zip-close plastic bag; add the chicken. Squeeze out the air and seal the bag; turn to coat the chicken. Refrigerate, turning the bag occasionally, at least 1 hour or up to overnight.

2. Combine the cabbage, carrots, the ¼ cup cilantro, the vinegar, oil, pepper, and the remaining ¼ teaspoon salt in a large bowl; toss well to coat.

3. Remove the chicken from the yogurt marinade; discard the marinade. Spray a large nonstick ridged grill pan with nonstick spray and set over medium-high heat. Add the chicken and cook until browned on the outside and cooked through, about 3 minutes on each side. Transfer the chicken to a cutting board; let rest about 5 minutes. Cut the chicken, on the diagonal, into thin slices.

4. Arrange the cabbage mixture on a large serving platter; top with the chicken and sprinkle with the remaining 2 tablespoons cilantro.

PER SERVING (1½ cups): 207 Cal, 7 g Fat, 2 g Sat Fat, 0 g Trans Fat, 69 mg Chol, 271 mg Sod, 8 g Carb, 2 g Fib, 27 g Prot, 81 mg Calc. *POINTS* value: *4*.

MAKES 4 SERVINGS

¾ cup **plain fat-free yogurt**

1½ teaspoons **ground cumin**

1 teaspoon minced peeled **fresh ginger**

1 **garlic clove**, minced

½ teaspoon **salt**

1 pound thin-sliced **chicken breast cutlets**

4 cups shredded **red cabbage**

¾ cup shredded **carrots**

¼ cup + 2 tablespoons chopped **fresh cilantro**

3 tablespoons **red-wine vinegar**

1 tablespoon **olive oil**

½ teaspoon **freshly ground pepper**

✓ Chicken Salad Provençal

Fingerling potatoes are small, narrow, finger-shaped potatoes with a thin golden skin and a delicious, moist, buttery texture. If you can't find fingerlings, use small red or white potatoes instead. Haricots verts are slender young green beans. Regular green beans may be substituted; simply slice them in half lengthwise. The potatoes and green beans can be prepared ahead of time and kept covered in the refrigerator for up to 2 days.

1. To make the dressing, combine the vinegar, oil, tarragon, mustard, pepper, and ¼ teaspoon of the salt in a small bowl; set aside.

2. Place the potatoes and enough water to cover in a large saucepan; bring to a boil. Reduce the heat and simmer, covered, until the potatoes are tender, about 15 minutes. With a slotted spoon, transfer the potatoes (reserving the water in the pot) to a large bowl.

3. Add the beans to the boiling water in the pot and cook until crisp-tender, about 4 minutes. Drain the beans and rinse under cold running water, then drain on layers of paper towels. Add beans to the potatoes.

4. Sprinkle the chicken with the oregano and the remaining ½ teaspoon salt. Spray a large nonstick skillet with nonstick spray and set over medium-high heat. Add the chicken and cook until browned on the outside and cooked through, about 3 minutes on each side. Transfer the chicken to a cutting board; let rest about 5 minutes. Cut the chicken, on the diagonal, into ¼-inch-thick slices.

5. Add the chicken, fennel, tomatoes, onion, and olives to the potato mixture. Add the dressing and toss gently to coat.

PER SERVING (1 cup): 311 Cal, 8 g Fat, 2 g Sat Fat, 0 g Trans Fat, 68 mg Chol, 617 mg Sod, 32 g Carb, 5 g Fib, 28 g Prot, 76 mg Calc. *POINTS* value: *6*.

MAKES 4 SERVINGS

- 2 tablespoons **cider vinegar**
- 1 tablespoon **extra-virgin olive oil**
- 1 tablespoon chopped **fresh tarragon**
- 1 teaspoon **Dijon mustard**
- ½ teaspoon **freshly ground pepper**
- ¾ teaspoon **salt**
- 1 pound **fingerling potatoes**, scrubbed and cut into ¼-inch-thick slices
- ½ pound **haricots verts**, trimmed
- 1 pound thin-sliced **chicken breast cutlets**
- 1 teaspoon **dried oregano**
- ½ **fennel bulb**, trimmed and thinly sliced
- ½ cup **grape or cherry tomatoes**, halved
- ½ **red onion**, thinly sliced
- 6 **kalamata olives**, pitted and coarsely chopped

Jerk Chicken and Sweet Potato Salad

When the weather is cool, you might like to roast the sweet potatoes instead of boiling them: Arrange the sweet potato pieces in one layer on an oiled baking sheet, spray them lightly with nonstick spray, and roast in a preheated 375°F oven until tender and browned, about 25 minutes.

1. Place the potatoes and enough water to cover in a large saucepan; bring to a boil. Reduce the heat and simmer, covered, until the potatoes are tender, 12–15 minutes. Drain the potatoes and transfer to a large bowl; let cool about 10 minutes. Add the pineapple, bell pepper, and cilantro.

2. Sprinkle the chicken with the jerk seasoning. Spray a large nonstick skillet with nonstick spray and set over medium-high heat. Add the chicken and cook until browned on the outside and cooked through, about 3 minutes on each side. Transfer the chicken to a cutting board; let rest about 5 minutes. Cut the chicken, on the diagonal, into thin slices.

3. Meanwhile, to make the dressing, whisk together the reserved ¼ cup pineapple juice, the soy sauce, sugar, ginger, and oil in a small bowl until blended; set aside.

4. Add the chicken to the potato mixture; drizzle with the dressing and toss gently to coat.

PER SERVING (scant 2 cups): 309 Cal, 5 g Fat, 1 g Sat Fat, 0 g Trans Fat, 68 mg Chol, 208 mg Sod, 39 g Carb, 4 g Fib, 27 g Prot, 61 mg Calc. *POINTS* value: *6*.

MAKES 4 SERVINGS

- 2 medium **sweet potatoes**, peeled and cut into 1½-inch pieces

- 1 (14-ounce) **can pineapple chunks**, drained (¼ cup juice reserved)

- 1 **red bell pepper**, seeded and diced

- ¼ cup chopped **fresh cilantro**

- 1 pound thin-sliced **chicken breast cutlets**

- 1 tablespoon **Caribbean jerk seasoning**

- 1 tablespoon **reduced-sodium soy sauce**

- 1 tablespoon packed **light brown sugar**

- 1 teaspoon minced peeled **fresh ginger**

- 1 teaspoon **Asian (dark) sesame oil**

Sesame Chicken Fingers and
Pickled Ginger–Rice Salad

Sesame Chicken Fingers and Pickled Ginger–Rice Salad

Want to save time making this crunchy and colorful salad? Buy packaged cut or salad bar-cut veggies. You can mix and match: Choose yellow bell pepper instead of red, broccoli florets instead of snow peas, and chopped red onion instead of scallions, if you like.

1. Preheat the oven to 450°F. Spray a small baking pan with nonstick spray.

2. Combine the cornflake crumbs and sesame seeds on a sheet of wax paper.

3. Combine the honey and 2 teaspoons of the soy sauce in a medium bowl; add the chicken and toss to coat. Dip the chicken, 1 piece at a time, into the crumb mixture, coating all sides. Place the chicken in the baking pan in one layer; lightly spray the chicken with nonstick spray. Bake, turning once, until the chicken is browned on the outside and cooked through, about 10 minutes.

4. Meanwhile, to make the dressing, whisk together the vinegar, ginger, ginger juice, cilantro, and the remaining 2 teaspoons soy sauce in a small bowl until blended; set aside.

5. Combine the rice, bell pepper, snow peas, carrots, and scallions in a large bowl. Add the chicken, drizzle with the dressing, and toss well to coat.

PER SERVING (1½ cups): 265 Cal, 5 g Fat, 1 g Sat Fat, 0 g Trans Fat, 34 mg Chol, 261 mg Sod, 36 g Carb, 3 g Fib, 18 g Prot, 43 mg Calc. *POINTS* value: *5.*

tip Pickled ginger is fresh ginger preserved in sweetened vinegar. Pungent, sweet, and fragrant, it can add a flavor boost to many dressings, dips, and sauces. You can find it in the ethnic section of large supermarkets and Asian groceries.

MAKES 4 SERVINGS

3 tablespoons **cornflake crumbs**

2 tablespoons **sesame seeds**

1 tablespoon **honey**

4 teaspoons **reduced-sodium soy sauce**

½ pound **skinless boneless chicken breasts**, cut into 2 x ½-inch strips

2 tablespoons **seasoned rice vinegar**

1 tablespoon **pickled ginger**, drained and chopped

1 tablespoon **pickled ginger juice**

3 tablespoons chopped **fresh cilantro**

2 cups **cooked white rice**

1 **red bell pepper**, seeded and diced

¼ pound **snow peas**, trimmed

½ **carrot**, cut into matchstick-thin strips

¼ cup chopped **scallions**

Mustard Chicken with Watercress and Belgian Endive

Dijon mustard does double duty here—it flavors the chicken deliciously *and* helps the bread crumbs adhere to the chicken. To save time cleaning and trimming watercress, look for it packaged in ¼-pound bags—it's triple-washed and the tough stems have been removed.

1. Preheat the oven to 450°F. Spray a small baking pan with nonstick spray.

2. Place the bread crumbs on a sheet of wax paper.

3. Combine the chicken and the 1 tablespoon mustard in a medium bowl. Dip the chicken, 1 piece at a time, into the crumbs, coating all sides. Place the chicken in the baking pan in one layer; lightly spray the chicken with nonstick spray. Bake, turning once, until the chicken is browned on the outside and cooked through, about 10 minutes.

4. Meanwhile, to make the dressing, whisk together the lemon juice, oil, capers, salt, pepper, and the remaining 2 teaspoons mustard in a small bowl; set aside.

5. Place the watercress, endive, and onion in a large bowl. Add the dressing and toss well to coat. Add the chicken and toss lightly. Serve at once.

PER SERVING (1 cup): 250 Cal, 9 g Fat, 2 g Sat Fat, 0 g Trans Fat, 68 mg Chol, 556 mg Sod, 14 g Carb, 2 g Fib, 28 g Prot, 96 mg Calc. *POINTS* value: *5*.

MAKES 4 SERVINGS

- ½ cup plain dry **bread crumbs**

- 1 pound **skinless boneless chicken breasts**, cut into 2 x ½-inch strips

- 1 tablespoon + 2 teaspoons **Dijon mustard**

- 3 tablespoons **fresh lemon juice**

- 1 tablespoon **extra-virgin olive oil**

- 1 tablespoon **capers**, drained

- ¼ teaspoon **salt**

- ½ teaspoon **freshly ground pepper**

- 1 bunch **watercress**, tough stems discarded

- 1 head **Belgian endive**, cored and cut into matchstick-thin strips

- ½ **red onion**, thinly sliced

Mustard Chicken
with Watercress and
Belgian Endive

Chicken, Penne, and Asparagus Salad

Chicken, Penne, and Asparagus Salad

Fresh basil, and lots of it, is key to this simple yet delicious meal. Use whatever green vegetable is fresh and in season. If asparagus is not available, sugar snap peas, snow peas, or broccoli florets are good alternatives. You can buy seasoning for poultry and meat, such as Old Bay seasoning, or regular poultry seasoning in the spice aisle of the supermarket.

1. Sprinkle the chicken with the seasoning. Spray a large nonstick skillet with nonstick spray and set over medium-high heat. Add the chicken and cook, turning occasionally, until browned on the outside and cooked through, about 8 minutes.

2. Meanwhile, cook the pasta according to package directions omitting the salt, if desired. With a small strainer or slotted spoon, transfer the pasta (reserving the water in the pot) to a colander. Rinse the pasta under cold running water; drain and transfer to a large bowl.

3. Add the asparagus to the same pot of boiling water and cook until crisp-tender, about 3 minutes. Rinse under cold running water to stop the cooking; drain and add to pasta. Add chicken, tomatoes, basil, cheese, garlic, oil, and salt; toss well to coat. Serve at once.

PER SERVING (1½ cups): 273 Cal, 8 g Fat, 2 g Sat Fat, 0 g Trans Fat, 39 mg Chol, 411 mg Sod, 29 g Carb, 3 g Fib, 21 g Prot, 136 mg Calc. *POINTS* value: *6*.

MAKES 4 SERVINGS

- ½ pound **skinless boneless chicken breasts**, cut into 2 x ½-inch strips

- 2 teaspoons **seasoning** for poultry and meat

- ¼ (1-pound) box **penne pasta** (about 1⅓ cups)

- 1 pound **asparagus**, trimmed and cut diagonally in thirds

- 2 medium **tomatoes**, chopped

- 1 cup chopped **fresh basil**

- ¼ cup (1 ounce) grated **Romano cheese**

- 2 **garlic cloves**, minced

- 1 tablespoon **extra-virgin olive oil**

- ¼ teaspoon **salt**

Chunky Chicken Gazpacho Salad

This recipe can easily be doubled for a large crowd and mostly prepared a day ahead. Simply make the dressing and keep it in a jar in the refrigerator; chop the vegetables and refrigerate in a bowl. Just before serving, cook the chicken then toss with the dressing and vegetables. If you prefer, serve this with round, baked tortilla chips and use them (instead of forks) as scoops to eat this crunchy, colorful salad. Six baked tortilla chips per serving will up the *POINTS* value by 1.

1. To make the dressing, whisk together the juice, vinegar, oil, jalapeño pepper, and garlic in a small bowl until blended; set aside.

2. Spray a large nonstick skillet with nonstick spray and set over medium-high heat. Add the chicken and sprinkle with the salt and ground pepper. Cook, turning occasionally, until browned on the outside and cooked through, about 8 minutes.

3. Combine the cucumber, tomatoes, red and yellow bell pepper, onion, and cilantro in a large bowl. Add the chicken, drizzle with the dressing, and toss to coat.

PER SERVING (1¾ cups): 206 Cal, 7 g Fat, 2 g Sat Fat, 0 g Trans Fat, 68 mg Chol, 222 mg Sod, 8 g Carb, 2 g Fib, 26 g Prot, 33 mg Calc. *POINTS* value: *4*.

tip If you like less heat, omit the jalapeño pepper and add a tablespoon of chopped canned mild green chiles instead.

MAKES 4 SERVINGS

½ cup **vegetable juice cocktail or tomato juice**

1 tablespoon **balsamic vinegar**

1 tablespoon **extra-virgin olive oil**

1 **jalapeño pepper**, seeded and minced (wear gloves to prevent irritation)

1 **garlic clove**, minced

1 pound **skinless boneless chicken breasts**, cut into ¾-inch pieces

⅛ teaspoon **salt**

½ teaspoon **freshly ground pepper**

½ large **seedless cucumber**, peeled and cut into ½-inch pieces

1 cup **cherry tomatoes**, halved

½ **red bell pepper**, seeded and diced

½ **yellow bell pepper**, seeded and diced

½ **red onion**, diced

½ cup chopped **fresh cilantro**

Moroccan Chicken Salad

Garam masala is an aromatic spice blend, which includes sweet spices and hot pepper. If you can't find it, you can make your own by combining a teaspoon each of ground cinnamon, cumin, coriander, and cardamom with ½ teaspoon black pepper or a pinch of cayenne. Most ground spices are best used within a few months. Purchase them in small quantities rather than in bulk, or buy them whole and grind them in a spice grinder as you need them.

1. To make the dressing, whisk together the orange juice, lemon juice, honey, mustard, oil, and ½ teaspoon of the garam masala in a small bowl until blended; set aside.

2. Sprinkle the chicken with the remaining ¾ teaspoon garam masala. Spray a large nonstick skillet with nonstick spray and set over medium-high heat.

Add the chicken and cook, turning occasionally, until browned and cooked through, about 10 minutes. Transfer the chicken to a cutting board; let rest about 5 minutes. Cut the chicken into 1-inch pieces.

3. Bring the water to a boil in a medium saucepan. Stir in the couscous; cover and remove from the heat. Let stand until all the liquid is absorbed, about 5 minutes. Transfer the couscous to a large bowl; fluff with a fork and let cool. Add the chicken, chickpeas, cucumber, carrot, currants, and scallions. Drizzle with the dressing and toss well to coat.

PER SERVING (1⅓ cups): 357 Cal, 8 g Fat, 2 g Sat Fat, 0 g Trans Fat, 35 mg Chol, 154 mg Sod, 52 g Carb, 6 g Fib, 21 g Prot, 63 mg Calc. *POINTS* value: *7*.

tip To keep the couscous light and fluffy, use a fork to lightly scrape the couscous as it falls into the bowl.

MAKES 6 SERVINGS

- ¼ cup **orange juice**
- 2 tablespoons **fresh lemon juice**
- 1 tablespoon **honey**
- 2 teaspoons **Dijon mustard**
- 2 teaspoons **olive oil**
- 1¼ teaspoons **garam masala**
- ¾ pound **skinless boneless chicken thighs**
- 2 cups **water**
- 1 cup **couscous**
- 1 (15½-ounce) **can chickpeas** (garbanzo beans), rinsed and drained
- ½ **cucumber**, peeled, seeded, and diced
- ½ cup shredded **carrot**
- ½ cup **dried currants or raisins**
- 3 tablespoons finely chopped **scallions**

Chicken and Quinoa Salad
with Dried Fruit

Chicken and Quinoa Salad with Dried Fruit

An ancient grain, quinoa has a light, delicate taste and can be substituted for most other grains. Considered to be a "super food," it contains all eight essential amino acids, making it a great source of complete protein. You can find quinoa in health-food markets.

1. To make the dressing, whisk together the vinegar, mirin, soy sauce, ginger, and oil in a small bowl until blended; set aside.

2. Bring the water to a boil in a medium saucepan; stir in quinoa. Reduce heat and simmer, covered, until all liquid is absorbed, about 20 minutes. Transfer the quinoa to a large bowl; let cool about 10 minutes.

3. Spray a large nonstick skillet with nonstick spray and set over medium-high heat. Add the chicken and cook, turning occasionally, until browned on the outside and cooked through, about 10 minutes. Transfer the chicken to a cutting board; let rest about 5 minutes. Cut the chicken into ¾-inch pieces.

4. Add the chicken to the quinoa. Stir in the scallions, cilantro, dates, currants, salt, and pepper. Drizzle with the dressing and toss well to coat.

PER SERVING (scant 1 cup): 309 Cal, 8 g Fat, 2 g Sat Fat, 0 g Trans Fat, 47 mg Chol, 337 mg Sod, 38 g Carb, 3 g Fib, 20 g Prot, 53 mg Calc. *POINTS* value: *6.*

tip When browning chicken in a skillet, make sure the heat is medium-high to high and add the pieces in one layer without touching each other. Also, don't "stir" the chicken, rather use tongs to turn the pieces. Low heat, overcrowding the pan, and stirring will cause the chicken to steam instead of brown.

MAKES 6 SERVINGS

3 tablespoons **seasoned rice vinegar**

2 tablespoons **mirin** (rice wine)

1 tablespoon **soy sauce**

2 teaspoons minced peeled **fresh ginger**

1 teaspoon **Asian (dark) sesame oil**

2 cups **water**

1 cup **quinoa**

1 pound **skinless boneless chicken thighs**

½ cup finely chopped **scallions**

½ cup chopped **fresh cilantro**

½ cup chopped **pitted dates**

¼ cup **dried currants**

½ teaspoon **salt**

½ teaspoon **freshly ground pepper**

Chicken Salad Adobo

Adobo seasoning is a traditional Mexican spice blend made from oregano, cumin, garlic, onion, and pepper. It perks up food by adding spice with little heat. We add a jalapeño pepper to the salad to make it spicy, but you can omit it if you like a gentler flavor. Adobo seasoning can be found in the spice section of most supermarkets. If you prefer, pinto beans or red kidney beans can be used in place of the black beans and diced papaya can be substituted for the mango.

1. To make the dressing, whisk together the orange zest, orange juice, vinegar, oil, honey, mustard, garlic, and salt in a small bowl until blended; set aside.

2. Sprinkle the chicken with the adobo seasoning. Spray a large nonstick skillet with nonstick spray and set over medium-high heat. Add the chicken and cook, turning occasionally, until browned on the outside and cooked through, about 8 minutes. Transfer the chicken to a large bowl. Stir in the beans, mango, bell pepper, onion, cilantro, and jalapeño pepper. Drizzle with the dressing and toss well to coat.

PER SERVING (scant 1 cup): 248 Cal, 8 g Fat, 2 g Sat Fat, 0 g Trans Fat, 47 mg Chol, 321 mg Sod, 23 g Carb, 4 g Fib, 21 g Prot, 63 mg Calc. *POINTS* value: *5*.

tip You can transform this salad into a delicious sandwich wrap by simply enclosing the chicken mixture in 3 (10-inch) fat-free flour tortillas. Cut each wrap in half on the diagonal and serve half a wrap per person. You'll increase the per-serving *POINTS* value by 2.

MAKES 6 SERVINGS

1 tablespoon grated **orange zest**

2 tablespoons **fresh orange juice**

1 tablespoon **wine vinegar**

2 teaspoons **olive oil**

1 teaspoon **honey**

1 teaspoon **Dijon mustard**

1 **garlic clove**, minced

⅛ teaspoon **salt**

1 pound **skinless boneless chicken thighs**, in 1-inch pieces

1 tablespoon **adobo seasoning**

1 (15½-ounce) **can black beans**, rinsed and drained

1 ripe **mango**, peeled and diced

1 **red bell pepper**, seeded and diced

½ **red onion**, finely chopped

½ cup chopped **fresh cilantro**

1 **jalapeño pepper**, seeded and minced

Layered Chicken Taco Salad

Show off this colorful, layered salad by serving it in a glass dish. Or layer the ingredients on a large round platter. If you tend to cook Mexican meals frequently, you might find it convenient to buy taco or chili seasoning in a 6¼-ounce can. Otherwise, it's available in individual packets.

1. Heat the oil in a large nonstick skillet over medium-high heat. Add the chicken, onion, and taco seasoning. Cook, breaking up the chicken with a wooden spoon, until browned, about 8 minutes. Stir in the tomato sauce and water; bring to a boil. Reduce the heat and simmer, uncovered, until the flavors are blended and the liquid evaporates, about 6 minutes. Remove the skillet from the heat; stir in the cheese and cilantro.

2. Spread the beans in the bottom of a 7 x 11-inch baking dish; top with a layer of the lettuce, then with the chicken mixture, salsa, and finally a layer of sour cream. Tuck the chips around the dish. Serve at once.

PER SERVING (¾ cup salad with 2 tortilla chips): 207 Cal, 5 g Fat, 1 g Sat Fat, 0 g Trans Fat, 47 mg Chol, 540 mg Sod, 19 g Carb, 4 g Fib, 22 g Prot, 109 mg Calc. *POINTS* value: *4*.

tip If you like, make individual open-face tacos by toasting 6 (6-inch) corn tortillas in a 400°F oven until crisp, about 7 minutes. Spread a scant 3 tablespoons of the refried beans onto the bottom of each tortilla and top each with the lettuce, chicken mixture, salsa, and sour cream.

MAKES 6 SERVINGS

- 2 teaspoons **canola oil**
- 1 pound ground **skinless lean chicken breast**
- 1 **onion**, chopped
- 2 tablespoons **taco or chili seasoning mix**
- 1 (8-ounce) **can no-salt added tomato sauce**
- ¼ cup **water**
- ¼ cup (1 ounce) **reduced-fat shredded cheddar cheese**
- ¼ cup chopped **fresh cilantro**
- 1 cup **fat-free refried beans**
- 3 cups shredded **iceberg lettuce**
- ½ cup **salsa verde** (green salsa)
- ¼ cup **fat-free sour cream**
- 12 **reduced-fat tortilla chips**

Grilled Chicken Sausage with Roasted Potato Salad

Gourmet-style chicken sausages are widely available in larger supermarkets. They are low in fat, fully cooked, and come in a variety of flavors ranging from sweet and mild to spicy and hot. Italian turkey sausage or low-fat kielbasa is also a delicious alternative. If you can't find small red potatoes, use larger ones and cut them into 1-inch pieces.

1. Preheat the oven to 425°F. Spray a nonstick roasting pan with nonstick spray.

2. To make the dressing, whisk together the vinegar, mustard, oil, garlic, ¼ teaspoon of the salt and ¼ teaspoon of the ground pepper in a small bowl until blended; set aside.

3. Combine the potatoes, onion, rosemary, and the remaining ½ teaspoon salt and ½ teaspoon ground pepper in a large bowl. Lightly spray the potato mixture with olive-oil nonstick spray; toss to coat. Arrange the potato mixture in the roasting pan in one layer. Roast, stirring occasionally, until the potatoes are tender and browned, about 40 minutes. Transfer the potatoes to a large bowl; set aside.

4. Spray a large nonstick skillet with nonstick spray and set over medium heat. Add the sausage and cook, covered, until lightly browned and just heated through, about 7 minutes. When the sausage is cool enough, cut diagonally into 1-inch pieces; add to the potatoes.

5. Add the peas, bell pepper, olives, and parsley to the potato mixture. Drizzle with the dressing and toss well to coat. Sprinkle with the cheese and serve at once.

PER SERVING (1⅓ cups): 241 Cal, 10 g Fat, 2 g Sat Fat, 0 g Trans Fat, 31 mg Chol, 1009 mg Sod, 26 g Carb, 5 g Fib, 13 g Prot, 50 mg Calc. *POINTS* value: *5.*

MAKES 6 SERVINGS

- 2 tablespoons **cider vinegar**
- 1 tablespoon **country-style mustard**
- 1 tablespoon **extra-virgin olive oil**
- 1 **garlic clove**, minced
- ¾ teaspoon **salt**
- ¾ teaspoon **freshly ground pepper**
- 1 pound small **red potatoes**, scrubbed and halved
- 1 large **red onion**, cut into ½-inch-thick wedges
- 1 tablespoon chopped **fresh rosemary**
- 1 (12-ounce) package **fully-cooked chicken sausage**
- 1 (10-ounce) box **frozen peas**, thawed
- 1 **yellow bell pepper**, seeded and thinly sliced
- 10 **kalamata olives**, pitted and chopped
- ¼ cup chopped **flat-leaf parsley**
- 3 tablespoons crumbled **reduced-fat goat cheese**

Grilled Chicken Sausage with
Roasted Potato Salad

Chicken and Slaw with Creamy Dressing

This quick and easy main-dish salad can be put together in under 15 minutes—especially if you use prepared coleslaw mix (shredded cabbage with a few shredded carrots), available in the produce section of most supermarkets. You can prepare this slaw several hours ahead and keep it covered in the refrigerator. Sprinkle the slaw with the bacon just before serving.

1. To make the dressing, whisk together the mayonnaise, mustard, vinegar, celery seed, and sugar in a small bowl until blended; set aside.

2. Combine the coleslaw mix, chicken, and tomato in a large bowl. Drizzle with the dressing and toss well to coat. Divide the mixture evenly among 4 plates and sprinkle with the bacon just before serving.

PER SERVING (1½ cups slaw with 1 slice crumbled bacon): 214 Cal, 7 g Fat, 2 g Sat Fat, 0 g Trans Fat, 63 mg Chol, 448 mg Sod, 14 g Carb, 3 g Fib, 25 g Prot, 77 mg Calc. *POINTS* value: *4*.

tip Skip the bacon and decrease the per-serving *POINTS* value by 1.

MAKES 4 SERVINGS

- 6 tablespoons **fat-free mayonnaise**
- 1 tablespoon **Dijon mustard**
- 1 tablespoon **cider vinegar**
- ¾ teaspoon **celery seed**
- 2 teaspoons **sugar**
- 1 (1-pound) bag **coleslaw mix** (about 4 cups)
- 2 cups chopped **cooked chicken breast**
- 1 **tomato**, cut into ½-inch pieces
- 4 slices **bacon**, crisp-cooked, drained, and crumbled

Chicken with Farfalle and Roasted Vegetable Salad

Roasting intensifies the flavor of vegetables by slightly caramelizing their natural sugars. Be sure to use a shallow roasting pan, large enough to accommodate the vegetables in one layer. Avoid overcrowding the pan or the vegetables will steam instead of brown. *And,* to ensure that they will all be cooked at the same time, cut the vegetables to about the same size.

1. Preheat the oven to 450°F. Spray a large shallow roasting pan with nonstick spray.

2. Spread the eggplant, zucchini, yellow squash, and onion in the pan. Lightly spray the vegetables with nonstick spray. Roast, stirring occasionally, until the vegetables are tender and browned, about 45 minutes. Let cool slightly.

3. Cook the pasta according to package directions omitting the salt, if desired; drain. Rinse under cold running water and drain again. Transfer the pasta to a large bowl. Add the roasted vegetables, chicken, tomatoes, basil, cheese, oil, and pepper; toss well to coat. Serve at once.

PER SERVING (generous 1⅓ cups): 306 Cal, 7 g Fat, 2 g Sat Fat, 0 g Trans Fat, 42 mg Chol, 230 mg Sod, 39 g Carb, 5 g Fib, 22 g Prot, 80 mg Calc. *POINTS* value: *6.*

MAKES 6 SERVINGS

- 1 (1-pound) **eggplant**, cut into 1-inch pieces
- 1 medium **zucchini**, cut into 1-inch pieces
- 1 medium **yellow squash**, cut into 1-inch pieces
- 1 **red onion**, cut into 1-inch pieces
- ½ (1-pound) box **farfalle (bow tie) pasta**
- 2 cups shredded **cooked chicken breast**
- ½ cup **cherry tomatoes**, halved
- ½ cup chopped **fresh basil**
- 3 tablespoons grated **Romano cheese**
- 1 tablespoon **extra-virgin olive oil**
- ½ teaspoon **freshly ground pepper**

Curried Chicken–Stuffed
Tomatoes

Curried Chicken–Stuffed Tomatoes

Stumped for something to serve friends coming for lunch? Let this elegant, no-cook dish be your answer. You can prepare the salad up to a day ahead and keep it refrigerated, ready to stuff into the tomato halves at the last minute. Adjust the amount of curry powder you use to suit your taste, but remember the flavors will develop if you keep the salad overnight.

1. Combine the chicken, celery, apple, raisins, mayonnaise, chutney, sour cream, lime juice, curry powder, and cumin in a large bowl; toss well to coat.

2. Cut each tomato horizontally in half. Scoop out the seeds and pulp leaving a quarter-inch border all around. Spoon the chicken mixture evenly (scant ½ cup) into each of the tomato halves.

3. Place a lettuce leaf on each of 4 plates; arrange 2 tomato halves on each lettuce leaf. Serve at once.

PER SERVING (2 stuffed tomato halves): 266 Cal, 6 g Fat, 2 g Sat Fat, 0 g Trans Fat, 60 mg Chol, 220 mg Sod, 34 g Carb, 4 g Fib, 22 g Prot, 61 mg Calc. *POINTS* value: *5*.

tip Be sure to cut a thin slice from the bottoms of the tomato halves before stuffing so they'll stand upright.

MAKES 4 SERVINGS

- 2 cups bite-size pieces **cooked chicken**
- 2 **celery** stalks, finely diced
- 1 **Granny Smith apple**, cored and finely chopped
- ½ cup **raisins**
- ¼ cup **fat-free mayonnaise**
- 2 tablespoons **mango chutney**
- 1 tablespoon **fat-free sour cream**
- 1 tablespoon **fresh lime juice**
- ½ tablespoons **curry powder**
- ½ teaspoon **ground cumin**
- 4 medium **tomatoes**
- 4 large **red or green leaf lettuce** leaves

 # Tzatziki Chicken Salad

You can make this delicious Greek dressing up to a day ahead and keep it in the refrigerator. It also makes a perfect accompaniment to grilled lamb or falafel (chickpea patties). Try serving this delicious chicken salad with warmed pita bread for a satisfying lunch (a small pita bread will up the *POINTS* value by 1).

1. To make the dressing, whisk together the yogurt, mint, lemon zest, lemon juice, garlic, and oil in a small bowl until blended; set aside.

2. Place the chicken, lettuce, tomato, onion, cucumber, and olives in a large bowl. Drizzle with the dressing and toss well to coat. Serve at once.

PER SERVING (1⅓ cups): 162 Cal, 4 g Fat, 1 g Sat Fat, 0 g Trans Fat, 58 mg Chol, 114 mg Sod, 6 g Carb, 1 g Fib, 21 g Prot, 87 mg Calc. *POINTS* value: *3*.

MAKES 6 SERVINGS

¾ cup **plain fat-free yogurt**

2 tablespoons chopped **fresh mint**

2 teaspoons grated **lemon zest**

1 tablespoon **fresh lemon juice**

1 **garlic clove**, minced

1 teaspoon **extra-virgin olive oil**

3 cups chopped **cooked chicken breast**

2 cups torn **romaine lettuce** leaves

1 **tomato**, chopped

1 **red onion**, finely chopped

½ **cucumber**, peeled, seeded, and diced

6 **kalamata olives**, pitted and chopped

Creole Turkey and Spicy Potato Salad

Spicy and delicious, this salad is great served with simple steamed green beans or steamed asparagus sprinkled with grated lemon zest.

1. To make the dressing, whisk together the mustard, mayonnaise, Creole seasoning, vinegar, and hot pepper sauce in a small bowl until blended; set aside.

2. Place the potatoes and enough water to cover in a large saucepan; bring to a boil. Reduce the heat and simmer, covered, until the potatoes are tender, about 20 minutes. Drain the potatoes and transfer to a large bowl; let cool about 10 minutes.

3. Spray a large nonstick skillet with nonstick spray and set over medium-high heat. Add the turkey and cook until browned on the outside and cooked through, about 4 minutes on each side. Transfer the turkey to a cutting board; let rest about 5 minutes. Cut the turkey into 1-inch pieces.

4. Add the turkey, bell pepper, celery, onion, and parsley to the potatoes. Drizzle with the dressing and toss well to coat. Serve at once, sprinkled with the bacon.

PER SERVING (1¾ cups salad with 2 teaspoons bacon): 294 Cal, 4 g Fat, 1 g Sat Fat, 0 g Trans Fat, 78 mg Chol, 489 mg Sod, 35 g Carb, 4 g Fib, 31 g Prot, 54 mg Calc. *POINTS* value: *5*.

tip Creole seasoning (a blend of spices) is available in the spice aisle of the supermarket. If you prefer to make your own, simply mix a tablespoon each of cayenne, ground black pepper, and paprika with a teaspoon each of dried oregano, thyme, and onion powder. Store in a jar with a tight-fitting lid for up to 3 months.

MAKES 4 SERVINGS

- ¼ cup **honey-Dijon mustard**
- 3 tablespoons **fat-free mayonnaise**
- 4 teaspoons **Creole seasoning**
- 1 tablespoon **cider vinegar**
- 4 drops **hot pepper sauce**
- 1 pound **red potatoes,** cut into 1½-inch pieces
- 4 (¼-pound) thin-sliced **turkey breast cutlets**
- 1 **green bell pepper,** seeded and chopped
- 1 **celery** stalk, finely chopped
- 1 small **red onion,** finely chopped
- ¼ cup chopped **flat-leaf parsley**
- 2 slices **bacon,** crisp-cooked, drained, and crumbled

Turkey Cobb Salad

Cobb salad originates from the Brown Derby restaurant in Hollywood, where, in 1937, the hungry owner Bob Cobb, used ingredients he had on hand, to create what was to become a famous and delicious main-course salad. We keep the dressing light and use turkey instead of chicken—otherwise it probably tastes very similar to the original.

1. To make the dressing, whisk together the vinegar, lemon juice, mustard, oil, pepper, and salt in a small bowl until blended; set aside.

2. Place the greens on a large serving platter. Arrange the turkey, tomatoes, and avocado alongside each other in rows on top of the greens. Sprinkle the salad with the egg whites, bacon, and blue cheese. Drizzle with the dressing and serve at once.

PER SERVING (generous 1 cup): 191 Cal, 11 g Fat, 2 g Sat Fat, 0 g Trans Fat, 44 mg Chol, 265 mg Sod, 6 g Carb, 3 g Fib, 18 g Prot, 57 mg Calc. *POINTS* value: *4*.

MAKES 6 SERVINGS

- 2 tablespoons **white-wine vinegar**
- 1 tablespoon **fresh lemon juice**
- 1 tablespoon **Dijon mustard**
- 4 teaspoons **olive oil**
- ¼ teaspoon **freshly ground pepper**
- ⅛ teaspoon **salt**
- 6 cups **mesclun greens**
- 2 cups bite-size pieces **cooked turkey breast**
- 2 **tomatoes**, diced
- 1 **avocado**, pitted and cut into ½-inch pieces
- 2 **hard-cooked egg whites**, finely chopped
- 3 slices **bacon**, crisp-cooked, drained, and crumbled
- 2 tablespoons crumbled **blue cheese**

Turkey Cobb Salad

Smoked Turkey and Crunchy Fruit Slaw

You can find cooked smoked turkey breast in the delicatessen section of the supermarket. Ask for a half-pound piece that you can cut into whatever size and shape pieces you like for this salad. Can't find jicama? Substitute an extra apple, a pear, or even pineapple chunks. If you like, sprinkle each serving of this tasty no-cook salad with a tablespoon of chopped toasted pecans and up the *POINTS* value by 1.

1. Combine the yogurt, preserves, lemon juice, and mustard in a large bowl. Add the turkey, jicama, apple, grapes, carrot, celery, and raisins; toss well to coat.

2. Place a lettuce leaf on each of 4 plates. Divide the turkey-slaw mixture evenly (about 1½ cups) onto each lettuce leaf. Serve at once.

PER SERVING (1 plate): 246 Cal, 2 g Fat, 1 g Sat Fat, 0 g Trans Fat, 28 mg Chol, 753 mg Sod, 45 g Carb, 7 g Fib, 13 g Prot, 106 mg Calc. *POINTS* value: *4*.

tip Jicama can sometimes be difficult to peel using a vegetable peeler. Here's an easy solution: Using a small paring knife and starting at the stem end, hold a piece of the skin with the blade of your knife and pull strips of the skin off by following the contour of the jicama. Continue all the way around until all of the skin is removed.

MAKES 4 SERVINGS

½ cup **plain fat-free yogurt**

3 tablespoons **apricot preserves**

2 teaspoons **fresh lemon juice**

1 teaspoon **Dijon mustard**

½ pound piece **cooked smoked turkey**, cut into bite-size pieces or strips

1 small **jicama**, peeled and cut into matchstick-thin strips

1 **apple**, cored and chopped

1 cup **seedless red or green grapes**, halved

1 **carrot**, cut into matchstick-thin strips

1 **celery** stalk, diced

¼ cup **golden raisins**

4 large **red or green leaf lettuce** leaves

Turkey Sausage, Mushroom, and Barley Salad

Traditionally known as a long-cooking grain, barley is now available in quick-cooking form, meaning this hearty salad can be made in minutes.

1. Heat 1 teaspoon of the oil in a large nonstick skillet over medium heat. Add the sausage and cook, covered, turning occasionally, until browned and cooked through, about 15 minutes. Transfer the sausage to a cutting board; let rest about 5 minutes. Cut the sausage into ¾-inch pieces.

2. Heat another 1 teaspoon oil in the same skillet over medium heat. Add the onion and garlic; cook, stirring occasionally, until softened and fragrant, about 5 minutes. Add the mushrooms and cook, stirring occasionally, until tender, about 5 minutes. Add the wine and bring to a boil. Reduce the heat and simmer, uncovered, until the liquid evaporates, about 3 minutes longer. Remove the skillet from the heat; stir in the thyme and set aside.

3. To make the dressing, whisk together the vinegar, mustard, and the remaining 2 teaspoons oil in a large bowl until blended; set aside.

4. Bring the water to a boil in a medium saucepan; add the barley. Reduce the heat and simmer, covered, until the barley is tender and the liquid is evaporated, 10–12 minutes.

5. Add the barley, sausage, and onion mixture to the dressing; toss well to coat.

PER SERVING (1 cup): 308 Cal, 13 g Fat, 3 g Sat Fat, 0 g Trans Fat, 44 mg Chol, 525 mg Sod, 32 g Carb, 6 g Fib, 17 g Prot, 39 mg Calc. *POINTS* value: *6*.

tip You can serve this salad at once while it is still warm, or cover and refrigerate it for up to a day and serve it chilled.

MAKES 6 SERVINGS

4 teaspoons **olive oil**

1 pound **Italian turkey sausage**

1 **onion**, thinly sliced

1 **garlic clove**, minced

½ pound fresh **shiitake mushrooms**, stems discarded, caps thinly sliced

¼ cup **dry white wine**

2 tablespoons chopped **fresh thyme**

3 tablespoons **white-wine vinegar**

2 teaspoons **Dijon mustard**

2 cups **water**

1 cup **quick-cooking barley**

Ginger Duck and Wild Rice Salad

Ginger Duck and Wild Rice Salad

Fresh duck is available from late spring to early winter. However, you can substitute thawed frozen duck or skinless boneless chicken thighs if you like. Alternatively, you can use up leftover holiday turkey in this recipe, stirring 1 cup chopped cooked turkey into the salad along with the dressing at the last minute and skipping the duck altogether.

1. To make the dressing, whisk together the soy sauce, orange juice, vinegar, honey, and sesame oil in a small bowl until blended; set aside.

2. Prepare the rice according to package directions, discarding the spice packet. Transfer the rice to a large bowl; set aside.

3. Heat the canola oil in a large nonstick skillet over medium heat. Add the ginger and garlic; cook, stirring frequently, until fragrant, about 1 minute. Add the duck and cook over medium-high heat, turning occasionally, until browned on the outside and cooked through, about 6 minutes.

4. Add the duck mixture to the rice. Stir in the cranberries, scallions, and pecans. Drizzle with the dressing and toss well to coat.

PER SERVING (1¼ cups): 326 Cal, 6 g Fat, 1 g Sat Fat, 0 g Trans Fat, 33 mg Chol, 294 mg Sod, 51 g Carb, 3 g Fib, 18 g Prot, 33 mg Calc. *POINTS* value: *6*.

tip We discard the spice packet that comes with the rice mix; not only is it high in sodium, but it will overpower the delicate balance of the dressing's flavor.

MAKES 4 SERVINGS

- 2 tablespoons **reduced-sodium soy sauce**
- 2 tablespoons **orange juice**
- 1 tablespoon **red-wine vinegar**
- 1 tablespoon **honey**
- 1 teaspoon **Asian (dark) sesame oil**
- 1 (6-ounce) box **long-grain and wild rice mix**, spice packet discarded
- 1 teaspoon **canola oil**
- 2 teaspoons minced peeled **fresh ginger**
- 1 **garlic clove**, minced
- ½ pound **skinless boneless duck breasts**, cut into 2 x ¼-inch strips
- ¼ cup **dried cranberries**
- 4 **scallions**, thinly sliced on the diagonal
- 2 tablespoons coarsely chopped **toasted pecans**

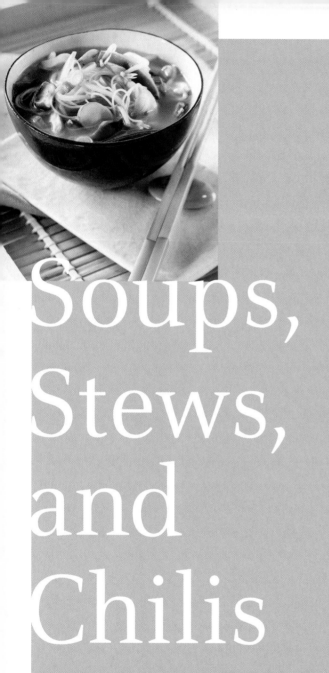

Soups, Stews, and Chilis

CHAPTER FOUR

Homemade Chicken Broth

Full of fresh, subtle, and comforting flavors, this broth can be enjoyed as a satisfying pick-me-up, or used where chicken broth is called for in any of our recipes. Pack the broth into 2-cup containers and refrigerate for up to 2 days or freeze for up to 3 months. You'll get about 5 cups of chicken from this recipe; you can use it in any of our recipes calling for cooked chicken. Wrap and refrigerate the chicken for up to 3 days or freeze for up to 4 months.

1. Bring the chicken, water, carrots, onions, celery, garlic, parsley, peppercorns, cloves, bay leaves, and salt to a boil in a large soup pot. Reduce the heat and simmer, covered, until the chicken is very tender and cooked through, about 2 hours.

2. Lift the chicken from the broth and set aside until cool enough to handle. Pull the chicken from the bones, then tear or cut into bite-size pieces.

3. Strain the broth through a large strainer (or a colander lined with cheesecloth) into a large bowl or pot. Discard the vegetables and spices in the strainer.

4. Let the broth cool at room temperature for about 1 hour, then cover and refrigerate until chilled, at least 4 hours or overnight. Remove any fat from surface of broth, then pack and refrigerate or freeze the broth.

PER SERVING (1 cup): 32 Cal, 0 g Fat, 0 g Sat Fat, 0 g Trans Fat, 0 mg Chol, 270 mg Sod, 4 g Carb, 0 g Fib, 3 g Prot, 12 mg Calc. *POINTS* value: *1*.

tip You can pick the vegetables out of the strainer, mash them lightly, and serve them as a tasty side dish.

MAKES 11 SERVINGS

1 (4½-pound) **chicken**, giblets discarded, chicken skinned

12 cups **water**

4 **carrots**, cut into 2-inch pieces

2 **onions**, cut into eighths

2 **celery** stalks, cut into 2-inch pieces

2 **garlic cloves**, minced

Handful **fresh parsley** sprigs

10 **black peppercorns**

4 **whole cloves**

3 **bay leaves**

1 teaspoon **salt**

Old-Fashioned Chicken Noodle Soup

When a little "TLC" is needed, this homey soup fits the bill. You'll get about 4 cups of cooked chicken from the recipe but you'll use only 2 cups of it in this soup. You might like to use the remaining chicken to make our speedy Thai Chicken Salad on page 266, another day.

1. Bring the chicken, water, carrots, celery, onions, bay leaves, salt, and pepper to a boil in a large soup pot. Reduce the heat and simmer, covered, until the chicken is tender and cooked through, about 45 minutes.

2. Lift the chicken from the soup and set aside until cool enough to handle. Pull the chicken from the bones, then tear or cut into bite-size pieces.

3. Discard the bay leaves. Add the noodles and return the soup to a boil. Reduce the heat and simmer, uncovered, until the noodles are tender, about 5 minutes. Add the tomato and thyme; simmer 5 minutes longer. Add the parsley and return 2 cups of the chicken to the soup; heat through, about 3 minutes.

PER SERVING (2 cups): 175 Cal, 4 g Fat, 1 g Sat Fat, 0 g Trans Fat, 47 mg Chol, 672 mg Sod, 21 g Carb, 4 g Fib, 15 g Prot, 58 mg Calc. *POINTS* value: *3*.

tip When removing the skin from raw chicken, use paper towels to help you get a good grip.

MAKES 6 SERVINGS ☛

1 (3-pound) **chicken**, cut into 8 pieces and skinned

7 cups **water**

6 **carrots**, cut into 1-inch pieces

3 **celery stalks**, cut into 1-inch pieces

2 **onions**, cut into eighths

2 **bay leaves**

2 teaspoons **salt**

½ teaspoon coarsely **ground black pepper**

2 cups **broad egg noodles**

1 large **tomato**, chopped

2 teaspoons **dried thyme**, crumbled

¼ cup chopped **flat-leaf parsley**

Paella Soup

We've used all the flavorful ingredients found in a traditional Spanish paella to make this delicious and hearty soup. If you prefer a milder taste, substitute an ounce of thinly sliced ham or prosciutto for the spicy chorizo.

1. Heat the oil in a nonstick soup pot or large Dutch oven over medium-high heat. Add the onion, bell pepper, and garlic; cook, stirring occasionally, until softened, about 8 minutes. Add the broth, tomatoes, and rice; bring to a boil, stirring once or twice. Reduce the heat and simmer, partially covered, until the rice is tender, about 20 minutes.

2. Add the chicken, shrimp, peas, oregano, saffron, and pepper to the pot; bring to a boil. Reduce the heat and simmer, uncovered, until the chicken is just cooked through and the shrimp are just opaque in the center, about 4 minutes. Stir in the chorizo and parsley; return to a boil. Reduce the heat and simmer about 3 minutes.

PER SERVING (2½ cups): 380 Cal, 11 g Fat, 3 g Sat Fat, 0 g Trans Fat, 94 mg Chol, 1087 mg Sod, 37 g Carb, 5 g Fib, 32 g Prot, 101 g Calc. *POINTS* value: *8*.

MAKES 4 SERVINGS ☞

- 1 tablespoon **extra-virgin olive oil**
- 1 large **red onion**, chopped
- 1 **red bell pepper**, seeded and chopped
- 3 **garlic cloves**, minced
- 6 cups **reduced-sodium chicken broth**
- 1 (14½-ounce) **can diced tomatoes**
- ½ cup **long-grain white rice**
- ½ pound **skinless boneless chicken breast**, cut into 2 x ¼-inch strips
- ½ pound **large shrimp**, peeled and deveined
- 1 cup **frozen peas**
- 1 teaspoon **dried oregano**
- ½ teaspoon **saffron threads**, lightly crushed
- ⅛ teaspoon **freshly ground pepper**
- 1 ounce **chorizo** or other hard cooked sausage, cut into very thin slices
- ¼ cup chopped **fresh parsley**

Paella Soup

Asian Chicken and Noodle Bowl

Asian Chicken and Noodle Bowl

If "dinner in a flash" sounds good to you, then try this recipe. You can prepare the chicken and vegetables in the time it takes to bring the broth to a boil, then simply add them to the soup with the few other ingredients, cook for 6 minutes, and it's ready. Rice stick noodles can be found in Asian markets and some supermarkets, but you can substitute capellini or vermicelli in this recipe, if you prefer.

1. Bring the broth to a boil in a Dutch oven. Add the chicken, noodles, snow peas, mushrooms, radishes, vinegar, soy sauce, oil, ginger, and garlic; return to a boil. Reduce the heat and simmer, stirring occasionally, until the chicken and noodles are cooked through, about 5 minutes.

2. Add the bean sprouts; return to a boil. Reduce the heat and simmer, about 1 minute. Serve the soup sprinkled with the scallions.

PER SERVING (generous 1½ cups): 400 Cal, 8 g Fat, 2 g Sat Fat, 0 g Trans Fat, 51 mg Chol, 942 mg Sod, 48 g Carb, 3 g Fib, 31 g Prot, 62 mg Calc. *POINTS* value: *8*.

tip For a spicy version of this soup, sprinkle in ⅛ to ¼ teaspoon crushed red pepper when you add the bean sprouts.

MAKES 4 SERVINGS ☛

6 cups **reduced-sodium chicken broth**

¾ pound **skinless boneless chicken breast**, cut into 2 x ¼-inch strips

1 (6¾-ounce) package **rice stick noodles**

¼ pound **fresh snow peas**, trimmed and sliced diagonally in half

¼ pound **fresh shiitake mushrooms**, stems discarded, caps sliced

½ cup sliced **radishes**

2 tablespoons **rice-wine vinegar**

1 tablespoon **reduced-sodium soy sauce**

2 teaspoons **dark (Asian) sesame oil**

1 teaspoon minced peeled **fresh ginger**

1 **garlic clove**, minced

½ cup **fresh bean sprouts**

3 **scallions** (white and light green portion only), thinly sliced

Mexicali Chicken Soup with Lime

This south-of-the-border rendition of chicken soup pairs the heat of minced chile pepper and the tang of fresh lime juice with the cooling effect of diced avocado and fresh cilantro.

1. Spray a nonstick Dutch oven with canola nonstick spray and set over medium-high heat. Add the chicken and cook, stirring occasionally, until browned, about 4 minutes. Transfer the chicken to a plate.

2. Add the onions, carrots, garlic, and chile pepper to the saucepan. Cook, stirring occasionally, until lightly browned, 5–6 minutes. Add the broth and bring to a boil. Reduce the heat and simmer, covered, until the flavors are blended, about 20 minutes. Return the chicken to the saucepan and simmer until cooked through, about 8 minutes.

3. Stir in the tomatoes, avocado, lime juice, cilantro, salt, and pepper; cook, stirring occasionally, until heated through, about 1 minute.

PER SERVING (1¾ cups): 244 Cal, 6 g Fat, 1 g Sat Fat, 0 g Trans Fat, 67 mg Chol, 924 mg Sod, 17 g Carb, 5 g Fib, 31 g Prot, 44 mg Calc. *POINTS* value: *5*.

tip Try serving this soup with toasted tortilla wedges. To make your own, preheat the broiler. Cut each of 4 (6-inch) corn tortillas into 4 wedges. Place the wedges on a baking sheet. Broil 4–5 inches from the heat until golden, about 45 seconds on each side; let cool. Four tortilla wedges for each serving will increase the *POINTS* value by 1.

MAKES 4 SERVINGS

1 pound **skinless boneless chicken breast,** cut into ½-inch pieces

2 **onions,** chopped

2 **carrots,** chopped

2 **garlic cloves,** minced

1 **serrano chile pepper,** seeded and minced (wear gloves to prevent irritation)

4½ cups **reduced-sodium chicken broth**

2 **plum tomatoes,** seeded and chopped

½ medium ripe **avocado,** peeled and diced

3 tablespoons **fresh lime juice**

3 tablespoons chopped **fresh cilantro**

¼ teaspoon **salt**

⅛ teaspoon **freshly ground pepper**

✓ Chicken and Barley Soup

This lovely concoction has the goodness of lots of fresh vegetables, comforting and soothing barley, and earthy fresh thyme. Consider making a double batch, as the soup freezes very well.

1. Spray a nonstick Dutch oven with canola nonstick spray and set over medium heat. Add the onion and cook, stirring frequently, until softened, about 4 minutes. Add the garlic and cook, stirring frequently, until fragrant, about 30 seconds.

2. Stir in the potatoes, carrots, celery, barley, and thyme; cook, stirring occasionally, until the vegetables begin to soften, about 4 minutes. Add the broth, salt, and pepper; bring to a boil. Reduce the heat and simmer until the vegetables are softened and the barley is cooked through, about 15 minutes.

3. Stir in the broccoli and chicken; return to a boil. Reduce the heat and simmer until the broccoli is fork-tender and the chicken is cooked through, about 5 minutes.

PER SERVING (about 1½ cups): 163 Cal, 1 g Fat, 0 g Sat Fat, 0 g Trans Fat, 21 mg Chol, 1,060 mg Sod, 24 g Carb, 5 g Fib, 15 g Prot, 38 mg Calc. *POINTS* value: *3*.

MAKES 6 SERVINGS 🍲

- 1 **red onion,** thinly sliced
- 1 **garlic clove,** minced
- ¾ pound (2 small) **sweet potatoes,** peeled and chopped
- 2 small **carrots,** halved lengthwise and thinly sliced
- 2 small **celery stalks with leaves,** thinly sliced
- ½ cup **quick-cooking barley**
- ¾ teaspoon **fresh thyme leaves**
- 8 cups **reduced-sodium chicken broth**
- ½ teaspoon **salt**
- ¼ teaspoon **freshly ground pepper**
- 2 cups small **broccoli florets**
- ½ pound **skinless boneless chicken breast,** cut into 2 x ¼-inch strips

☑ Creamy Chicken and Corn Avgolemono Soup

This substantial soup, inspired by the Greek classic, can be ready in minutes. Eggs, quickly whisked in, make it creamy, while fresh lemon juice (don't use bottled lemon juice—it just doesn't cut it) adds zing. If fresh corn is not available, frozen petite white corn is especially sweet and good. You might like to serve this soup with a slice of fresh pumpernickel bread; just remember to deduct it from your weekly *POINTS* Allowance value by 2.

1. Bring the broth to a boil in a large saucepan. Add the chicken and corn; return to a boil. Reduce the heat and simmer, uncovered, until the chicken is just cooked through, about 5 minutes.

2. Meanwhile, lightly beat the eggs, lemon juice, parsley, and pepper in a small bowl. Stir about 2 tablespoons of the hot broth into the egg mixture. Gradually pour the egg mixture into the simmering soup and cook, stirring constantly, until the egg forms shreds, about 1 minute. Serve the soup sprinkled with the scallions.

PER SERVING (scant 1½ cups): 211 Cal, 6 g Fat, 2 g Sat Fat, 0 g Trans Fat, 140 mg Chol, 553 mg Sod, 17 g Carb, 2 g Fib, 23 g Prot, 42 mg Calc. *POINTS* value: *4*.

MAKES 4 SERVINGS

- 4 cups **reduced-sodium chicken broth**

- ½ pound **skinless boneless chicken breast,** cut into 2 x ¼-inch strips

- 2 cups fresh or frozen **corn kernels**

- 2 large **eggs**

- 3 tablespoons **fresh lemon juice**

- 3 tablespoons chopped **fresh parsley**

- ⅛ teaspoon **freshly ground pepper**

- 2 **scallions** (white and light green portion only), thinly sliced

✓ Chicken Scotch Broth

Scotch broth is traditionally made with lamb, barley, and a variety of vegetables but chicken makes a nice alternative to lamb here. Fresh thyme adds lively flavor to the gentle flavors of the barley, mushrooms, and peas.

1. Heat the oil in a nonstick Dutch oven over medium heat. Add the onion and cook, stirring occasionally, until golden, 7–10 minutes. Add the broth, barley, carrots, parsnips, salt, and pepper; bring to a boil. Add the chicken; return to a boil. Reduce the heat and simmer, covered, until the chicken is cooked through and the barley is tender, about 40 minutes.

2. Lift the chicken from the soup and set aside until cool enough to handle. Pull the chicken from the bones, then tear or cut into bite-size pieces.

3. Add the mushrooms, peas, and thyme to the pot; return to a boil. Reduce the heat and simmer, covered, until the vegetables are tender, about 10 minutes. Return the chicken to the soup and heat through.

PER SERVING (1½ cups): 372 Cal, 10 g Fat, 3 g Sat Fat, 0 g Trans Fat, 59 mg Chol, 777 mg Sod, 39 g Carb, 9 g Fib, 31 g Prot, 77 mg Calc. *POINTS* value: *7*.

tip Most soups containing grains, such as barley, tend to thicken on standing, so add a little water when reheating.

MAKES 6 SERVINGS ☛

- 1 teaspoon **canola oil**
- 1 large **onion**, chopped
- 6 cups **reduced-sodium chicken broth**
- ¾ cup **pearl barley**, rinsed
- 3 **carrots**, thinly sliced
- 2 **parsnips**, peeled and diced
- ½ teaspoon **salt**
- ¼ teaspoon **freshly ground pepper**
- 1¼ pounds **skinless bone-in chicken thighs**
- 1 (10-ounce) **package cremini or baby bella mushrooms**, halved or quartered if large
- 1½ cups **frozen peas**
- 1½ tablespoons chopped **fresh thyme**, or 1½ teaspoons dried

☑ Mulligatawny Soup

Skinless boneless chicken chunks stay moist and tender when dropped into a simmering soup, such as this, for only a few minutes until they are just cooked through. Garam masala—an aromatic Indian blend of coriander and other sweet spices, dried chiles, and black pepper—is added towards the end of cooking to give fresh, spicy flavor to the soup. Cream is often stirred in to traditional mulligatawny, but plain yogurt makes a healthy alternative here.

1. Heat the oil in a Dutch oven over medium heat. Add the onion and garlic; cook, stirring occasionally, until golden, 7–10 minutes. Add the curry powder and cook, stirring constantly, until fragrant, about 1 minute.

2. Stir in the broth, potatoes, carrots, and cauliflower; bring to a boil. Reduce the heat and simmer, uncovered, until the vegetables are tender, about 15 minutes.

3. Add the chicken, cilantro, garam masala, and salt; return to a boil. Reduce the heat and simmer, covered, until the chicken is cooked through, about 5 minutes. Serve with the yogurt.

PER SERVING (scant 2 cups soup with 1 tablespoon yogurt): 309 Cal, 11 g Fat, 3 g Sat Fat, 0 g Trans Fat, 53 mg Chol, 835 mg Sod, 24 g Carb, 4 g Fib, 28 g Prot, 88 mg Calc. *POINTS* value: *6*.

MAKES 4 SERVINGS 🍳

- 2 teaspoons **canola oil**
- 1 **onion**, chopped
- 3 **garlic cloves**, minced
- 2 teaspoons **curry powder**
- 5 cups **reduced-sodium chicken broth**
- 2 medium **Yukon Gold potatoes**, peeled and diced (about 1½ cups)
- 2 **carrots**, diced (about 1 cup)
- 2 cups small **cauliflower florets**
- ¾ pound **skinless boneless chicken thighs**, cut into ½-inch chunks
- ¼ cup chopped **fresh cilantro or parsley**
- 1 teaspoon **garam masala**
- ¼ teaspoon **salt**
- ¼ cup **plain fat-free yogurt**

Matzo Ball Soup

Matzo ball soup is a favorite to serve at Passover. For this special occasion—if you have the time—we recommend using our Homemade Chicken Broth to best accommodate the delicate matzo balls.

1. To make the matzo balls, combine the matzo meal, salt, and pepper in a medium bowl. Combine the eggs, seltzer water, and oil in a small bowl. Add the egg mixture to the matzo meal mixture and stir until just blended. Cover and refrigerate, about 20 minutes.

2. Bring the broth, carrots, and shallot to a boil in a Dutch oven or large pot. Reduce the heat and simmer, covered, until the carrots are partially tender, about 5 minutes.

3. With wet hands, shape the matzo mixture into 12 balls. Carefully drop the balls, one at a time, into the simmering soup. Simmer, uncovered, until the matzo balls are cooked through, about 20 minutes, stirring in the peas during the last 5 minutes. Stir in the chicken and simmer until heated through, about 2 minutes. Stir in the parsley just before serving.

PER SERVING (1 cup soup with 2 matzo balls): 207 Cal, 6 g Fat, 2 g Sat Fat, 0 g Trans Fat, 99 mg Chol, 654 mg Sod, 16 g Carb, 2 g Fib, 20 g Prot, 40 mg Calc. *POINTS* value: *4*.

tip Matzo ball soup is often served without chicken. If you omit it here you will be cutting the per-serving *POINTS* value by 1.

MAKES 6 SERVINGS

½ cup **matzo meal**

¼ teaspoon **salt**

⅛ teaspoon **freshly ground pepper**

2 large **eggs**, lightly beaten

⅓ cup **seltzer water or water**

2 teaspoons **canola oil**

6 cups **Homemade Chicken Broth**, page 94 or canned reduced-sodium chicken broth

2 **carrots**, very thinly sliced

1 **shallot**, finely chopped

1 cup **fresh or frozen peas**, thawed

1½ cups shredded **cooked chicken breast**

2 tablespoons chopped **fresh parsley**

Tuxedo Meatball Soup with Escarole

Small bow tie pasta adds elegance to an everyday soup, chock-full of tender, savory meatballs, while escarole and basil add great color, texture, and flavor to this comforting Italian favorite.

1. Heat the oil in a nonstick Dutch oven over medium heat. Add the onion and garlic; cook, stirring frequently, until softened, about 5 minutes. Transfer half of the onion mixture to a medium bowl; set aside.

2. To the remaining onion mixture in the Dutch oven, add the broth, tomatoes, and pasta; bring to a boil. Reduce the heat and simmer, uncovered, about 2 minutes.

3. Meanwhile, to the onion mixture in the bowl, add the chicken, bread crumbs, egg, salt, and pepper; mix well. Shape into 24 meatballs.

4. Add the meatballs to the simmering mixture in the Dutch oven; return to a boil, stirring occasionally. Reduce the heat and simmer, partially covered, until the meatballs and pasta are cooked through, about 10 minutes. Gently stir in the escarole and basil; return to a simmer and cook, partially covered, about 3 minutes. Serve with the Parmesan cheese.

PER SERVING (1½ cups soup with 1 tablespoon cheese): 329 Cal, 9 g Fat, 3 g Sat Fat, 0 g Trans Fat, 86 mg Chol, 1020 mg Sod, 32 g Carb, 4 g Fib, 30 g Prot, 191 mg Calc. **POINTS** value: **7**.

MAKES 6 SERVINGS

- 2 teaspoons **olive oil**
- 1 large **onion**, chopped
- 3 **garlic cloves**, minced
- 5 cups **reduced-sodium chicken broth**
- 1 (28-ounce) **can peeled tomatoes**, broken up
- 1 cup small **egg bow ties or small elbow macaroni**
- 1 pound **ground skinless lean chicken breast**
- ⅓ cup **seasoned dry bread crumbs**
- 1 large **egg**, lightly beaten
- ½ teaspoon **salt**
- ¼ teaspoon **freshly ground pepper**
- 1 small bunch **escarole**, cleaned and chopped (about 8 cups)
- ¼ cup coarsely chopped **fresh basil**
- 6 tablespoons **shredded Parmesan cheese**

**Tuxedo Meatball Soup
with Escarole**

Caramelized Onion and
Chicken Soup au Gratin

Caramelized Onion and Chicken Soup au Gratin

Much like the well-loved French onion soup, this version is made heartier with the addition of chicken. Comté cheese (from the Franche-Comté region of France) crowns the soup deliciously. It is from the Gruyère family of cheeses and melts beautifully, making it perfect for gratins such as this.

1. Melt the butter and oil in a nonstick Dutch oven over medium-high heat. Add the onions and cook, stirring occasionally, until translucent, about 8 minutes. Reduce the heat to medium-low and cook, stirring occasionally, until golden brown and well softened, about 12 minutes.

2. Add the broth, wine, thyme, and pepper; bring to a boil. Reduce the heat and simmer, uncovered, about 25 minutes. Add the chicken and simmer until heated through, about 2 minutes.

3. Preheat the broiler. Place the bread rounds on a baking sheet and broil 5 inches from the heat until toasted, about 2 minutes on each side.

4. Place 4 bread rounds in each of 4 ovenproof soup bowls. Add the soup (a generous 2 cups in each bowl) and sprinkle evenly with the cheese.

5. Place the bowls on the baking sheet and broil 5 inches from the heat until the cheese melts and is golden brown, about 3 minutes.

PER SERVING (1 bowl): 360 Cal, 12 g Fat, 5 g Sat Fat, 0 g Trans Fat, 60 mg Chol, 1025 mg Sod, 29 g Carb, 3 g Fib, 31 g Prot, 211 mg Calc. *POINTS* value: *8*.

tip If you don't have ovenproof soup bowls, you can use small casserole dishes for broiling and serving this soup.

MAKES 4 SERVINGS

- 1 teaspoon **butter**

- 1 teaspoon **canola oil**

- 3 **Vidalia onions**, halved lengthwise, then thinly sliced crosswise

- 6 cups **reduced-sodium chicken broth**

- ¼ cup **dry white wine**

- 1 teaspoon chopped fresh **thyme**, or ¼ teaspoon dried

- ⅛ teaspoon **freshly ground pepper**

- 1½ cups chopped **cooked chicken breast**

- ½ (10-ounce) **French baguette**, cut into 16 rounds

- ½ cup (2 ounces) shredded **Comté, Gruyère, or Jarlsberg cheese**

South-of-the-Border Bean and Chicken Soup

It's surprising how spicy this soup is. If you like your food less fiery, cut the chipotle chili powder in half. If heat is your thing, by all means add more. You can use chicken breast or dark meat or a combination of the two. Be aware that dark meat has a few extra calories.

1. Heat the oil in a nonstick Dutch oven over medium heat. Add the onion and garlic; cook, stirring occasionally, until golden, about 8 minutes.

2. Add the broth, beans, tomatoes, corn, chili powder, and cumin; bring to a boil. Reduce the heat and simmer, covered, until the flavors are blended, about 5 minutes.

3. Add the chicken, cilantro, and lime juice; simmer, stirring frequently, until heated through, about 3 minutes. Serve the soup with the sour cream.

PER SERVING (1¾ cups soup with 1 tablespoon sour cream): 305 Cal, 5 g Fat, 1 g Sat Fat, 0 g Trans Fat, 30 mg Chol, 569 mg Sod, 44 g Carb, 10 g Fib, 23 g Prot, 130 mg Calc. *POINTS* value: *6*.

tip For really fresh cumin flavor, you can toast and grind your own cumin seeds. Here's how: Toast 2 tablespoons of cumin seeds in a small skillet over medium heat, tossing them frequently, until they are fragrant, 3 to 4 minutes. Transfer them to a plate to cool, then grind them in a spice grinder or coffee grinder. The ground, toasted cumin will keep in a sealed jar for 2 to 3 months.

MAKES 4 SERVINGS

- 1 teaspoon **canola oil**
- 1 large **onion**, chopped
- 2 **garlic cloves**, minced
- 2 cups **reduced-sodium chicken broth**
- 1 (15½-ounce) **can pinto beans**, rinsed and drained
- 1 (14½-ounce) **can diced tomatoes with green chiles** (no added sugar)
- 2 cups fresh or frozen **corn kernels**
- 1 teaspoon **chipotle chili powder**
- 1 teaspoon **ground cumin**
- 1 cup chopped **cooked chicken**
- 3 tablespoons chopped **fresh cilantro**
- 2 teaspoons **fresh lime juice**
- ¼ cup **fat-free sour cream**

Cornish Hens au Vin

Fresh small white or red onions (about ¾ inch in diameter) are often available in markets, loose or in net bags, during the holiday season and are a delicious alternative to frozen whole small onions. You might like to serve this dish with steamed fresh green beans.

1. Rub the hens with the garlic then sprinkle with the flour, salt, and pepper; set aside. Heat a large nonstick Dutch oven over medium-high heat. Add the bacon and cook, stirring occasionally, until browned, about 5 minutes; transfer to paper towels to drain.

2. Add the hens, 2 halves at a time, to the Dutch oven and cook over medium-high heat until lightly browned, about 3 minutes on each side. Transfer to a plate and set aside.

3. Add the shallots to the Dutch oven and cook, stirring frequently, until golden, about 3 minutes. Add the carrots and onions; cook, stirring occasionally, about 2 minutes. Add the broth, wine, and potatoes; bring to a boil, stirring to scrape the browned bits from the bottom of the Dutch oven. Return the hens to the Dutch oven. Reduce the heat and simmer, covered, about 20 minutes. Add the mushrooms and simmer until the hens are cooked through and the vegetables are tender, about 15 minutes longer. Stir in the parsley, marjoram, and bacon just before serving.

PER SERVING (½ Cornish hen with generous 1 cup vegetables and sauce): 321 Cal, 8 g Fat, 2 g Sat Fat, 0 g Trans Fat, 106 mg Chol, 555 mg Sod, 32 g Carb, 5 g Fib, 29 g Prot, 73 mg Calc. *POINTS* value: *6.*

tip Use poultry shears, regular kitchen scissors, or a meat cleaver to cut the hens in half. After pulling off the skin, be sure to remove as much of the excess fat as possible, then rinse and pat the hen halves dry with paper towels.

MAKES 4 SERVINGS ☛

- 2 (1¼-pound) **Cornish game hens**, halved and skinned

- 2 **garlic cloves**, minced

- 2 tablespoons **all-purpose flour**

- ½ teaspoon **salt**

- ¼ teaspoon **freshly ground pepper**

- 1 slice **thick-cut bacon**, chopped

- 3 **shallots**, chopped

- 3 **carrots**, cut into ½-inch chunks

- 1 cup frozen whole small **onions**

- 1 cup **reduced-sodium chicken broth**

- ⅓ cup **dry white wine**

- ¾ pound small **red or white potatoes**, scrubbed and cut in half

- ½ pound fresh **white or baby Portobello mushrooms**, halved

- ¼ cup chopped **fresh parsley**

- 2 tablespoons chopped **fresh marjoram**, or 2 teaspoons dried

Gingered Chicken and Sweet Potato Soup

A package of cooked, carved chicken pieces—available in most supermarkets in a variety of flavors such as Southwestern, lemon-pepper, and oven-roasted—makes this recipe unbelievably easy. We find the mildly flavored oven-roasted chicken is delicious in this sweet potato soup.

1. Heat the oil in a nonstick Dutch oven or large saucepan over medium-high heat. Add the onion and cook, stirring frequently, until softened, about 8 minutes. Add the garlic, ginger, and jalapeño pepper; cook, stirring constantly, until fragrant, about 2 minutes.

2. Add the sweet potatoes and 3 cups of the broth to the Dutch oven; bring to a boil. Reduce the heat and simmer, covered, until the potatoes are tender, about 20 minutes. Remove the pan from the heat and let the mixture cool for about 15 minutes.

3. Transfer the mixture in batches, if necessary, to a food processor or blender and puree. Return the soup to the Dutch oven. Stir in the remaining 3 cups broth, the chicken, and lime juice; bring to a boil. Reduce the heat and simmer until heated through, about 3 minutes. Divide the soup among 6 bowls, swirl a tablespoon of the half-and-half on top of each bowl, and sprinkle with the cilantro.

PER SERVING (1¾ cups soup with 1 tablespoon half-and-half): 275 Cal, 6 g Fat, 2 g Sat Fat, 0 g Trans Fat, 42 mg Chol, 112 mg Sod, 36 g Carb, 4 g Fib, 19 g Prot, 79 mg Calc. *POINTS* value: *5*.

MAKES 6 SERVINGS

- 2 teaspoons **olive oil**

- 1 large **Vidalia onion**, chopped

- 3 **garlic cloves**, minced

- 1½ tablespoons minced peeled **fresh ginger**

- 1 small **jalapeño pepper**, seeded and chopped (wear gloves to prevent irritation)

- 3 large (about 2 pounds) **sweet potatoes**, peeled and cut into 1-inch chunks

- 6 cups **low-sodium chicken broth**

- 1 (10-ounce) **package carved roasted skinless chicken breast pieces**

- 2 teaspoons **fresh lime juice**

- 6 tablespoons **fat-free half-and-half**

- 2 tablespoons chopped **fresh cilantro or parsley**

Gingered Chicken and
Sweet Potato Soup

Thai Chicken with Spinach

Thai Chicken with Spinach

Like many of us, you've probably enjoyed good Thai food in restaurants. Here's an easy way to enjoy unique Thai flavors at home. The tasty ingredients combine to make a subtle but distinctly Thai dish.

1. Bring the coconut milk, garlic, ginger, paprika, soy sauce, fish sauce, lime zest, and crushed red pepper to a boil in a large saucepan. Cook, stirring occasionally, over medium-high heat until the flavors are blended and the mixture thickens slightly, about 8 minutes.

2. Add the chicken; reduce the heat and simmer, covered, until just cooked through, about 10 minutes. Add the spinach, basil, oil, sugar, and salt; return to a boil. Reduce the heat and simmer, uncovered, stirring occasionally, until the spinach wilts, about 2 minutes. Serve with the rice and sprinkle with the coconut.

PER SERVING (1 piece chicken, scant ½ cup sauce, ½ cup rice, and 1 teaspoon coconut): 355 Cal, 10 g Fat, 6 g Sat Fat, 0 g Trans Fat, 68 mg Chol, 991 mg Sod, 36 g Carb, 4 g Fib, 31 g Prot, 78 mg Calc. *POINTS* value: *7*.

MAKES 4 SERVINGS

- 1 cup **light (reduced-fat) coconut milk**
- 2 **garlic cloves**, minced
- 2 tablespoons minced peeled **fresh ginger**
- 1 tablespoon **paprika**
- 1 tablespoon **reduced-sodium soy sauce**
- 1 tablespoon **Asian fish sauce** (nam pla)
- 1 teaspoon grated **lime zest**
- ¼ teaspoon **crushed red pepper**
- 4 (¼-pound) **skinless boneless chicken breast halves**
- 1 (6-ounce) bag washed **baby spinach leaves**
- 3 tablespoons chopped **fresh basil or cilantro**
- 1 teaspoon **Asian (dark) sesame oil**
- 1 tablespoon packed **brown sugar**
- ½ teaspoon **salt**
- 2 cups hot **cooked white rice**
- 4 teaspoons **unsweetened shredded coconut**

Braised Chicken with Peanut Sauce

Peanut butter stews are very popular in Africa and they can vary greatly in spiciness. Ours is quite mild with a little heat coming from the crushed red pepper and the curry powder. The curry powder also provides an interesting depth of flavor. You might like to add a package of frozen cut green beans to the stew, along with the peanut butter, to make it a complete meal.

1. Heat the oil in a nonstick Dutch oven over medium-high heat. Add the chicken and cook until lightly browned, about 2 minutes on each side. Transfer to a plate.

2. Add the onion and garlic to the Dutch oven and cook, stirring occasionally, until golden, about 7 minutes. Add the bell pepper, cumin, curry powder, oregano, and crushed red pepper; cook, stirring occasionally, until fragrant, about 2 minutes.

3. Add the broth and tomato paste; bring to a boil, stirring to scrape any browned bits from the bottom of the pan. Add the chicken. Reduce the heat and simmer, covered, until the chicken is cooked through, about 15 minutes.

4. Combine the peanut butter with some of the liquid from the Dutch oven; mix to form a smooth paste. Stir the peanut butter mixture into the Dutch oven and bring to a simmer, stirring constantly. Stir in the lemon juice. Serve with the rice and sprinkle with the peanuts.

PER SERVING (1 piece chicken, scant ½ cup sauce, ½ cup rice, and ½ tablespoon peanuts): 391 Cal, 12 g Fat, 2 g Sat Fat, 0 g Trans Fat, 68 mg Chol, 734 mg Sod, 38 g Carb, 3 g Fib, 33 g Prot, 55 mg Calc. *POINTS* value: *8*.

MAKES 6 SERVINGS ☛

- 2 teaspoons **olive oil**
- 6 (¼-pound) **skinless boneless chicken breast halves**
- 1 large **onion**, chopped
- 2 **garlic cloves**, minced
- 1 **yellow bell pepper**, seeded and chopped
- ½ teaspoon **ground cumin**
- ½ teaspoon **curry powder**
- ½ teaspoon **dried oregano**
- ¼ teaspoon **crushed red pepper**
- 1 cup **reduced-sodium chicken broth**
- ½ (6-ounce) **can tomato paste**
- ¼ cup **reduced-fat creamy peanut butter**
- 2 teaspoons **lemon juice**
- 3 cups hot **cooked white rice**
- 3 tablespoons chopped **unsalted dry-roasted peanuts**

Country Captain Chicken

This spicy favorite of the American south is said to have been brought from India by a sea captain involved in the spice trade. Try serving it with fragrant basmati rice (½ cup cooked will up the *POINTS* value by 2) and mango chutney (1 tablespoon will up the *POINTS* value by 1).

1. Heat 1 teaspoon of the oil in a nonstick Dutch oven over medium-high heat. Add the chicken and cook, turning occasionally, until browned, about 6 minutes; transfer to a bowl.

2. Add the remaining 1 teaspoon oil to the Dutch oven and set over medium-high heat. Add the onion, bell pepper, and garlic; cook, stirring frequently, until lightly browned, about 8 minutes. Add the flour, curry powder, salt, cinnamon, and allspice; cook, stirring constantly, until fragrant, about 1 minute.

3. Add the tomatoes, broth, currants, coconut, and the browned chicken; bring to a boil. Reduce the heat and simmer, covered, stirring once or twice, until the chicken is cooked through and the flavors are blended, about 15 minutes. Stir in the parsley and serve sprinkled with the almonds.

PER SERVING (scant 1 cup stew with 1 teaspoon almonds): 261 Cal, 12 g Fat, 4 g Sat Fat, 0 g Trans Fat, 59 mg Chol, 337 mg Sod, 15 g Carb, 3 g Fib, 23 g Prot, 69 mg Calc. *POINTS* value: **6.**

tip To toast almonds, place them in a small, dry skillet over medium-low heat. Cook, shaking the pan and stirring constantly, until lightly browned and fragrant, 3 to 4 minutes. Watch them carefully when toasting; almonds can burn quickly. Transfer the almonds to a plate to cool.

MAKES 6 SERVINGS

- 2 teaspoons **olive oil**
- 2¼ pounds **skinless boneless chicken thighs**, cut into 1-inch pieces
- 1 large **onion**, chopped
- 1 **green bell pepper**, seeded and chopped
- 3 **garlic cloves**, minced
- 2 tablespoons **all-purpose flour**
- 2–3 teaspoons **Madras curry powder**
- ¼ teaspoon **salt**
- ¼ teaspoon **cinnamon**
- ¼ teaspoon **ground allspice**
- 1 (14½-ounce) **can diced tomatoes**
- 1 cup **reduced-sodium chicken broth**
- ¼ cup **dried currants**
- 3 tablespoons **unsweetened shredded coconut**
- 2 tablespoons chopped **fresh parsley**
- 2 tablespoons **toasted sliced almonds**

Brunswick Drumstick Stew

Brunswick Stew originated in Brunswick county, Virginia, in the early 1800s, where it was first made with rabbit, onions, tomatoes, lima beans, corn, and okra. We substitute skinless chicken for rabbit and use super-convenient frozen vegetables and canned tomatoes. The one constant: This dish is just as delicious today as it was then.

1. Cook the bacon in a nonstick Dutch oven over medium heat until crisp, about 3 minutes. Drain the bacon on paper towels and set aside. Add the drumsticks to the Dutch oven and cook until lightly browned, about 2 minutes on each side; transfer the drumsticks to a plate.

2. Add the onion to the Dutch oven and cook over medium heat, stirring occasionally, until softened, about 8 minutes. Add the flour and cook, stirring constantly, until lightly browned, about 1 minute. Add the tomatoes, broth, Worcestershire sauce, salt, and pepper; bring to a boil, stirring constantly, until the sauce thickens slightly. Add the chicken. Reduce the heat and simmer, covered, about 20 minutes.

3. Add the lima beans, corn, and okra; return to a boil. Reduce the heat and simmer, covered, until the chicken is cooked through and the vegetables are tender, about 10 minutes. Stir in the bacon.

4. Meanwhile, toss the bread crumbs with the butter in a small bowl. Serve the stew sprinkled with the buttered crumbs.

PER SERVING (1 drumstick, scant 1 cup vegetables and sauce, and 1 tablespoon buttered crumbs): 284 Cal, 9 g Fat, 3 g Sat Fat, 0 g Trans Fat, 71 mg Chol, 570 mg Sod, 28 g Carb, 6 g Fib, 24 g Prot, 79 mg Calc. *POINTS* value: *6*.

MAKES 6 SERVINGS

- 2 slices **thick-cut bacon,** chopped
- 6 (5-ounce) **skinless chicken drumsticks**
- 1 **Vidalia onion,** chopped
- 1 tablespoon **all-purpose flour**
- 1 (14½-ounce) **can diced tomatoes**
- 1 cup **reduced-sodium chicken broth**
- 1 tablespoon **Worcestershire sauce**
- ½ teaspoon **salt**
- ⅛ teaspoon **freshly ground pepper**
- 1 (10-ounce) package **frozen baby lima beans**
- 1 (10-ounce) package **frozen corn kernels**
- 1 cup **frozen cut okra**
- 1 slice **whole-wheat bread,** made into crumbs
- 1 teaspoon melted **butter**

Brunswick
Drumstick Stew

Chicken Stew with Dumplings

Chicken Stew with Dumplings

Nothing is as likely to please and comfort the whole family as this everyday, gently flavored chicken and vegetable stew with dumplings. Tarragon goes particularly well with chicken, but you could substitute an equal amount of oregano or ½ teaspoon thyme, if you prefer.

1. To make the chicken stew, spray a nonstick Dutch oven with nonstick spray and set over medium-high heat. Add the chicken; sprinkle with the salt and pepper and cook, turning occasionally, until browned, about 6 minutes. Add the onion; cook, stirring frequently, until softened, about 4 minutes. Add the flour and cook, stirring constantly, until lightly browned, about 1 minute. Stir in the broth and potato; bring to a boil. Reduce the heat and simmer, covered, until the chicken and potatoes are cooked through, about 15 minutes. Stir in the peas and carrots and the tarragon; return to a boil. Reduce the heat and simmer 2 minutes.

2. Meanwhile, to make the dumplings, combine the flour, baking powder, and salt in a medium bowl. Add the milk, butter, and parsley; stir until a soft dough forms.

3. Drop the dough, by 8 rounded tablespoonfuls onto the simmering stew. Cover the Dutch oven and simmer about 8 minutes. Uncover and simmer until the dumplings have doubled in size and are cooked through, about 3 minutes longer.

PER SERVING (scant 1 cup stew with 2 dumplings): 414 Cal, 12 g Fat, 4 g Sat Fat, 0 g Trans Fat, 76 mg Chol, 1136 mg Sod, 42 g Carb, 4 g Fib, 33 g Prot, 202 mg Calc. *POINTS* value: *8*.

MAKES 4 SERVINGS ☛

- 1 pound **skinless boneless chicken thighs,** cut into 1-inch chunks
- ½ teaspoon **salt**
- ¼ teaspoon **freshly ground pepper**
- 1 **onion,** chopped
- 1 tablespoon **all-purpose flour**
- 2 cups **reduced-sodium chicken broth**
- 1 large (about 10-ounce) **Yukon Gold potato,** diced
- 1 cup **frozen peas and carrots**
- 1 teaspoon **dried tarragon**

Dumplings:

- ¾ cup **all-purpose flour**
- 1½ teaspoons **baking powder**
- ½ teaspoon **salt**
- ½ cup **fat-free milk**
- 2 teaspoons melted **butter**
- 2 tablespoons chopped **fresh parsley**

Chili Verde

Tomatillos are small green tomatoes with papery husks or coverings, which need to be removed. They can be found in Latin American markets and occasionally in the produce section of some large supermarkets. If you can't find fresh tomatillos, you can substitute 2 (11-ounce) cans tomatillos, drained and broken up. If using the canned version, omit the salt in this recipe—canned tomatillos have salt added. We add a teaspoon of sugar to this chili, since tomatillos have a tendency to be a little tart.

1. Heat the oil in a large nonstick Dutch oven over medium-high heat. Add the onion, bell peppers, garlic, and jalapeño pepper; cook, stirring frequently, until softened, about 10 minutes. Add the chicken and cook, turning occasionally, until browned, about 6 minutes.

2. Add the oregano, sugar, cumin, and salt; cook, stirring constantly, until fragrant, about 1 minute. Stir in the tomatillos, chiles, and broth; bring to a boil. Reduce the heat and simmer, uncovered, until the flavors are blended and the chili thickens slightly, about 20 minutes. Stir in the beans; return to a boil. Reduce the heat and simmer until heated through, about 1 minute.

3. Serve the chili in bowls; top with the sour cream and red onion and serve with the chips.

PER SERVING (scant 1 cup chili with 1 tablespoon each sour cream and red onion, and ¼ cup tortilla chips): 240 Cal, 5 g Fat, 1 g Sat Fat, 0 g Trans Fat, 35 mg Chol, 407 mg Sod, 30 g Carb, 7 g Fib, 20 g Prot, 88 mg Calc. *POINTS* value: *4*.

tip For a flavor boost stir in ¼ cup chopped fresh cilantro with the beans.

MAKES 6 SERVINGS

2 teaspoons **canola oil**

1 large **onion**, chopped

2 **green bell peppers**, seeded and chopped

3 **garlic cloves**, minced

1 **jalapeño pepper**, seeded and minced

¾ pound **skinless boneless chicken breast**, cut into ½-inch pieces

2 teaspoons **oregano**

1 teaspoon **sugar**

1 teaspoon **cumin**

¼ teaspoon **salt**

1 pound **fresh tomatillos**, chopped

1 (4½-ounce) **can chopped green chiles**

½ cup **reduced-sodium chicken broth**

1 (15½-ounce) **can cannellini beans**, rinsed and drained

6 tablespoons **fat-free sour cream**

6 tablespoons finely chopped **red onion**

1½ cups **baked tortilla chips**

Serious Chicken and Chorizo Chili

If you like your chili spicy, bordering on the incendiary, this recipe is for you. The combination of spicy chorizo sausage, milder ancho chile peppers and spicy, hot habañero chile peppers give this zesty dish a unique blend of flavors. Habañero and serrano chile peppers are very hot, but you can substitute the milder jalapeño pepper if you prefer. Wear gloves to prevent irritation when handling habañero chili peppers and be very careful not to touch your face, especially your eyes—hot peppers can burn and irritate.

1. Soak the ancho chiles in one cup boiling water in a bowl, about 30 minutes. Drain and discard the liquid; finely chop the chiles and set aside.

2. Heat a nonstick Dutch oven over medium heat. Add the chorizo and cook until browned, about 5 minutes. Add the onion, celery, and garlic; cook, stirring occasionally, until softened, about 6 minutes.

3. Add the tomatoes, chicken, corn, salt, cumin, sugar, habañero pepper, and the ancho chiles; bring to a boil. Reduce the heat and simmer, partially covered, until the flavors are blended and the chili thickens slightly, about 40 minutes. Stir in the cilantro.

4. Serve the chili in bowls with the rice; top with the sour cream and red onion.

PER SERVING (1 cup chili, ⅓ cup rice, and 1 tablespoon each sour cream and onion): 361 Cal, 14 g Fat, 5 g Sat Fat, 0 g Trans Fat, 64 mg Chol, 1100 mg Sod, 34 g Carb, 4 g Fib, 26 g Prot, 120 mg Calc. *POINTS* value: *8*.

tip Use only 2 ounces of chorizo sausage in this recipe and you'll reduce the per-serving *POINTS* value by 1.

MAKES 6 SERVINGS

- 2 **dried ancho chile peppers**
- ¼ pound **chorizo sausage**, thinly sliced
- 1 large **onion**, chopped
- 3 **celery stalks**, chopped
- 2 **garlic cloves**, chopped
- 1 (28-ounce) **can Italian peeled tomatoes**, broken up
- 1 pound **skinless boneless chicken thighs**, cut into ½-inch pieces
- 1 cup fresh or frozen **corn kernels**
- 1 teaspoon **salt**
- 1 teaspoon **cumin**
- ½ teaspoon **sugar**
- 1–2 **habañero chile peppers**, seeded and minced
- 2 tablespoons chopped **fresh cilantro**
- 2 cups hot **cooked white rice**
- 6 tablespoons **light sour cream**
- 6 tablespoons chopped **red onion or scallions**

Cincinnati 5-Way Chili

Greek immigrants opened the first chili parlor in Cincinnati many years ago and the idea caught on—in a big way! Today, traditional Cincinnati 5-way chili is served on an oval plate, on a bed of spaghetti, topped with chili, then warm red kidney beans, chopped raw onion, and shredded cheese. Cincinnati chili parlors also serve chili plain (1-way), with cheese (2-way), with onions and cheese (3-way), or with spaghetti, onions, and cheese (4-way). If you like a zestier chili, substitute hot salsa for the mild, and jalapeño Jack cheese for the regular Monterey Jack cheese.

1. Heat the oil in a nonstick Dutch oven over medium-high heat. Add the onion and garlic; cook, stirring frequently, until golden, about 7 minutes. Stir in the chili powder, cumin, and allspice; cook, stirring constantly, until fragrant, about 1 minute. Add the turkey and cook, breaking it up with a wooden spoon, until browned, about 5 minutes.

2. Add the salsa, tomato sauce, and chocolate; bring to a boil. Reduce the heat and simmer, partially covered, until the flavors are blended and the chili thickens slightly, about 20 minutes.

3. Meanwhile, cook the spaghetti according to package directions omitting the salt, if desired; drain. Put the beans in a microwavable bowl; cover and microwave on High until heated through, about 2 minutes. Divide the spaghetti among 6 plates. Spoon the chili evenly over the spaghetti, top with the beans, then sprinkle with the onion and cheese.

PER SERVING (about ⅔ cup spaghetti, ¾ cup chili, ¼ cup beans, and 1 tablespoon each onion and cheese): 385 Cal, 5 g Fat, 2 g Sat Fat, 0 g Trans Fat, 55 mg Chol, 934 mg Sod, 54 g Carb, 7 g Fib, 31 g Prot, 124 mg Calc. *POINTS* value: *7*.

MAKES 6 SERVINGS

- 1 teaspoon **canola oil**
- 1 **onion**, chopped
- 3 **garlic cloves**, chopped
- 1 tablespoon **chili powder**
- 1 teaspoon **ground cumin**
- ¼ teaspoon **ground allspice**
- 1 pound **ground skinless lean turkey breast**
- 1 (16-ounce) **jar mild chunky salsa**
- 1 (8-ounce) **can tomato sauce**
- ½ ounce **bittersweet chocolate**, grated
- ½ pound **spaghetti**
- 1 (15½-ounce) **can red kidney beans**, rinsed and drained
- 6 tablespoons chopped **red onion**
- 6 tablespoons **shredded reduced-fat Monterey Jack cheese**

Turkey and Vegetable Chili

Here's a basic chili, stretched with plenty of vegetables and seasoned with chili powder and jalapeño pepper. Jalapeño peppers are the most popular chile peppers used in North America. They are medium-hot and readily available in the produce section of most supermarkets.

1. Heat the oil in a nonstick Dutch oven over medium heat. Add the turkey and cook, breaking it up with a wooden spoon, until browned, about 5 minutes. Add the onion, garlic, and jalapeño pepper; cook, stirring frequently, until softened and fragrant, about 4 minutes.

2. Add the tomatoes, water, eggplant, zucchini, chili powder, cumin, salt, sugar, and oregano; bring to a boil. Reduce the heat and simmer, covered, stirring occasionally, until the vegetables are well softened and the flavors are blended, about 40 minutes.

3. Divide the chili among 6 shallow bowls; top evenly with the sour cream and a few sliced scallions. Serve the chili with the chips, lettuce, and tomatoes in bowls on the side.

PER SERVING (generous 1 cup chili, 1 tablespoon sour cream, ¼ cup tortilla chips, and vegetables): 231 Cal, 6 g Fat, 2 g Sat Fat, 0 g Trans Fat, 56 mg Chol, 683 mg Sod, 25 g Carb, 6 g Fib, 22 g Prot, 108 mg Calc. *POINTS* value: *4*.

MAKES 6 SERVINGS

- 1 tablespoon **olive oil**
- 1 pound **ground skinless lean turkey breast**
- 1 large **onion**, chopped
- 2 **garlic cloves**, minced
- 1 **jalapeño pepper**, seeded and minced
- 1 (28-ounce) **can crushed tomatoes**
- ½ cup **water**
- 1 small **eggplant**, diced
- 2 **zucchini**, diced
- 1–2 teaspoons **chili powder**
- 1 teaspoon **cumin**
- 1 teaspoon **salt**
- 1 teaspoon **sugar**
- ½ teaspoon **oregano**
- 6 tablespoons **light sour cream**
- 4 **scallions**, thinly sliced
- 1½ cups **baked tortilla chips**
- 2 cups shredded **romaine lettuce**
- 2 cups chopped **tomatoes**

Corn Bread–Topped Red Chili

Chilis can range in spiciness from gentle warmth to five-alarm; this falls between the two, but with an added smoky flavor from chipotle chili powder—one of the new ground chili powders available in the gourmet section of the spice aisle.

1. Heat the oil in a nonstick Dutch oven over medium-high heat. Add the onion, bell pepper, garlic, and jalapeño pepper; cook, stirring frequently, until softened, about 8 minutes. Add the chicken and cook, turning occasionally, until lightly browned, about 8 minutes.

2. Add the chili powder and oregano; cook, stirring constantly, until fragrant, about 1 minute. Stir in the tomatoes; bring to a boil. Reduce the heat and simmer, covered, until the flavors are blended and the chili thickens slightly, about 20 minutes. Rinse and drain the beans, then stir into the chili and cook until heated through. Transfer the mixture to a 2-quart shallow baking dish.

3. Preheat the oven to 400°F.

4. To make the corn bread, combine the cornmeal, flour, baking powder, sugar, and salt in a medium bowl. Combine the milk and egg substitute in a small bowl. Stir the milk mixture into the cornmeal mixture until just blended. Stir in the cheese. Spoon the batter in 6 spoonfuls on top of the casserole. Bake, uncovered, until the chili is bubbly and the corn bread is golden, about 15 minutes.

PER SERVING (about ¾ cup chili with 1 piece corn bread): 304 Cal, 6 g Fat, 2 g Sat Fat, 0 g Trans Fat, 39 mg Chol, 670 mg Sod, 40 g Carb, 7 g Fib, 23 g Prot, 203 mg Calc. *POINTS* value: *6*.

tip You can make the chili, without the topping, up to 2 days ahead of time, and keep it in the refrigerator. When you're ready to serve it, reheat the chili, make the corn bread mixture, spoon it on top of the hot chili, and bake as directed above.

MAKES 6 SERVINGS

2 teaspoons **canola oil**

1 large **onion**, chopped

1 **red bell pepper**, seeded and chopped

2 **garlic cloves**, minced

1 **red jalapeño pepper**, seeded and chopped

¾ pound **skinless boneless chicken breast**, cut into ½-inch pieces

2 teaspoons **chipotle chili powder**

1 teaspoon **oregano**

1 (28-ounce) **can Italian peeled tomatoes**

1 (15½-ounce) **can red kidney beans**

⅔ cup **yellow cornmeal**

⅓ cup **all-purpose flour**

2 teaspoons **baking powder**

1 teaspoon **sugar**

¼ teaspoon **salt**

¼ cup **fat-free milk**

¼ cup **fat-free egg substitute**

¼ cup (1 ounce) **shredded sharp cheddar cheese**

Corn Bread–Topped Red Chili

Easy Chili con Queso

Here's a simple and mild chili for the whole family. You can adjust the amount of chili seasoning you use to suit even the youngest child. If your family enjoys spicy food, try substituting jalapeño Jack cheese for the Monterey Jack.

1. Heat the oil in a large nonstick saucepan over medium heat. Add the onion and cook, stirring frequently, until softened, about 5 minutes. Add the chili seasoning and cook, stirring constantly, until fragrant, about 1 minute. Add the tomatoes; bring to a boil. Reduce the heat and simmer, uncovered, until the flavors are blended, about 3 minutes. Add the corn and chicken; return to a simmer and cook, about 2 minutes.

2. Meanwhile, spray a 7-inch nonstick skillet with nonstick spray and set over medium-high heat. Add the tortillas, 1 at a time, and cook until lightly toasted, 1–2 minutes on each side. Cut each tortilla into 4 triangles.

3. Remove the saucepan from the heat and add the cheese. Stir until the cheese melts. Serve the chili with the toasted tortilla triangles.

PER SERVING (1 cup chili with 4 tortilla triangles): 290 Cal, 9 g Fat, 3 g Sat Fat, 0 g Trans Fat, 40 mg Chol, 459 mg Sod, 36 g Carb, 4 g Fib, 19 g Prot, 179 mg Calc. *POINTS* value: *6*.

tip If you don't want to take the time to toast tortillas, you can serve this chili with low-fat baked tortilla chips.

MAKES 4 SERVINGS

- 1 teaspoon **canola oil**
- 1 large **onion**, chopped
- 1–2 teaspoons **chili seasoning mix**
- 1 (14½-ounce) **can diced tomatoes**
- 2 cups fresh or frozen **corn kernels**
- 1 cup chopped **cooked chicken**
- 4 (6-inch) **flour tortillas**
- ½ cup (2 ounces) **shredded reduced-fat Monterey Jack cheese**

Chili Pronto

Canned and frozen products plus already cooked chicken and packaged tortilla chips make this chili a breeze to assemble. Chili and taco seasonings—both convenient and tasty blends of chile peppers, salt, cumin, oregano, and garlic—can be used interchangeably. They can be found in 1 to 2 ounce packages in the Mexican aisle of supermarkets.

1. Combine the tomatoes, bell peppers, mixed vegetables, chiles, and chili seasoning in a nonstick saucepan; bring to a boil. Reduce the heat and simmer, uncovered, until the flavors are blended and the vegetables are softened, about 10 minutes. Add the chicken and cook, stirring occasionally, until heated through, about 3 minutes.

2. Divide the chili among 4 bowls. Top with the sour cream and scallions and serve with the chips.

PER SERVING (scant 1 cup chili, 1 tablespoon sour cream, and ½ cup tortilla chips): 235 Cal, 4 g Fat, 1 g Sat Fat, 0 g Trans Fat, 46 mg Chol, 635 mg Sod, 30 g Carb, 6 g Fib, 20 g Prot, 124 mg Calc. *POINTS* value: *4*.

MAKES 4 SERVINGS

- 1 (14½-ounce) **can chili-style chunky tomatoes**

- 1 (10-ounce) package **frozen diced green bell peppers**

- 1 (9-ounce) package **frozen mixed vegetables**

- 1 (4½-ounce) **can chopped mild green chiles**

- 1 tablespoon **chili or taco seasoning mix**

- 1½ cups chopped cooked **chicken**

- ¼ cup **fat-free sour cream**

- 2 **scallions** (white and light green portions only), thinly sliced

- 2 cups **baked tortilla chips**

Skillet and Wok Dinners

CHAPTER FIVE

Hunter-Style Chicken

Hunter-Style Chicken

"Hunter-style" refers to a dish cooked with onions, peppers, mushrooms, and tomatoes. You might be more familiar with its Italian name—cacciatore, which means hunter. It's delicious over cooked pasta (1 cup cooked whole-wheat pasta per serving will increase the **POINTS** value by 3).

1. Sprinkle the chicken with the salt and ground pepper. Heat 2 teaspoons of the oil in a large nonstick skillet over medium-high heat. Add the chicken and cook until browned, 3–4 minutes on each side. Transfer the chicken to a plate and set aside.

2. Add the remaining 1 teaspoon oil to the same skillet and heat over medium-high heat. Add the onion and garlic; cook, stirring occasionally, until softened, about 3 minutes. Add the bell peppers, mushrooms, and celery; cook, stirring occasionally, until softened, 5–6 minutes. Return the chicken to the skillet; add the pasta sauce and stir to coat. Bring the mixture to a boil. Reduce the heat and simmer, covered, until the chicken is cooked through and the vegetables are tender, about 20 minutes.

PER SERVING (1 piece chicken with scant ½ cup vegetables and sauce): 203 Cal, 8 g Fat, 2 g Sat Fat, 0 g Trans Fat, 48 mg Chol, 510 mg Sod, 16 g Carb, 2 g Fib, 18 g Prot, 33 mg Calc. **POINTS** value: *4*.

tip For a richer, mellower flavor, make this recipe a day or two before serving and keep it in the refrigerator. The standing time allows the flavors to develop. When you're ready to serve it, simply reheat in a large, nonstick skillet, covered, over medium-low heat until heated through, about 15 minutes. Be sure to stir it occasionally to avoid scorching the sauce.

MAKES 8 SERVINGS ☞

1 (2½–3-pound) **chicken**, cut into 8 pieces and skinned

½ teaspoon **salt**

¼ teaspoon **freshly ground pepper**

3 teaspoons **olive oil**

1 **onion**, chopped

3 **garlic cloves**, minced

2 **assorted color bell peppers**, seeded and cut into ½-inch pieces

¼ pound **fresh white mushrooms**, sliced

1 **celery stalk**, chopped

1 (1-pint) container refrigerated **fresh pasta sauce**

Braised Chicken Breasts with Dried Figs and Apricots

Calimyrna figs have grown in Turkey for centuries and were first introduced to California in 1880, where they had their first successful crop in 1899. Full of chewy sweetness, these dried figs add a honey-like flavor to this sauce.

1. Combine the flour, ½ teaspoon of the salt, and ⅛ teaspoon of the pepper in a zip-close plastic bag. Add the chicken and shake to coat.

2. Heat the oil in a large nonstick skillet over medium-high heat. Add the chicken and cook until browned, 3–4 minutes on each side. Add the shallot and garlic; cook, stirring constantly, until fragrant, about 1 minute. Add the wine, stirring to scrape the brown bits from the skillet. Add the broth, figs, apricots, sugar, tarragon, and the remaining ½ teaspoon salt and ⅛ teaspoon pepper; bring to a boil. Reduce the heat and simmer, covered, until the chicken is cooked through, 20–25 minutes. Transfer the chicken to a serving plate. Increase the heat to high and bring the sauce to a boil. Cook until slightly thickened, about 5 minutes. Serve the sauce over the chicken.

PER SERVING (1 piece chicken with ⅓ cup sauce): 358 Cal, 8 g Fat, 2 g Sat Fat, 0 g Trans Fat, 74 mg Chol, 728 mg Sod, 42 g Carb, 6 g Fib, 30 g Prot, 96 mg Calc. *POINTS* value: *7.*

tip You can make this chicken and sauce one or two days before serving and keep it refrigerated—the flavors of the fruits will blend and permeate the chicken, making for an even more flavorful dish.

MAKES 4 SERVINGS ☛

- 1½ tablespoons **all-purpose flour**
- 1 teaspoon **salt**
- ¼ teaspoon **freshly ground pepper**
- 2 (¾-pound) **bone-in chicken breast halves,** skinned and cut in half the short way
- 1 tablespoon **olive oil**
- 1 large **shallot,** chopped
- 2 **garlic cloves,** minced
- ¾ cup **dry white wine**
- ½ cup **reduced-sodium chicken broth**
- 8 dried **Calimyrna figs,** halved
- ½ cup **dried apricots**
- 1 tablespoon **sugar**
- 2 teaspoons **dried tarragon**

Chipotle-Marinated Chicken Breasts with Chimichurri

Chimichurri is a tangy Argentinean sauce made with olive oil, herbs, garlic, vinegar, and salt. It is commonly served with meats but it is also delicious with vegetables. The sauce goes very well with this smoky, chipotle-flavored chicken. You can find chipotle chilis en adobo in cans in specialty-food stores and in the ethnic section of most supermarkets.

1. Combine 2 of the garlic cloves, the chipotles, honey, and cumin in a zip-close plastic bag; add the chicken. Squeeze out the air and seal the bag; turn to coat the chicken. Refrigerate, turning the bag occasionally, at least 4 hours or up to overnight.

2. Sprinkle the chicken with ½ teaspoon of the salt. Heat 1 teaspoon of the oil in a large nonstick skillet over medium-high heat. Add the chicken and cook until browned, 3–4 minutes on each side. Add the broth and bring to a boil. Reduce the heat and simmer, covered, about 10 minutes. Uncover the chicken and increase the heat to medium. Cook, turning twice, until the chicken is cooked through, 12–15 minutes. Discard any liquid left in the skillet.

3. Meanwhile to make the chimichurri sauce, combine the remaining 1 garlic clove, 3 teaspoons oil, and ¼ teaspoon salt with the vinegar and cilantro; mix well. Serve the chimichurri with the chicken.

PER SERVING (1 piece chicken with 2 tablespoons chimichurri): 198 Cal, 7 g Fat, 2 g Sat Fat, 0 g Trans Fat, 74 mg Chol, 387 mg Sod, 4 g Carb, 0 g Fib, 27 g Prot, 20 mg Calc. *POINTS* value: *5*.

tip To store the leftover chipotle chiles en adobo, transfer them to a small jar or airtight container and refrigerate for up to a month.

MAKES 8 SERVINGS

- 3 **garlic cloves**, minced
- 2 **chipotles en adobo**, finely chopped
- 2 tablespoons **honey**
- 1 teaspoon **ground cumin**
- 2 (¾-pound) **bone-in chicken breast halves**, skinned and cut in half the short way
- ¾ teaspoon **salt**
- 4 teaspoons **olive oil**
- 1 cup **reduced-sodium chicken broth**
- ¼ cup **white-wine vinegar**
- 3 tablespoons chopped **fresh cilantro**

Simmered Chicken with Soy-Ginger Sauce

Chicken breasts are infused with flavor while they gently simmer, then sit for a few minutes, in this fragrant broth. The soy-ginger sauce adds a bright finish. If you have leftover chicken and soy-ginger sauce, cut the cold chicken into cubes and toss with the sauce, a little low-fat mayonnaise, and chopped red bell pepper for an Asian-influenced chicken salad.

1. Heat 2 teaspoons of the oil in a large nonstick skillet over medium-high heat. Add the chicken and cook until browned, 3–4 minutes on each side. Transfer the chicken to a plate.

2. Add 4 of the scallions and the 1 tablespoon ginger to the skillet and cook, stirring constantly, until fragrant, about 1 minute. Add the broth and 2 tablespoons of the soy sauce; bring to a boil. Reduce the heat and simmer, covered, about 4 minutes. Add the chicken and return to a gentle simmer; cook, covered, about 12 minutes. Turn off the heat and let the chicken sit in the liquid about 10 minutes longer. With a slotted spoon, lift the chicken from the liquid onto a serving plate. Discard the liquid.

3. Combine the remaining 1 teaspoon oil, 1 scallion, 2 teaspoons ginger, 1 tablespoon soy sauce, the vinegar, and honey in a small bowl; mix well. Serve with the chicken.

PER SERVING (1 piece chicken with 1½ tablespoons sauce): 205 Cal, 6 g Fat, 1 g Sat Fat, 0 g Trans Fat, 74 mg Chol, 299 mg Sod, 10 g Carb, 0 g Fib, 28 g Prot, 22 mg Calc. *POINTS* value: *5*.

MAKES 4 SERVINGS 🍳

3 teaspoons **Asian (dark) sesame oil**

2 (¾-pound) **bone-in chicken breast halves**, skinned and cut in half the short way

5 **scallions**, finely chopped

1 tablespoon + 2 teaspoons grated peeled **fresh ginger**

1 cup **reduced-sodium chicken broth**

3 tablespoons **reduced-sodium soy sauce**

3 tablespoons **rice vinegar**

5 teaspoons **honey**

Chicken Sauté with Lemon-Caper Sauce

This delicately flavored chicken and sauce is delicious served over wide egg noodles. A cup of cooked noodles per serving will increase the *POINTS* value by 3.

1. Sprinkle the chicken with ¼ teaspoon of the salt and ⅛ teaspoon of the pepper.

2. Melt the 1 tablespoon butter in a large nonstick skillet over medium-high heat. Add the chicken and cook until lightly browned, about 2 minutes on each side. Add the broth, lemon juice, capers, and oregano; bring to a simmer. Reduce the heat and simmer, turning the chicken once to coat with the sauce, until the chicken is cooked through, about 2 minutes.

3. Remove the skillet from the heat and swirl in the remaining 1 teaspoon butter, ¼ teaspoon salt, and ⅛ teaspoon pepper.

PER SERVING (1 piece chicken with generous 1 tablespoon sauce): 182 Cal, 8 g Fat, 3 g Sat Fat, 0 g Trans Fat, 79 mg Chol, 477 mg Sod, 1 g Carb, 0 g Fib, 26 g Prot, 19 mg Calc. *POINTS* value: *4*.

tip If you don't have a large enough skillet to brown the chicken without overcrowding the pan, you may want to brown it in two batches. Then simply return all of the chicken to the skillet with the broth and seasonings and continue with the recipe.

MAKES 4 SERVINGS

4 (¼-pound) **skinless boneless chicken breast halves**, pounded to ⅛-inch thickness

½ teaspoon **salt**

¼ teaspoon **freshly ground pepper**

1 tablespoon + 1 teaspoon **unsalted butter**

½ cup **reduced-sodium chicken broth**

¼ cup **fresh lemon juice**

1 tablespoon drained **capers**

½ teaspoon **dried oregano**

☑ Chicken and Mixed Mushroom Sauté

Old-fashioned mushroom sauces would often include butter or cream, but now that intensely flavored wild mushrooms are readily available, you no longer have to rely on those vices to deliver great flavor. We use skinless boneless chicken breast halves in this recipe, but it would be equally delicious with turkey cutlets. Steamed spinach would make an excellent accompaniment.

1. Heat the oil in a large nonstick skillet over medium-high heat. Add the chicken and cook until browned, about 3 minutes on each side. Transfer the chicken to a plate.

2. Add the mushrooms, garlic, shallot, and thyme to the skillet. Cook, stirring occasionally, until the mushrooms are golden and softened, about 8 minutes. Add the broth, chicken, salt, and pepper; bring to a boil. Reduce the heat to medium-low and simmer, turning the chicken occasionally, until the chicken is cooked through, about 8 minutes.

3. Transfer the chicken to a serving plate; cover to keep warm. Increase the heat to high and bring the mushroom mixture to a boil. Cook until the liquid is reduced to about 1¼ cups, about 4 minutes. Spoon the mushroom mixture over the chicken.

Per serving (1 piece chicken with 5 tablespoons mushroom mixture): 186 Cal, 6 g Fat, 1 g Sat Fat, 0 g Trans Fat, 63 mg Chol, 581 mg Sod, 6 g Carb, 1 g Fib, 27 g Prot, 21 mg Calc. *POINTS* value: *4*.

tip If sliced shiitake mushrooms are available at your supermarket, by all means use them (you will need about a 4-ounce package). You can also use a similar size package of assorted sliced wild mushrooms, which can include oyster, baby bella, and shiitake mushrooms.

MAKES 4 SERVINGS ☞

1 tablespoon **olive oil**

4 (¼-pound) **skinless boneless chicken breast halves**

½ pound **fresh white mushrooms**, sliced

1 (5-ounce) package **fresh shiitake mushrooms**, stems discarded, caps sliced

2 **garlic cloves**, minced

1 medium **shallot**, chopped

½ teaspoon **dried thyme**

1½ cups **reduced-sodium chicken broth**

½ teaspoon **salt**

¼ teaspoon **freshly ground pepper**

Pan-Grilled Jerk Chicken Breasts

Chicken breasts marinate in an eclectic combination of scallions, bay leaves, jalapeño pepper, vinegar, allspice, thyme, and cayenne, then are grilled until tender and juicy.

1. Put the scallions, bay leaves, jalapeños, garlic, oil, vinegar, allspice, thyme, salt, and cayenne in a small food processor; pulse until a thick paste forms. Place the paste in a zip-close plastic bag; add the chicken. Squeeze out the air and seal the bag; turn to coat the chicken. Refrigerate, turning the bag occasionally, at least 2 hours or overnight.

2. Spray a ridged grill pan or large nonstick skillet with nonstick spray and set over medium heat. Add the chicken and cook, turning occasionally, until cooked through, 10–12 minutes.

PER SERVING (1 chicken breast half): 160 Cal, 6 g Fat, 1 g Sat Fat, 0 g Trans Fat, 63 mg Chol, 202 mg Sod, 2 g Carb, 1 g Fib, 23 g Prot, 26 mg Calc. *POINTS* value: *4*.

MAKES 4 SERVINGS

3 **scallions**, chopped

2 **bay leaves**, crumbled

1 to 2 **jalapeño peppers**, seeded and chopped (wear gloves to prevent irritation)

1 to 2 **garlic cloves**, chopped

1 tablespoon **canola oil**

2 teaspoons **apple-cider vinegar**

½ teaspoon **ground allspice**

½ teaspoon **dried thyme**, crumbled

¼ teaspoon **salt**

¼ teaspoon **cayenne**

4 (¼-pound) **skinless boneless chicken breast halves**

Wild Mushroom and Goat Cheese–Stuffed Chicken Breasts

You can make the filling and stuff the chicken breasts the day before and keep them covered in the refrigerator. Serve with rice cooked in broth, then spinkled with parsley or thyme and toasted sliced almonds, and some steamed asparagus.

1. Heat 2 teaspoons of the oil in a large nonstick skillet over medium-high heat. Add the garlic; cook until fragrant, about 30 seconds. Add the mushrooms, herbes de Provence, ¼ teaspoon of the salt, and ⅛ teaspoon of the pepper; cook, stirring occasionally, until the mushrooms are golden, 5–6 minutes. Transfer the mixture to a bowl; add the goat cheese and stir until combined. Let the mixture cool completely.

2. Make a pocket in the side of each chicken breast by inserting a sharp paring knife into the thickest part, then gently cutting back and forth until a small chamber has opened in the side. Do not cut through to the back or the sides of the breasts. Enlarge the pockets gently with your fingers. Fill each pocket with 2 tablespoons of the mushroom-cheese mixture.

3. Wipe out the skillet. Add the remaining 1 teaspoon oil and heat over medium heat. Add the chicken and sprinkle with the remaining ½ teaspoon salt and ⅛ teaspoon pepper. Cook until the chicken is browned on the outside and cooked through, 7–8 minutes on each side. Cut each chicken breast into 4 or 5 slices, transfer to a serving plate, and keep warm.

4. Add the shallot to the skillet and cook until fragrant, about 30 seconds. Add the broth and sherry; bring to a boil. Reduce the heat and simmer about 3 minutes. Meanwhile, dissolve the cornstarch in the cold water in a small bowl. Stir the cornstarch mixture into the skillet and cook, stirring constantly, until the mixture bubbles and thickens, about 1 minute. Serve the sauce over the chicken.

PER SERVING (1 stuffed chicken breast with 3 tablespoons sauce): 252 Cal, 10 g Fat, 4 g Sat Fat, 0 g Trans Fat, 75 mg Chol, 652 mg Sod, 7 g Carb, 1 g Fib, 30 g Prot, 52 mg Calc. **POINTS** value: **6.**

MAKES 4 SERVINGS ☛

- 3 teaspoons **extra-virgin olive oil**
- 2 **garlic cloves**, minced
- ½ pound **fresh shiitake mushrooms**, stems discarded, caps finely chopped
- ¾ teaspoon **herbes de Provence**
- ¾ teaspoon **salt**
- ¼ teaspoon **freshly ground pepper**
- 2 ounces **reduced-fat goat cheese**, softened
- 4 (¼-pound) **skinless boneless chicken breast halves**
- 1 **shallot**, chopped
- ¾ cup **reduced-sodium chicken broth**
- 6 tablespoons **dry sherry**
- 1 teaspoon **cornstarch**
- 2 teaspoons cold **water**

Wild Mushroom and Goat
Cheese–Stuffed Chicken Breasts

Honey-Balsamic Chicken

Lightly pounding the chicken breasts helps to tenderize them and indirectly adds flavor by exposing more surface area of the chicken to the honey-balsamic marinade. To ease up on the cleanup, sandwich the chicken breast halves between sheets of plastic wrap or wax paper before pounding with a meat mallet or the base of a heavy saucepan.

1. Combine the chicken, vinegar, lemon juice, honey, and 2 teaspoons of the oil in a bowl; toss well to coat and set aside for 15 minutes.

2. Heat the remaining 2 teaspoons oil in a large nonstick skillet over medium-high heat. Add the garlic and cook, stirring constantly, until fragrant, about 15 seconds. Add the chicken and sprinkle with ¼ teaspoon of the salt and ⅛ teaspoon of the pepper. Cook until lightly browned, 1–2 minutes on each side.

3. Add the broth, wine, raisins, and the remaining ¼ teaspoon salt and ⅛ teaspoon pepper to the skillet; bring to a boil. Reduce the heat and simmer, covered, until the chicken is cooked through, 10–12 minutes. Transfer the chicken to a serving plate and keep warm. Bring the mixture in the skillet to a boil over high heat and cook until the sauce reduces to about ½ cup, about 4 minutes. Serve the chicken with the sauce.

PER SERVING (1 piece chicken with 2 tablespoons sauce): 247 Cal, 8 g Fat, 2 g Sat Fat, 0 g Trans Fat, 68 mg Chol, 422 mg Sod, 16 g Carb, 1 g Fib, 26 g Prot, 25 mg Calc. *POINTS* value: *5*.

MAKES 4 SERVINGS 🍳

- 4 (¼-pound) **skinless boneless chicken breast halves**, lightly pounded
- 1 tablespoon **balsamic vinegar**
- 1 tablespoon **fresh lemon juice**
- 1 tablespoon **honey**
- 4 teaspoons **olive oil**
- 1 **garlic clove**, minced
- ½ teaspoon **salt**
- ¼ teaspoon **freshly ground pepper**
- ½ cup **reduced-sodium chicken broth**
- ½ cup **dry white wine**
- ⅓ cup **golden raisins**

Thai Red Curry Chicken

Thai cooks are fond of combining spicy, pungent, and sweet flavors with meats, poultry, and fish. In this easy skillet dinner, the spicy ginger and red curry paste balance the pungent fish sauce and sweet brown sugar. Steamed brown basmati rice, with its nutty flavor and chewy texture, makes a satisfying accompaniment to the richly flavored, saucy chicken (½ cup cooked rice per serving will increase the *POINTS* value by 2).

1. Heat the oil in a large nonstick skillet over medium-high heat. Sprinkle the chicken with the salt and add to the skillet. Cook the chicken until browned on the outside and cooked through, 4–5 minutes on each side. Transfer the chicken to a plate and keep warm.

2. Reduce the heat under the skillet to medium then add the scallions, ginger, and garlic; cook, stirring constantly, until fragrant, about 30 seconds. Add the coconut milk, curry paste, fish sauce, sugar, and lime juice; bring to a boil. Reduce the heat and simmer, stirring occasionally, until the mixture begins to thicken, 5–6 minutes. Add the chicken and simmer until heated through, about 1 minute longer. Serve, sprinkled with the cilantro, if using.

PER SERVING (1 piece chicken with 2 tablespoons sauce): 223 Cal, 10 g Fat, 3 g Sat Fat, 0 g Trans Fat, 68 mg Chol, 368 mg Sod, 10 g Carb, 2 g Fib, 27 g Prot, 33 mg Calc. *POINTS* value: *5*.

tip Thai red curry paste is quite spicy. For a tamer version of this dish, use only 1 teaspoon.

MAKES 8 SERVINGS

- 2 teaspoons **canola oil**
- 4 (¼-pound) **skinless boneless chicken breast** halves, lightly pounded
- ¼ teaspoon **salt**
- 2 **scallions**, chopped
- 2 teaspoons grated peeled **fresh ginger**
- 2 **garlic cloves**, minced
- ¾ cup **light (reduced-fat) coconut milk**
- 1 tablespoon **Thai red curry paste**
- 1 tablespoon **Asian fish sauce** (nam pla)
- 1 tablespoon packed **dark brown sugar**
- 2 teaspoons **fresh lime juice**
- 2 tablespoons chopped **fresh cilantro** (optional)

Kung Pao Chicken

Kung Pao Chicken

This Chinese favorite gets a burst of exquisite flavor from sake (Japanese rice wine), hoisin sauce, fresh ginger, and crushed red pepper. Our version is moderately spicy, but, traditionally, this dish can be quite fiery. Simply add extra crushed red pepper if you like your recipes fiery.

1. Combine the broth, sake, hoisin sauce, soy sauce, cornstarch, and honey in a bowl; mix well.

2. Heat a large nonstick skillet or wok over medium-high heat until a drop of water sizzles. Pour in 2 teaspoons of the oil and swirl to coat the pan, then add the chicken. Stir-fry until the chicken is cooked through, 4–5 minutes. Transfer the chicken to a plate.

3. Add the remaining 1 teaspoon oil to the skillet and swirl to coat the pan. Add the scallions, ginger, and crushed red pepper; stir-fry until fragrant, about 30 seconds. Add the water chestnuts and peanuts; stir-fry until heated through, about 1 minute. Add the broth mixture and cook, stirring constantly, until the mixture bubbles and thickens, about 1 minute. Add the chicken and cook until heated through, about 1 minute longer.

PER SERVING (¾ cup): 345 Cal, 12 g Fat, 2 g Sat Fat, 0 g Trans Fat, 68 mg Chol, 593 mg Sod, 29 g Carb, 2 g Fib, 30 g Prot, 48 mg Calc. *POINTS* value: *8*.

tip A pound of sea scallops or large deveined shrimp would make a nice alternative to the chicken.

MAKES 8 SERVINGS

- ½ cup **reduced-sodium chicken broth**
- ⅓ cup **sake or mirin** (rice wine)
- 3 tablespoons **hoisin sauce**
- 2 tablespoons **reduced-sodium soy sauce**
- 2 tablespoons **cornstarch**
- 2 tablespoons **honey**
- 3 teaspoons **Asian (dark) sesame oil**
- 1 pound **skinless boneless chicken breasts**, cut into ½-inch pieces
- 2 **scallions**, chopped
- 1 tablespoon grated peeled **fresh ginger**
- ¼ teaspoon **crushed red pepper**
- 1 (8-ounce) **can sliced water chestnuts**, drained
- 1¼ cup **unsalted dry-roasted peanuts**

Mediterranean Lemon Chicken with Artichokes and Orzo

Fresh lemon juice really makes this dish. For additional lemon flavor, and if you have time, grate the zest from the lemon before you juice it and stir the zest into the orzo just before serving. Or, serve the dish with lemon wedges.

1. Cook the orzo according to package directions, omitting the salt, if desired; drain and transfer to a large bowl. Stir in the feta cheese and olives; cover and keep warm.

2. Sprinkle the chicken with the salt and pepper. Spray a large nonstick skillet with nonstick spray and set over medium-high heat. Add the chicken and cook until browned, 3–4 minutes on each side. Transfer the chicken to a plate.

3. Add the artichoke hearts, garlic, and oregano to the skillet; cook, stirring constantly, until fragrant, about 1 minute. Return the chicken to the skillet and add the broth and lemon juice; bring to a boil. Reduce the heat and simmer, covered, until the chicken is cooked through, about 20 minutes.

4. Transfer the chicken to a plate. Pour 1 cup of the artichoke sauce over the orzo and toss well. Divide the orzo among 6 plates and place 1 chicken leg on each plate. Serve with the remaining sauce.

PER SERVING (1 chicken leg, ½ cup orzo mixture, and scant ¼ cup sauce): 365 Cal, 10 g Fat, 4 g Sat Fat, 0 g Trans Fat, 91 mg Chol, 864 mg Sod, 32 g Carb, 5 g Fib, 36 g Prot, 127 mg Calc. *POINTS* value: *7*.

MAKES 6 SERVINGS

6 ounces **orzo**

2 ounces **reduced-fat feta cheese**

8 **pitted kalamata olives**, sliced

6 (½-pound) **whole chicken legs**, skinned

¾ teaspoon **salt**

¼ + ⅛ teaspoon **freshly ground pepper**

1 (1¼-pound) **can artichoke hearts** in brine, drained and quartered

3 **garlic cloves**, minced

1½ teaspoons **fresh oregano** leaves, or ½ teaspoon dried

1 cup **reduced-sodium chicken broth**

2 tablespoons **fresh lemon juice**

Mediterranean Lemon Chicken
with Artichokes and Orzo

☑ Osso Buco–Style Chicken

Italian osso buco is traditionally prepared with veal shanks that are braised with tomatoes, vegetables, and garlic. We discovered this dish also works beautifully with whole chicken legs—which is much easier on the pocketbook. The flavor of the chicken and sauce only improves when made ahead (refrigerate, covered, for up to 3 days), so it's a great choice for entertaining. Serve with whole-wheat spaghetti and a simple green salad.

1. Heat the oil in a large deep nonstick skillet or Dutch oven over medium-high heat. Add 3 chicken legs and cook until browned, about 4 minutes on each side. Transfer the chicken to a plate. Repeat with the remaining chicken.

2. Add the onion, carrot, celery, garlic, oregano, and crushed red pepper to the skillet. Cook, stirring occasionally, until the vegetables begin to soften, about 4 minutes. Stir in the broth, stirring constantly to scrape the brown bits from the bottom of the pan. Stir in the tomatoes, salt, and chicken; bring to a boil. Reduce the heat to medium-low and simmer, covered, until the chicken is cooked through and very tender, about 40 minutes.

PER SERVING (1 whole chicken leg with ½ cup sauce): 267 Cal, 11 g Fat, 3 g Sat Fat, 0 g Trans Fat, 96 mg Chol, 522 mg Sod, 13 g Carb, 3 g Fib, 31 g Prot, 73 mg Calc. *POINTS* value: *6*.

tip Gremolata, a mixture of parsley, lemon zest, and garlic, is the traditional garnish for osso buco. It would also make a terrific *POINTS*-free topper for this chicken dish. To prepare, combine 2 tablespoons chopped fresh parsley, 1 garlic clove, minced, and ½ teaspoon grated lemon zest in a small bowl.

MAKES 6 SERVINGS ☞

- 2 teaspoons **extra-virgin olive oil**

- 6 (7-ounce) **whole chicken legs**, skinned

- 1 **onion**, chopped

- 1 **carrot**, chopped

- 1 **celery stalk**, chopped

- 3 **garlic cloves**, minced

- 1 teaspoon **dried oregano**

- ⅛ teaspoon **crushed red pepper**

- ½ cup **reduced-sodium chicken broth**

- 1 (28-ounce) **can crushed tomatoes** (no added sugar)

- ½ teaspoon **salt**

☑ Chicken Tagine

Tagine is a stew-like dish from Morocco that's typically prepared with meat or poultry and vegetables, garlic, and olives. Seasonings can vary— in this version we opt for a refreshing blend of fresh ginger, saffron, lemon juice, and cilantro. Try serving with couscous (½ cup cooked couscous will up the *POINTS* value by 2).

1. Heat the oil in a large nonstick skillet over medium-high heat. Add the chicken and cook, stirring occasionally, until lightly browned, about 3 minutes. Transfer the chicken to a plate.

2. Add the okra, onion, garlic, ginger, and saffron to the skillet; cook, stirring occasionally, until the onion starts to soften, about 5 minutes. Stir in the broth and lemon juice; bring to a boil. Reduce the heat, stir in the chicken, and simmer, covered, until the chicken is cooked through, about 7 minutes. Uncover and cook until the liquid is slightly reduced, about 3 minutes longer. Remove the skillet from the heat; stir in the olives, cilantro, salt, and pepper.

PER SERVING (1 cup): 207 Cal, 8 g Fat, 1 g Sat Fat, 0 g Trans Fat, 63 mg Chol, 568 mg Sod, 10 g Carb, 3 g Fib, 25 g Prot, 85 mg Calc. *POINTS* value: *4.*

tip Saffron comes either powdered or in threads. While the threads are more costly, powdered saffron loses its flavor more readily and is often blended with less expensive powders such as turmeric. Buying powdered saffron won't save money in the long run, because more will be needed for the same flavor impact, so the threads are definitely worth the investment.

MAKES 4 SERVINGS ☛

1 tablespoon **sunflower oil**

1 pound **skinless boneless chicken breast**, cut into 1-inch pieces

1 (10-ounce) package **frozen whole okra**

1 **onion**, chopped

3 **garlic cloves**, minced

1 tablespoon minced peeled **fresh ginger**

¼ teaspoon **saffron threads**, lightly crushed

¾ cup **reduced-sodium chicken broth**

2 tablespoons **fresh lemon juice**

12 **pimiento-stuffed olives**, halved

3 tablespoons chopped **fresh cilantro**

¼ teaspoon **salt**

¼ teaspoon **freshly ground pepper**

Tomato and Red Wine–Braised Chicken Legs

Fresh orange zest adds piquancy to this deliciously flavored stew, which is easily doubled for a crowd or to freeze half for another day. The chicken and sauce will keep in the refrigerator for up to 3 days or in the freezer for up to 3 months. To reheat, simmer in a covered skillet, with a little water if necessary, until the chicken is thoroughly heated through, about 15 minutes. If frozen, let the chicken and sauce thaw overnight in the refrigerator before reheating.

1. Sprinkle the chicken with ½ teaspoon of the salt and ⅛ teaspoon of the pepper. Heat the oil in a large nonstick skillet over medium-high heat. Add the chicken and cook until browned, 3–4 minutes on each side. Transfer the chicken to a plate.

2. Add the garlic to the skillet and cook, stirring constantly, until fragrant, about 30 seconds. Add the tomatoes and wine; bring to a boil. Reduce the heat and simmer, uncovered, about 5 minutes. Return the chicken to the skillet and add the remaining ¼ teaspoon salt and ⅛ teaspoon pepper; return to a boil. Reduce the heat and simmer, covered, until the chicken is cooked through and pulls easily from the bones, 35–40 minutes.

3. Transfer the chicken to a plate; cover with foil to keep warm. Return the tomato mixture in the skillet to a boil. Reduce the heat to medium and cook, uncovered, until slightly thickened, about 8 minutes. Return the chicken to the skillet, then stir in the parsley and orange zest.

4. Meanwhile, cook the pasta according to package directions, omitting the salt, if desired; drain. Divide the pasta among 4 plates, then top with a chicken leg and the sauce.

PER SERVING (1 cup pasta, 1 chicken leg, and ½ cup sauce): 437 Cal, 11 g Fat, 3 g Sat Fat, 0 g Trans Fat, 132 mg Chol, 828 mg Sod, 47 g Carb, 4 g Fib, 37 g Prot, 119 mg Calc.
POINTS value: *9*.

MAKES 4 SERVINGS

- 4 (½-pound) **whole chicken legs**, skinned
- ¾ teaspoon **salt**
- ¼ teaspoon **freshly ground pepper**
- 1 teaspoon **olive oil**
- 2 **garlic cloves**, minced
- 1 (28-ounce) **can Italian-seasoned crushed tomatoes**
- ½ cup **dry red wine**
- 3 tablespoons chopped **fresh parsley**
- 2 teaspoons grated **orange zest**
- 8 ounces **pappardelle or extra-wide noodles**

Drumstick Osso Buco

Osso buco is a rich stew traditionally made with veal shanks. We substitute lean skinless chicken drumsticks for the veal in this recipe, but we keep the deliciously flavorful vegetables and garlicky wine broth. You could use skinless chicken thighs instead of drumsticks. Whether drumsticks or thighs, be sure to use bone-in chicken for the best flavor.

1. Sprinkle the chicken with ½ teaspoon of the salt and ⅛ teaspoon of the pepper. Heat 1 teaspoon of the oil in a large nonstick skillet over medium-high heat. Add the chicken and cook until browned, 3–4 minutes on each side. Transfer the chicken to a plate.

2. Heat the remaining 1 teaspoon oil in the same skillet. Add the onion, carrot, celery, and garlic; cook, stirring frequently, until the vegetables begin to soften, about 5 minutes. Add the wine and simmer 30 seconds. Add the tomatoes, basil, oregano, and the remaining ¼ teaspoon salt and ⅛ teaspoon pepper; bring to a boil. Reduce the heat and simmer, covered, about 10 minutes. Add the chicken and simmer, covered, until the chicken is cooked through, about 25 minutes. Serve with the rice.

PER SERVING (½ cup rice, 2 drumsticks, and ½ cup sauce): 317 Cal, 7 g Fat, 2 g Sat Fat, 0 g Trans Fat, 102 mg Chol, 985 mg Sod, 32 g Carb, 3 g Fib, 30 g Prot, 87 mg Calc. *POINTS* value: *6*.

MAKES 8 SERVINGS

- 8 (¼-pound) **skinless chicken drumsticks**
- ¾ teaspoon **salt**
- ¼ teaspoon **freshly ground pepper**
- 2 teaspoons **extra-virgin olive oil**
- 1 **onion**, finely chopped
- 1 **carrot**, finely chopped
- 1 **celery stalk**, finely chopped
- 3 **garlic cloves**, minced
- ½ cup **dry red wine**
- 1 (14½-ounce) **can diced tomatoes**
- ½ teaspoon **dried basil**
- ½ teaspoon **dried oregano**
- 2 cups hot **cooked white rice**

☑ Cajun Chicken and Okra Stir-Fry

Okra plants were brought to the New World during the slave trade. It has become a southern staple and is frequently battered and deep-fried, or used in gumbo or stir-fries, as both a thickening agent and a vegetable.

1. Heat a large nonstick skillet or wok over medium-high heat until a drop of water sizzles. Pour in 1 teaspoon of the oil and swirl to coat the pan, then add the chicken, salt, and pepper. Stir-fry until the chicken is browned and cooked through, 4–5 minutes. Transfer the chicken to a plate.

2. Add the remaining 1 teaspoon oil to the same skillet and swirl to coat the pan. Add the bell pepper, onion, celery, and garlic; stir-fry until crisp-tender, about 2 minutes. Add the okra and stir-fry until tender, about 4 minutes. Add the chicken, tomatoes, and oregano; bring to a boil. Reduce the heat and simmer until the mixture thickens slightly, about 4 minutes longer.

PER SERVING (1 cup): 222 Cal, 6 g Fat, 2 g Sat Fat, 0 g Trans Fat, 94 mg Chol, 508 mg Sod, 15 g Carb, 4 g Fib, 27 g Prot, 111 mg Calc. *POINTS* value: *4*.

tip Cornbread makes a terrific accompaniment. One portion of most cornbread mixes with increase the *POINTS* value by 3.

MAKES 4 SERVINGS

- 2 teaspoons **olive oil**
- 1 pound **skinless boneless chicken thighs**, cut into 1-inch pieces
- ¼ teaspoon **salt**
- ⅛ teaspoon **freshly ground pepper**
- 1 **green bell pepper**, seeded and chopped
- 1 **onion**, chopped
- 1 **stalk celery**, chopped
- 2 **garlic cloves**, minced
- 1 cup **frozen okra**, cut into ½-inch pieces
- 1 (14½-ounce) **can diced tomatoes with jalapeños** (no added sugar)
- 1 teaspoon **dried oregano**

Cajun Chicken and Okra Stir-Fry

Korean-Style Chicken

Korean-Style Chicken

Korean food is often associated with spicy-hot dishes. This traditional marinade does have a bit of a kick, but it also gives a sweet-tart flavor to the chicken. If you want more heat, serve this with *kimchi*, the extremely hot and pungent fermented vegetables offered in Korean restaurants and available in Asian markets.

1. Combine the scallions, mirin, vinegar, sugar, soy sauce, 1 teaspoon of the oil, and the crushed red pepper in a zip-close plastic bag; add the chicken. Squeeze out the air and seal the bag; turn to coat the chicken. Refrigerate, turning the bag occasionally, at least 2 hours or up to overnight.

2. Lift the chicken from the marinade and pat dry with paper towels. Discard the marinade. Heat the remaining 1 teaspoon oil in a large nonstick skillet over medium heat. Add the chicken and cook until lightly browned, about 2 minutes on each side. Add the broth; bring to a boil. Reduce the heat and simmer, covered, turning once, until the chicken is cooked through and the liquid is syrupy, about 10 minutes. Turn the chicken to coat with the liquid.

PER SERVING (1 chicken thigh): 211 Cal, 11 g Fat, 3 g Sat Fat, 0 g Trans Fat, 71 mg Chol, 190 mg Sod, 2 g Carb, 0 g Fib, 25 g Prot, 29 mg Calc. *POINTS* value: *5*.

tip For added flavor, prick the chicken all over with the tip of a sharp knife and marinate it for 24 hours.

MAKES 8 SERVINGS

- 2 **scallions**, chopped
- 3 tablespoons **mirin** (rice wine)
- 2 tablespoons **rice vinegar**
- 2 tablespoons **sugar**
- 2 tablespoons **reduced-sodium soy sauce**
- 2 teaspoons **Asian (dark) sesame oil**
- ½ teaspoon **crushed red pepper**
- 4 (¼-pound) **skinless boneless chicken thighs**
- ½ cup **reduced-sodium chicken broth**

Safe Cooking and Serving Tips

According to the National Chicken Council, many foodborne illnesses in the home are caused by cooking or reheating foods at too low a temperature for too short a time, and keeping foods at room temperature for too long, especially in the summer months. For more information about poultry safety, visit the Web site eatchicken.com. Meantime, follow these simple guidelines.

• Always cook chicken thoroughly, not medium or rare. We recommend using an instant-read meat thermometer. The internal temperature should reach 180°F for whole chicken or turkey and bone-in thighs and drumsticks, 170°F for bone-in breasts, and 165°F for boneless parts, and burgers and meatloaves made from ground chicken or turkey. For burgers, insert the thermometer into the side of the burger.

• Check that the chicken is cooked through by piercing it with a fork; the juices should run clear— not pink. This tip works best if not using a thermometer (in casseroles and skillet meals for example).

• Never leave cooked chicken at room temperature for more than 2 hours. If not eaten immediately, cooked chicken should be kept either hot or refrigerated.

• Don't stuff an uncooked bird in advance—stuff it just before you place it in the oven.

• Transfer the stuffing of a cooked, stuffed chicken or turkey to a separate container before refrigerating.

• Cooked, cut-up chicken is at its best refrigerated for no longer than 2 days—whole cooked chicken, 3 days.

• Reheat leftovers the smart way: Cover to retain moisture and be sure that the chicken is heated all the way through.

• Bring gravies to a rolling boil before serving.

Sunshine Chicken Sauté

This delightful dish is a fusion of Tex-Mex flavors and traditional Chinese stir-fry techniques. You can serve it with warmed flour tortillas (a 6 to 7-inch fat-free flour tortilla will up the *POINTS* value by 1) or with rice (½ cup cooked rice will up the *POINTS* value by 2). A simple green salad makes a perfect side.

1. Combine the chicken, cumin, and ½ teaspoon of the salt in a medium bowl; mix well.

2. Heat a large nonstick skillet or wok over medium-high heat until a drop of water sizzles. Pour in 2 teaspoons of the oil and swirl to coat the pan, then add the chicken. Stir-fry until the chicken is browned and cooked through, 4–5 minutes. Transfer the chicken to a plate.

3. Add the remaining 1 teaspoon oil to the same skillet and swirl to coat the pan. Add the garlic and jalapeño; stir-fry until fragrant, about 30 seconds. Add the mixed vegetables and stir-fry until crisp-tender, about 1 minute. Add the orange juice, lime juice, and remaining ¼ teaspoon salt; cook, stirring occasionally, until the vegetables are tender, about 2 minutes. Add the chicken and cook until heated through, about 1 minute.

PER SERVING (1 cup): 261 Cal, 13 g Fat, 3 g Sat Fat, 0 g Trans Fat, 71 mg Chol, 530 mg Sod, 10 g Carb, 3 g Fib, 26 g Prot, 68 mg Calc. *POINTS* value: *6*.

MAKES 4 SERVINGS

- 1 pound **skinless boneless chicken thighs**, cut into ½-inch pieces

- 1 teaspoon **ground cumin**

- ¾ teaspoon **salt**

- 3 teaspoons **canola oil**

- 3 **garlic cloves**, minced

- 1 **jalapeño pepper**, seeded and finely chopped (wear gloves to prevent irritation)

- 1 (12-ounce) **bag mixed vegetables** for stir-fry (carrots, snow peas, red bell pepper, and broccoli)

- ⅔ cup **orange juice**

- 2 tablespoons **fresh lime juice**

Moo Shu Chicken

Moo shu dishes—savory meat (usually pork) and vegetables rolled in a thin pancake—are a favorite in Chinese cuisine. We've substituted chicken for the pork and conveniently stuff the filling into flour tortillas. If you are so inclined, a crêpe or thin pancake would make this recipe a touch more authentic.

1. Heat a large nonstick skillet or wok over medium-high heat until a drop of water sizzles. Pour in the oil and swirl to coat the pan, then add the chicken, onion, ginger, and garlic. Stir-fry until the chicken is browned and cooked through, 4–5 minutes.

2. Add the cabbage, mushrooms, and carrot; stir-fry until the carrot is crisp-tender, about 5 minutes. Add the hoisin sauce and cook, stirring constantly, until heated through, about 1 minute longer. Remove the skillet from the heat.

3. Heat the tortillas according to package directions. Spoon ½ cup of the chicken mixture on each tortilla. Roll up the tortillas and serve at once.

PER SERVING (1 filled tortilla): 400 Cal, 11 g Fat, 3 g Sat Fat, 0 g Trans Fat, 71 mg Chol, 732 mg Sod, 43 g Carb, 4 g Fib, 31 g Prot, 127 mg Calc. *POINTS* value: *8.*

MAKES 4 SERVINGS

1 teaspoon **canola oil**

1 pound **skinless boneless chicken thighs,** cut into thin strips

1 small **onion,** thinly sliced

1 tablespoon grated peeled **fresh ginger**

2 **garlic cloves,** minced

¼ small head **napa cabbage,** shredded, about 2 cups

¼ pound **fresh white mushrooms,** sliced

1 **carrot,** cut into matchstick-thin sticks

3 tablespoons **hoisin sauce**

4 (8-inch) **fat-free flour tortillas**

Moo Shu Chicken

Arroz con Pollo

Arroz con pollo is a traditional dish that varies in its components from one region to another throughout Spain, the Caribbean, and Latin America. It is a popular one-pot dinner made with simple, flavorful ingredients. Chicken, rice, onion, garlic, and tomatoes are the common base and a variety of vegetables such as bell peppers, peas, and olives can be added according to family traditions.

1. Sprinkle the chicken with ¼ teaspoon of the salt and ⅛ teaspoon of the pepper. Heat 1 teaspoon of the oil in a large nonstick skillet over medium-high heat. Add the chicken and cook until browned, 3–4 minutes on each side. Transfer the chicken to a plate.

2. Heat the remaining 1 teaspoon oil in the same skillet. Add the bell peppers, onion, and garlic; cook, stirring frequently, until the vegetables begin to soften, about 7 minutes. Add the rice and saffron; cook, stirring constantly, about 1 minute. Add the tomatoes, broth and chicken; bring to a boil, stirring occasionally. Reduce the heat and simmer, covered, until the liquid is absorbed and the chicken is cooked through, about 20 minutes. Stir in the peas, olives, and remaining ½ teaspoon salt and ⅛ teaspoon pepper. Cook, stirring occasionally, until heated through, about 1 minute. Remove the skillet from the heat and let stand, covered, about 5 minutes.

PER SERVING (1 chicken thigh with 1⅓ cups rice mixture): 450 Cal, 12 g Fat, 3 g Sat Fat, 0 g Trans Fat, 57 mg Chol, 1042 mg Sod, 56 g Carb, 5 g Fib, 28 g Prot, 100 mg Calc. *POINTS* value: *9*.

MAKES 4 SERVINGS ☛

- 4 (5-ounce) **skinless bone-in chicken thighs**
- ¾ teaspoon **salt**
- ¼ teaspoon **freshly ground pepper**
- 2 teaspoons **extra-virgin olive oil**
- 2 **assorted color bell peppers**, seeded and chopped
- 1 **onion**, chopped
- 3 **garlic cloves**, minced
- 1 cup **long-grain white rice**
- ½ teaspoon **saffron threads**, lightly crushed
- 1 (14½-ounce) **can diced tomatoes**
- 1 cup **reduced-sodium chicken broth**
- 1 cup **frozen peas**
- 12 small **stuffed green olives**

Spiced Chicken-Currant Patties with Yogurt Sauce

Make this a totally Greek-café experience and serve these aromatic, slightly sweet patties in pita bread (½ large pita would up the **POINTS** value by 1) with slices of red onion and tomato.

1. To make the yogurt sauce, combine the yogurt, garlic, the 1½ teaspoons oil, ¼ teaspoon of the salt, and ⅛ teaspoon of the pepper in a small bowl.

2. Combine the chicken, bread crumbs, currants, tomato paste, coriander, oregano, cinnamon, and remaining ½ teaspoon salt and ⅛ teaspoon pepper in a large bowl; mix well. Shape the mixture into 4 (½-inch-thick) patties.

3. Heat the remaining 1 tablespoon oil in a large nonstick skillet over medium heat. Add the patties and cook until browned and an instant-read thermometer inserted in the side of a patty registers 165°F, about 6 minutes on each side. Serve the patties with the yogurt sauce.

PER SERVING (1 patty with 2 tablespoons yogurt sauce): 274 Cal, 9 g Fat, 2 g Sat Fat, 0 g Trans Fat, 69 mg Chol, 671 mg Sod, 18 g Carb, 1 g Fib, 28 g Prot, 113 mg Calc. **POINTS** value: **6**.

MAKES 4 SERVINGS

- ½ cup **plain fat-free yogurt**
- ½ **garlic clove**, minced
- 1½ teaspoon + 1 tablespoon **extra-virgin olive oil**
- ¾ teaspoon **salt**
- ¼ teaspoon **freshly ground pepper**
- 1 pound **ground skinless lean chicken breast**
- ⅓ cup plain dry **bread crumbs**
- ¼ cup **dried currants**
- 2 tablespoons **tomato paste**
- 1 teaspoon **coriander**
- 1 teaspoon **dried oregano**
- ½ teaspoon **cinnamon**

Sausage and Penne with
Vodka-Tomato Sauce

Sausage and Penne with Vodka-Tomato Sauce

Vodka sauce is traditionally made with heavy cream, which is very high in fat. We've lightened the dish by making it with a little milk and Romano cheese. If you can't find Mediterranean-style chicken sausage you might like to try artichoke-and-garlic chicken sausage in this recipe.

1. Cook the pasta according to package directions, omitting the salt, if desired.

2. Meanwhile, heat 1 teaspoon of the oil in a large nonstick skillet over medium-high heat. Add the sausage and cook, turning occasionally, until browned, about 4 minutes. Transfer the sausage to a plate.

3. Meanwhile, heat the remaining 2 teaspoons oil in the same skillet. Add the onion and garlic; cook, stirring frequently, until softened, about 3 minutes. Add the tomatoes and vodka; bring to a boil. Reduce the heat and simmer, uncovered, about 2 minutes. Add the sausage and milk; simmer until heated through, about 2 minutes. Remove the skillet from the heat and stir in the cheese. Serve with the pasta.

PER SERVING (1 cup pasta with scant ½ cup sauce): 235 Cal, 8 g Fat, 2 g Sat Fat, 0 g Trans Fat, 26 mg Chol, 574 mg Sod, 28 g Carb, 2 g Fib, 12 g Prot, 83 mg Calc. *POINTS* value: *5*.

MAKES 6 SERVINGS

- 6 ounces **penne pasta**
- 3 teaspoons **extra-virgin olive oil**
- 1 (9-ounce) package fully cooked **Mediterranean-style chicken sausage**, cut into ½-inch pieces
- 1 **onion**, chopped
- 2 **garlic cloves**, minced
- 1 (14½-ounce) **can Italian-seasoned diced tomatoes**
- 1 tablespoon **vodka**
- 3 tablespoons **fat-free milk**
- 3 tablespoons grated **Romano cheese**

Chicken, Shrimp, and Kielbasa Paella

Originating in Valencia, this famous saffron-infused rice dish is rich with chicken, seafood, sausages, and flavorful seasonings. If you like paella, it may be worth investing in a paella pan—a shallow round pan with splayed sides and two brightly colored red or green handles—to cook and serve this delicious favorite.

1. Heat the oil in a large nonstick skillet over medium-high heat. Add the chicken and cook until browned, 3–4 minutes on each side. Transfer the chicken to a plate. Add the shrimp to the skillet and cook until browned, $1\frac{1}{2}$ minutes on each side; transfer to a separate plate. Add the kielbasa to the skillet and cook until browned, about 3 minutes on each side; transfer to the plate with the chicken.

2. Add the onion, bell pepper, and garlic to the skillet; cook, stirring occasionally, until softened, about 4 minutes. Add the tomatoes, broth, rice, olives, saffron, and cayenne; bring to a boil. Add the chicken and kielbasa; return to a boil. Reduce the heat and simmer, covered, about 15 minutes.

3. Add the shrimp to the skillet and simmer, covered, until the chicken and kielbasa are cooked through and the shrimp are opaque in the center, about 7 minutes. Fluff the mixture with a fork and stir in the cilantro, if using.

PER SERVING ($1\frac{1}{3}$ cups): 299 Cal, 8 g Fat, 2 g Sat Fat, 0 g Trans Fat, 94 mg Chol, 587 mg Sod, 27 g Carb, 2 g Fib, 29 g Prot, 59 mg Calc. *POINTS* value: *6*.

MAKES 6 SERVINGS ☞

- 1 tablespoon **extra-virgin olive oil**
- 2 ($\frac{3}{4}$-pound) **bone-in chicken breast halves**, skinned and cut in half the short way
- $\frac{1}{2}$ pound **extra-large shrimp**, peeled and deveined
- $\frac{1}{4}$ pound **turkey kielbasa**, cut into $\frac{1}{4}$-inch-thick slices
- 1 **onion**, chopped
- 1 **green bell pepper**, seeded and chopped
- 3 **garlic cloves**, minced
- 1 ($14\frac{1}{2}$-ounce) **can diced tomatoes**, drained
- $1\frac{1}{4}$ cups **reduced-sodium chicken broth**
- $\frac{3}{4}$ cup **long-grain white rice**
- 8 small **stuffed green olives**, sliced
- $\frac{1}{2}$ teaspoon **saffron threads**, crushed
- $\frac{1}{8}$ teaspoon **cayenne**
- 3 tablespoons chopped **fresh cilantro** (optional)

Turkey Paprikash

You'll want to soak up every bit of the wonderful sauce in this dish, so you might like to serve it over noodles ($\frac{1}{2}$ cup per serving will increase the *POINTS* value by 2) or serve with a slice of high-fiber bread (1 slice will increase the *POINTS* value by 1).

1. Sprinkle the turkey with $\frac{1}{2}$ teaspoon of the salt and $\frac{1}{8}$ teaspoon of the pepper. Melt 2 teaspoons of the butter in a large nonstick skillet over medium-high heat. Add the turkey and cook, turning occasionally, until browned and cooked through, about 5 minutes. Transfer the turkey to a plate.

2. Melt the remaining 2 teaspoons butter in the same skillet. Add the celery, carrots, onion, and garlic; cook, stirring occasionally, until softened, about 6 minutes. Add the flour and cook, stirring constantly, until the flour is golden, about 1 minute. Stir in the broth, wine, paprika, and remaining $\frac{1}{4}$ teaspoon salt and $\frac{1}{8}$ teaspoon pepper; bring to a boil. Reduce the heat and simmer, uncovered, until the mixture bubbles and thickens and the vegetables are tender, about 5 minutes. Add the turkey and simmer, stirring occasionally, until heated through, about 2 minutes. Remove the skillet from the heat and stir in the sour cream.

PER SERVING (1 cup): 250 Cal, 6 g Fat, 3 g Sat Fat, 0 g Trans Fat, 86 mg Chol, 732 mg Sod, 15 g Carb, 2 g Fib, 32 g Prot, 113 mg Calc. *POINTS* value: *5.*

MAKES 4 SERVINGS ☛

- 1 pound **skinless boneless turkey breast**, cut into $\frac{1}{2}$-inch pieces
- $\frac{3}{4}$ teaspoon **salt**
- $\frac{1}{4}$ teaspoon **freshly ground pepper**
- 4 teaspoons **unsalted butter**
- 2 **celery stalks**, chopped
- 2 **carrots**, chopped
- 1 **onion**, chopped
- 1 **garlic clove**, minced
- 3 tablespoons **all-purpose flour**
- $1\frac{1}{2}$ cups **reduced-sodium chicken broth**
- $\frac{1}{2}$ cup **dry white wine**
- 1 tablespoon **paprika**
- $\frac{1}{2}$ cup **fat-free sour cream**

Turkey and Bell Pepper Roulades

Roulades—stuffed and rolled thin slices of meat—are surprisingly easy to assemble and make a wonderful presentation. Try serving these with couscous that has been tossed with orange zest, lemon zest, and a splash of olive oil.

1. Heat 2 teaspoons of the oil in a large nonstick skillet. Add the red and green bell peppers, the onion, ¼ teaspoon of the salt, and ⅛ teaspoon of the pepper; cook, stirring occasionally, until softened, about 5 minutes. Remove the skillet from the heat and let cool about 10 minutes.

2. Gently pound the turkey cutlets to ¼-inch thickness with a meat mallet or heavy saucepan. Sprinkle with the remaining ¼ teaspoon salt and ⅛ teaspoon pepper and arrange on a work surface with the short sides nearest you. Divide the bell pepper mixture into 4 portions and place each portion crosswise on the side of the turkey closest to you. Roll up, jelly-roll style, and secure each with a wooden pick.

3. Wipe out the skillet, add the remaining 2 teaspoons oil, and heat over medium-high heat. Add the turkey rolls and cook, turning occasionally, until browned, about 4 minutes. Add the broth, lemon juice, mustard, and Worcestershire sauce; bring to a boil. Reduce the heat and simmer, covered, until the turkey is cooked through, about 7 minutes. Transfer the turkey rolls to a serving plate and keep warm. Increase the heat to high and boil the mixture in the skillet rapidly until slightly reduced, about 4 minutes. Remove the skillet from the heat and stir in the sour cream. Serve the sauce with the turkey rolls.

PER SERVING (1 turkey roll with ¼ cup sauce): 215 Cal, 8 g Fat, 2 g Sat Fat, 0 g Trans Fat, 81 mg Chol, 516 mg Sod, 6 g Carb, 1 g Fib, 29 g Prot, 43 mg Calc. **_POINTS_** value: **5**.

MAKES 4 SERVINGS ☛

- 4 teaspoons **extra-virgin olive oil**
- 1 small **red bell pepper**, seeded and cut into thin strips
- 1 small **green bell pepper**, seeded and cut into thin strips
- 1 **onion**, thinly sliced
- ½ teaspoon **salt**
- ¼ teaspoon **freshly ground pepper**
- 4 (¼-pound) **turkey breast cutlets**
- 1 cup **reduced-sodium chicken broth**
- 1 tablespoon **fresh lemon juice**
- 1 teaspoon **Dijon mustard**
- 1 teaspoon **Worcestershire sauce**
- ¼ cup **light sour cream**

Turkey Cutlets Parmesan

This one-skillet dish, traditionally made with chicken cutlets instead of turkey cutlets, is a family favorite. To keep it traditional, serve it with spaghetti and a green salad.

1. Gently pound the turkey cutlets to a scant ¼-inch thickness with a meat mallet or heavy saucepan.

2. Lightly beat the egg whites in a medium bowl. Spread the bread crumbs on a plate. Spread the flour on a second plate. Working with 1 piece of turkey at a time, dip both sides into the flour; shake off excess flour. Then dip the turkey into the egg whites and then into the bread crumbs to coat; set aside. Repeat with remaining cutlets, flour, egg whites, and bread crumbs.

3. Heat the oil in a large nonstick skillet over medium-high heat. Add the coated turkey cutlets and cook until browned and cooked through, about 3 minutes on each side. Reduce the heat and pour the pasta sauce over the cutlets. Top each cutlet with 2 tablespoons of the mozzarella cheese and 1 tablespoon of the Parmesan cheese. Cover and simmer until the sauce is hot and the cheese melts, about 4 minutes.

PER SERVING (1 cutlet with about ⅓ cup sauce): 318 Cal, 9 g Fat, 4 g Sat Fat, 0 g Trans Fat, 88 mg Chol, 666 mg Sod, 20 g Carb, 1 g Fib, 37 g Prot, 232 mg Calc. *POINTS* value: *7*.

tip Turkey cutlets are softer than chicken cutlets and require more care when pounding. Place the cutlets between two pieces of wax paper or plastic wrap and, with a firm but gentle motion, pound the cutlets in an outward motion from the center.

MAKES 4 SERVINGS

- 4 (¼-pound) **turkey breast cutlets**
- 2 **egg whites**
- ⅓ cup **Italian seasoned dry bread crumbs**
- 3 tablespoons **all-purpose flour**
- 1 tablespoon **extra-virgin olive oil**
- 2⅔ cups **fat-free prepared tomato-basil pasta sauce**
- ½ cup (2 ounces) **shredded part-skim mozzarella cheese**
- ¼ cup (1 ounce) grated **Parmesan cheese**

Hunan Orange Turkey

If you love Chinese orange duck with its sweet, spicy, and savory flavors, you'll love this dish. Hot cooked rice makes a good carrier for the sauce (½ cup cooked white or brown rice per serving will increase the *POINTS* value by 2).

1. Combine the orange juice, soy sauce, cornstarch, honey, and crushed red pepper in a small bowl; stir until smooth.

2. Heat a large nonstick skillet or wok over medium-high heat until a drop of water sizzles. Pour in 2 teaspoons of the oil and swirl to coat the pan, then add the turkey and stir-fry until browned and cooked through, about 4 minutes. Transfer the turkey to a plate.

3. Heat the remaining 2 teaspoons oil in the same skillet. Add the bell pepper and ginger; stir-fry until fragrant, about 2 minutes. Add the snow peas and stir-fry until the vegetables are crisp-tender, about 1 minute. Add the turkey and the orange juice mixture. Cook, stirring constantly, until the mixture bubbles and thickens, about 1 minute.

PER SERVING (1 cup): 265 Cal, 6 g Fat, 1 g Sat Fat, 0 g Trans Fat, 75 mg Chol, 452 mg Sod, 24 g Carb, 2 g Fib, 28 g Prot, 35 mg Calc. *POINTS* value: *5*.

MAKES 4 SERVINGS

1 cup **orange juice**

3 tablespoons **reduced-sodium soy sauce**

2 tablespoons **cornstarch**

2 tablespoons **honey**

¼ teaspoon **crushed red pepper**

4 teaspoons **Asian (dark) sesame oil**

1 pound **turkey breast cutlets,** cut into ½-inch pieces

1 **red bell pepper,** seeded and cut into ½-inch pieces

1 tablespoon grated peeled **fresh ginger**

¼ pound **fresh snow peas,** trimmed and halved

Hunan Orange Turkey

Turkey Fajitas with
Nectarine Salsa

Turkey Fajitas with Nectarine Salsa

Salsa is best made fresh, right before you use it. If you would like to make it ahead, simply chop the fruit and vegetables the night before and toss them together with the lime juice, cilantro, and salt just before serving.

1. To make the nectarine salsa, finely chop ¼ of the red onion and place in a medium bowl. Slice the remaining ¾ onion and set aside. To the chopped onion, add the nectarines, 1 of the jalapeños, the cilantro, lime juice, and ¼ teaspoon of the salt; mix well.

2. Heat 1 teaspoon of the oil in a large nonstick skillet over medium-high heat. Add the turkey; sprinkle with the ground pepper and the remaining ½ teaspoon salt. Cook, stirring occasionally, until browned and cooked through, about 4 minutes. Transfer turkey to a plate.

3. Heat the remaining 2 teaspoons oil in the same skillet over medium-high heat. Add the reserved sliced onion, remaining jalapeño, and the bell peppers; cook, stirring occasionally, until softened and light golden, about 8 minutes. Add the turkey and cook until heated through, about 1 minute.

4. Meanwhile, warm the tortillas according to package directions. Divide the turkey mixture evenly among the tortillas (about ¾ cup filling on each) and top with salsa (about ½ cup on each). Roll up and serve at once.

PER SERVING (1 fajita): 370 Cal, 5 g Fat, 1 g Sat Fat, 0 g Trans Fat, 56 mg Chol, 946 mg Sod, 55 g Carb, 5 g Fib, 26 g Prot, 83 mg Calc. *POINTS* value: *7*.

MAKES 4 SERVINGS

- 1 large **red onion**
- 4 **nectarines**, about 1 pound, pitted and cut into ¼-inch dice
- 2 small **jalapeño peppers**, seeded and chopped (wear gloves to prevent irritation)
- 1 tablespoon chopped **fresh cilantro**
- 1 tablespoon **fresh lime juice**
- ¾ teaspoon **salt**
- 3 teaspoons **extra-virgin olive oil**
- ¾ pound **turkey breast cutlets**, cut into 2 x ¼-inch strips
- ¼ teaspoon **freshly ground pepper**
- 2 **assorted color bell peppers**, seeded and cut into thin strips
- 4 (8-inch) **fat-free flour tortillas**

Turkey Picadillo with Toasted Tortillas

Picadillo is a classic Mexican dish, traditionally made with ground pork. We substitute ground turkey with winning results.

1. Spray a large nonstick skillet with nonstick spray and set over medium-high heat. Add the turkey and cook, breaking up the turkey with a wooden spoon, until browned, about 5 minutes. Add the onion, bell pepper, garlic, and cumin; cook, stirring occasionally, until the vegetables are softened, about 5 minutes. Add the broth, raisins, and capers; bring to a boil. Reduce the heat and simmer, uncovered, until the broth is nearly evaporated, about 2 minutes. Add the tomatoes, salt, and pepper; cook, stirring occasionally, until the mixture thickens slightly, about 3 minutes.

2. Meanwhile, heat a small nonstick skillet over medium heat. Add the tortillas, 1 at a time, and cook until lightly toasted, about 2 minutes on each side. Serve the toasted tortillas with the turkey mixture.

PER SERVING (¾ cup turkey mixture with 1 tortilla): 246 Cal, 2 g Fat, 1 g Sat Fat, 0 g Trans Fat, 75 mg Chol, 509 mg Sod, 27 g Carb, 3 g Fib, 30 g Prot, 82 mg Calc. *POINTS* value: *4*.

MAKES 4 SERVINGS

- 1 pound **ground skinless lean turkey breast**
- 1 **onion,** cut into ¼-inch dice
- 1 **red bell pepper,** seeded and cut into ¼-inch pieces
- 2 **garlic cloves,** minced
- ¾ teaspoon **ground cumin**
- ½ cup **reduced-sodium chicken broth**
- ¼ cup **golden raisins**
- 1 tablespoon drained **capers**
- 2 **tomatoes,** seeded and chopped, about 1 cup
- ½ teaspoon **salt**
- ¼ teaspoon **freshly ground pepper**
- 4 (6-inch) **corn tortillas**

Saigon Turkey in Lettuce Leaves

Nam pla (fish sauce) is a *must* have ingredient in Southeast Asian countries, where it is used like soy sauce is used in Japan and China. Don't be put off by the strong aroma of fish sauce: Its exotic taste makes the sauce authentic (and very delicious). It is found in the Asian section of large supermarkets and in Asian-food markets.

1. Cook the noodles according to package directions. Drain the noodles and rinse under cold water; chop into small pieces.

2. Combine the lime juice, fish sauce, and sugar in a small bowl; mix well to dissolve the sugar.

3. Spray a large nonstick skillet with nonstick spray and set over medium-high heat. Add the turkey and cook, breaking up the turkey with a wooden spoon, until browned, about 5 minutes. Add the ginger and cook, stirring constantly, until fragrant, about 2 minutes. Transfer the mixture to a medium bowl and let cool about 2 minutes. Add the cucumber, scallion, cilantro, the chopped noodles, and the lime juice mixture; mix well.

4. To serve, place 2 lettuce leaves on each of 4 plates. Fill each lettuce leaf with ⅓ cup of the turkey mixture. Serve at once.

PER SERVING (2 lettuce leaves with ⅔ cup turkey mixture): 139 Cal, 1 g Fat, 0 g Sat Fat, 0 g Trans Fat, 56 mg Chol, 196 mg Sod, 11 g Carb, 1 g Fib, 21 g Prot, 26 mg Calc. *POINTS* value: *3*.

tip For the best flavor, serve this while the turkey mixture is still warm.

MAKES 4 SERVINGS

1 ounce **cellophane noodles**

2 tablespoons **fresh lime juice**

1 tablespoon **Asian fish sauce** (nam pla)

1 tablespoon **sugar**

¾ pound **ground skinless lean turkey breast**

1 tablespoon grated peeled **fresh ginger**

½ medium **cucumber**, peeled, seeded, and chopped, about 1 cup

1 **scallion**, finely chopped

2 tablespoons chopped **fresh cilantro or mint**

8 Boston **lettuce leaves**

Sautéed Duck with Pears and Apples

This flavorful fall dish lends itself perfectly to being served with a side of mashed, cooked butternut or acorn squash (1 cup mashed with no added butter or oil will up the *POINTS* value by 1). You can find *demi-glace* sauce in gourmet stores and in the meat department of some large supermarkets.

1. Sprinkle the duck with ½ teaspoon of the salt and ⅛ teaspoon of the pepper. Melt 2 teaspoons of the butter in a large nonstick skillet over medium-high heat. Add the duck and cook until browned and just cooked through, about 4 minutes on each side. Cut each duck breast into 4 slices, transfer to a plate, and keep warm.

2. Wipe out the skillet and melt the remaining 2 teaspoons butter. Add the pears, apple, sugar, and thyme; cook, stirring frequently, until the fruit is light golden, about 4 minutes. Add the brandy and cook 1 minute. Add the apple juice and demi-glace; bring to a boil. Reduce the heat and simmer, uncovered, until slightly thickened, about 4 minutes.

3. Dissolve the cornstarch in the water; add to the skillet, stirring constantly. Cook and stir until the mixture bubbles and thickens, about 1 minute. Stir in remaining ¼ teaspoon salt and ⅛ teaspoon pepper. Serve the sauce with the duck breasts.

PER SERVING (1 duck breast with generous ⅓ cup sauce): 270 Cal, 5 g Fat, 3 g Sat Fat, 0 g Trans Fat, 77 mg Chol, 498 mg Sod, 28 g Carb, 3 g Fib, 24 g Prot, 31 mg Calc. *POINTS* value: *5*.

tip Duck skin is somewhat more difficult to remove than chicken skin. A thin, tough membrane helps to hold the skin in place. Use the tip of a sharp knife to help carefully peel back the skin, slicing the membrane near the breast meat as you go.

MAKES 4 SERVINGS ☛

- 4 (4–5-ounce) **skinless boneless duck breasts**
- ¾ teaspoon **salt**
- ¼ teaspoon **freshly ground pepper**
- 4 teaspoons **unsalted butter**
- 2 **pears**, peeled, cored, and cut into ½-inch cubes
- 1 **Golden Delicious apple**, peeled, cored, and cut into ½-inch cubes
- 1 tablespoon **sugar**
- ½ teaspoon **dried thyme**
- ¼ cup **brandy**
- ¾ cup **apple juice**
- ⅓ cup **prepared duck demi-glace sauce**
- 2 teaspoons **cornstarch**
- 1 tablespoon cold **water**

**Sautéed Duck with
Pears and Apples**

Turkey Sausage and Mushroom Risotto

Mushrooms give an earthy taste to this risotto. While we've used regular white mushrooms, feel free to substitute fresh shiitake or baby bella mushrooms for richer flavor.

1. Bring the broth to a boil in a medium saucepan. Reduce the heat and keep at a simmer.

2. Heat 1 teaspoon of the oil in a large nonstick skillet over medium-high heat. Add the sausage and cook, breaking up the sausage with a wooden spoon, until browned and cooked through, about 5 minutes. Add the mushrooms and oregano; cook, stirring frequently, until the mushrooms are tender, about 4 minutes. Add ¼ cup of the Madeira and cook until it is absorbed, about 1 minute. Transfer the mixture to a bowl.

3. Heat the remaining 2 teaspoons oil in the same skillet over medium-high heat. Add the shallot and garlic; cook, stirring constantly, until fragrant, about 1 minute. Add the rice and cook, stirring, until it is lightly toasted, about 2 minutes. Add the remaining ½ cup Madeira and stir until it is almost absorbed, about 1 minute. Add the broth, 1 cup at a time, stirring until it is absorbed before adding more, until the rice is just tender. The cooking time should be about 20 minutes from the first addition of broth. Add the sausage mixture, cheese, and pepper; cook, stirring, until heated through, about 1 minute. Serve at once.

PER SERVING (1 cup): 400 Cal, 12 g Fat, 4 g Sat Fat, 0 g Trans Fat, 37 mg Chol, 865 mg Sod, 48 g Carb, 1 g Fib, 21 g Prot, 115 mg Calc. *POINTS* value: *9*.

MAKES 6 SERVINGS

- 5–6 cups **reduced-sodium chicken broth**
- 3 teaspoons **extra-virgin olive oil**
- ¾ pound **turkey sausage**, casings removed, sausage crumbled
- ½ pound **fresh white mushrooms**, sliced
- 1 teaspoon **dried oregano**
- ¾ cup **Madeira wine**
- 1 **shallot**, chopped
- 3 **garlic cloves**, minced
- 1½ cups **Arborio rice**
- ⅓ cup grated **Parmesan cheese**
- ¼ teaspoon **freshly ground pepper**

Hoisin Duck Stir-Fry

This versatile stir-fry is delicious made with duck, but it also lends itself well to lean pork tenderloin, skinless boneless chicken breasts or thighs, or shrimp.

1. Combine the broth, hoisin sauce, soy sauce, and cornstarch in a small bowl; mix well.

2. Heat a large nonstick skillet or wok over medium-high heat until a drop of water sizzles. Pour in 2 teaspoons of the oil and swirl to coat the pan, then add the duck and stir-fry until browned and cooked through, about 4 minutes. Transfer the duck to a plate.

3. Heat the remaining 2 teaspoons oil in the same skillet. Add the scallions and ginger; stir-fry until fragrant, about 30 seconds. Add the green beans and stir-fry until crisp-tender, about 3 minutes. Add the tomatoes and stir-fry 1 minute. Add the duck and the broth mixture. Cook, stirring constantly, until the mixture bubbles and thickens, about 1 minute.

PER SERVING (1 cup): 232 Cal, 7 g Fat, 1 g Sat Fat, 0 g Trans Fat, 66 mg Chol, 659 mg Sod, 16 g Carb, 3 g Fib, 27 g Prot, 61 mg Calc. *POINTS* value: *5*.

MAKES 4 SERVINGS 🖝

- ⅔ cup **reduced-sodium chicken broth**
- ¼ cup **hoisin sauce**
- 2 tablespoons **reduced-sodium soy sauce**
- 3 teaspoons **cornstarch**
- 4 teaspoons **Asian (dark) sesame oil**
- 1 pound **skinless boneless duck breasts**, cut into thin strips
- 3 **scallions**, chopped
- 1 tablespoon grated peeled **fresh ginger**
- ½ pound **fresh green beans**, trimmed
- 1 cup **cherry tomatoes**, halved

Pan-Seared Quail with Dried
Cranberry Chutney

Pan-Seared Quail with Dried Cranberry Chutney

Quail are small game birds that are tender and flavorful. You can buy them at a specialty butcher shop. Removing the skin on the quail helps cut the fat in the recipe—keep in mind that the skin on the wing tips will not come off, so you might want to discard them. Try serving with steamed broccolini and a cooked wild rice mix.

1. With a sharp knife, split each quail along the backbone and press down on the breasts to flatten; remove the skin. Combine 1 tablespoon of the sugar, the soy sauce, and five-spice powder in a zip-close plastic bag. Add the quail. Squeeze out the air and seal the bag; turn to coat the quail. Refrigerate, turning the bag occasionally, at least 2 hours or up to overnight.

2. To make the chutney, heat 1 teaspoon of the oil in a medium nonstick skillet over medium heat. Add the onion and ginger; cook, stirring frequently, until softened, about 3 minutes. Add the remaining 4 tablespoons sugar, the orange juice, cranberries, and cherries; bring to a boil. Reduce the heat and simmer, stirring occasionally, until thickened, about 8 minutes. Stir in ¼ teaspoon of salt and ⅛ teaspoon of pepper.

3. Remove the quail from the marinade and pat dry with paper towels. Discard the marinade. Sprinkle the quail with the remaining ¼ teaspoon salt and ⅛ teaspoon pepper. Heat the remaining 2 teaspoons oil in a large nonstick skillet over medium heat. Add the quail and cook, breast-side down, 5 minutes. Turn the quail over and reduce the heat to medium-low. Cover the skillet and simmer until the quail is cooked through, about 8 minutes. Serve with the chutney.

PER SERVING (1 quail with ¼ cup chutney): 392 Cal, 11 g Fat, 3 g Sat Fat, 0 g Trans Fat, 64 mg Chol, 635 mg Sod, 51 g Carb, 3 g Fib, 25 g Prot, 64 mg Calc. *POINTS* value: *8*.

tip The chutney can be made up to 1 week ahead and kept refrigerated in an airtight container.

MAKES 4 SERVINGS

- 4 (5-ounce) **whole quail**
- 5 tablespoons **sugar**
- 2 tablespoons **reduced-sodium soy sauce**
- ½ teaspoon **five-spice powder**
- 3 teaspoons **canola oil**
- 1 small **onion**, finely chopped
- 1 tablespoon grated peeled **fresh ginger**
- 1 cup **orange juice**
- ½ cup **dried cranberries**
- ½ cup **dried pitted tart cherries**
- ½ teaspoon **salt**
- ¼ teaspoon **freshly ground pepper**

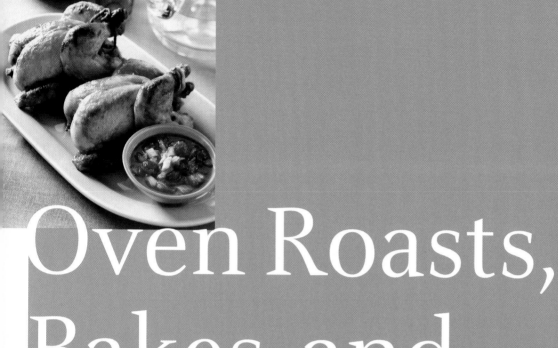

Oven Roasts, Bakes, and Casseroles

CHAPTER SIX

☑ Chicken Baked in a Salt Crust

Talk about dramatic: a whole chicken, roasted under a salt dome, which is cracked open with a mallet before serving. Truth is, this ancient way of roasting—probably via Sicily—doesn't add as much salty flavor as you might think. And it's a great way to seal in the chicken's natural juices. You'll need to use a coarse salt, such as kosher salt and take care removing the crust so you don't get salt crumbs mixed in with the cooked chicken.

1. Preheat the oven to 350°F.

2. Combine the salt and water in a large bowl, stirring until a thick paste forms.

3. Place 3 cups of this salt mixture in the bottom of a large roasting pan, spreading it out to about 6 inches larger than the chicken you will be roasting. Pack the salt dough down, then cover it completely with a double layer of about 18 overlapping grape leaves, leaving a 1-inch border of salt exposed at the edges.

4. Place the lemon inside the chicken cavity, then place the chicken on top of the grape leaves. Fold the grape leaves up to cover parts of the chicken. Use remaining grape leaves to cover chicken entirely, creating a grape-leaf "shell" to protect the meat from the salt.

5. Mound the remaining salt dough onto the grape-leaf covered chicken, shaping the crust to the bird's natural contours. Seal all cracks, but take care not to move the grape leaves underneath.

6. Roast until a meat thermometer inserted in a thigh (throught the salt crust) registers 180°F, about 1 hour and 40 minutes. Let the chicken stand about 10 minutes.

7. Crack the salt crust with a meat mallet or a clean hammer, then remove the crust in chunks, making sure it doesn't crumble onto the meat. Remove the grape leaves. Transfer chicken to a carving board and carve.

PER SERVING (⅛ of chicken): 168 Cal, 6 g Fat, 2 g Sat Fat, 0 g Trans Fat, 78 mg Chol, 369 mg Sod, 0 g Carb, 0 g Fib, 26 g Prot, 13 mg Calc. *POINTS* value: *4*.

MAKES 8 SERVINGS ☛

6 pounds **kosher salt**

3 cups **water**

1 (16-ounce) **jar grape leaves**, rinsed

3 **lemons**, cut into quarters

1 (4-pound) **chicken**, giblets discarded, chicken skinned

Chicken Baked in a Salt Crust

✔ Herbed Roast Chicken

Roast chicken is one of life's simplest—and best—pleasures. We give mouthwatering, fresh herb flavor to this oven roaster with a fragrant rub (a ground mixture of fresh herbs and a small amount of oil or liquid) spread over the meat, under the skin. The secret to keeping the chicken moist is to roast it at a fairly low temperature, which also gives the herbs time to infuse the meat with great flavor.

1. Preheat the oven to 325°F.

2. Place the ¼ cup parsley, the ¼ cup tarragon, the sage, garlic, oil, salt, and pepper in a mini food processor, a spice grinder, or a clean coffee grinder. Pulse until the mixture forms a coarse paste, scraping down the sides of the bowl as necessary.

3. Using a sharp paring knife, make a few small slits in the skin of the chicken thighs and legs. Slip your fingers under these slits to open pockets between the skin and the meat. Also slip your fingers under the skin covering the breast to create large pockets over both breast halves. Rub the spice mixture into the meat under the skin. Place the remaining sprigs of parsley and tarragon inside the body cavity. If desired, tie the legs closed with kitchen string to help hold the shape of the bird during roasting.

4. Place the chicken, breast-side up, in a large roasting pan. Roast until an instant-read thermometer inserted in a thigh registers 180°F, about 1 hour and 20 minutes. Transfer the chicken to a carving board and let stand about 10 minutes before carving. Remove the skin before eating.

PER SERVING (⅛ of chicken): 168 Cal, 8 g Fat, 2 g Sat Fat, 0 g Trans Fat, 70 mg Chol, 216 mg Sod, 1 g Carb, 0 g Fib, 23 g Prot, 24 mg Calc. *POINTS* value: *4*.

tip To carve a chicken, gently pry the wings off the bird and discard the tips. Next, use a sharp carving knife to slice the meat from both halves of the breast. Then remove the thighs and drumsticks. The thigh meat can be sliced off the bones in long, spear-like pieces.

MAKES 8 SERVINGS

¼ cup packed **flat-leaf parsley** leaves + 2 stems parsley

¼ cup packed **fresh tarragon** leaves + 2 stems tarragon

¼ cup packed **fresh sage** leaves

2 **garlic cloves**, minced

1 tablespoon **olive oil**

½ teaspoon **salt**

¼ teaspoon **freshly ground pepper**

1 (4-pound) **chicken**, giblets discarded

Tuscan Baked Chicken Breasts

It doesn't take much to replicate the fresh, light taste that has made Tuscan cooking an international favorite—just a little lemon zest, fresh rosemary, and some aromatic olive oil. Although you needn't use expensive extra-virgin olive oil for this recipe, do use a bottle that's very "nosey"—that is, one that smells like premium green olives. You might like to serve these flavorful breasts with a salad of watercress, grapefruit segments, and balsamic vinegar.

1. Preheat the oven to 400°F.

2. Toss the chicken pieces, garlic, rosemary, lemon zest, oil, crushed red pepper, and salt in a zip-close plastic bag until the chicken is coated with the spices.

3. Place the chicken pieces on a rimmed baking sheet. Bake 30 minutes. Increase the oven temperature to 450°F. Sprinkle the vinegar over the chicken. Continue baking until the chicken is browned and an instant-read thermometer inserted in a breast registers 170°F, about 10 minutes longer. Transfer the chicken to a platter and let stand about 5 minutes. Meanwhile, skim any visible fat from the pan juices. Serve the pan juices with the chicken.

PER SERVING (1 piece chicken with 2 teaspoons juices): 168 Cal, 5 g Fat, 1 g Sat Fat, 0 g Trans Fat, 74 mg Chol, 265 mg Sod, 1 g Carb, 0 g Fib, 27 g Prot, 18 mg Calc. *POINTS* value: *4*.

tip Lemon zest, lemon rind—what's the difference? The zest is actually the top thin "skin" of the rind, where most of the flavorful lemon oil is located. It includes no white pith, which is bitter and astringent. A specially designed lemon zester will take off the thinnest layer of zest by running tiny rings over the lemon's surface. If you use a box grater to remove the lemon zest, don't press down too heavily; simply run the lemon lightly over the surface.

MAKES 6 SERVINGS

- 3 (¾-pound) **bone-in chicken breast halves**, skinned and cut in half the short way

- 3 **garlic cloves**, slivered

- 2 tablespoons chopped **fresh rosemary**

- 2 teaspoons grated **lemon zest**

- 2 teaspoons **olive oil**

- ½ teaspoon **crushed red pepper**

- ½ teaspoon **salt**

- 1 tablespoon **balsamic vinegar**

**Sweet-and-Sour
Glazed Chicken**

Sweet-and-Sour Glazed Chicken

Here's a flavorful chicken dish that makes an easy dinner any night of the week, thanks to a no-fuss, Asian-inspired marinade. You might like to serve this with a wild-and-white rice mix and steamed greens.

1. Combine the pineapple, soy sauce, honey, lemon juice, ginger, garlic, and jalapeño pepper in a large zip-close plastic bag; add the chicken. Squeeze out the air and seal the bag; turn to coat the chicken. Refrigerate, turning the bag occasionally, at least 4 hours or up to overnight.

2. Preheat the oven to 375°F.

3. Place a rack in a roasting pan. Lift the chicken pieces from the marinade and place on the rack (reserve the marinade). Bake the chicken until browned and an instant-read thermometer inserted in a thigh registers 180°F, about 45 minutes, basting with the reserved marinade twice during the first 30 minutes of cooking.

4. Combine the cornstarch and water in a small bowl until smooth. Transfer the chicken to a serving platter; cover and keep warm. Remove the rack from the pan and with a spoon, skim off any fat from the pan juices. Pour the pan juices into a saucepan and simmer over medium heat until the juices are reduced by half, about 2 minutes. Add the cornstarch mixture and cook, stirring constantly, until the mixture bubbles and thickens, about 10 seconds. Serve chicken with sauce.

PER SERVING (1 piece chicken with 2 tablespoons sauce): 199 Cal, 6 g Fat, 2 g Sat Fat, 0 g Trans Fat, 78 mg Chol, 210 mg Sod, 8 g Carb, 0 g Fib, 26 g Prot, 18 mg Calc. *POINTS* value: *4*.

tip The chicken pieces need to be marinated for a minimum of 4 hours, but if you get a chance to combine the marinade and chicken the night before, the fruity-ginger flavors will really shine through.

MAKES 8 SERVINGS

½ cup **canned crushed pineapple** in juice

2 tablespoons **reduced-sodium soy sauce**

2 tablespoons **honey**

2 tablespoons **fresh lemon juice**

1 tablespoon grated peeled **fresh ginger**

1 **garlic clove**, minced

1 small **jalapeño pepper**, seeded and minced (wear gloves to prevent irritation)

1 (4-pound) **chicken**, cut into 8 pieces and skinned

½ teaspoon **cornstarch**

2 teaspoons **water**

Couscous-Stuffed Chicken Breasts

Couscous, fig jam, thyme, and ginger give an international flair to everyday chicken breasts.

1. Bring broth to a boil in a small saucepan; remove from the heat. Stir in the couscous; cover and let stand until all the liquid is absorbed, about 5 minutes.

2. Meanwhile, using a sharp paring knife, make a pocket in each piece of chicken, starting at the thickest part of the cut side of each breast. Do not cut all the way through the breast; rather, once you have an opening, use you fingers to enlarge the pocket until it will hold about ¼ cup stuffing. Set the breasts aside.

3. Preheat the oven to 375°F. Spray a flameproof 9-inch square baking pan with nonstick spray.

4. Fluff the couscous with a fork. Add the raisins, scallion, thyme, salt, and pepper; mix well. Let the mixture cool about 5 minutes. Pack ¼ cup of the mixture into each of the breast pockets. Place the breasts in the baking pan.

5. Combine 3 tablespoons of the water, the fig jam, and ginger in a small bowl; brush half of this mixture over the chicken breasts. Bake 25 minutes. Baste with the remaining fig glaze, then continue baking until the chicken is deeply browned and an instant-read thermometer inserted in a breast registers 170°F, about 20 minutes longer.

6. Transfer the chicken to a serving platter and keep warm. Skim any visible fat from the pan juices. Place the baking pan over medium heat, mix in the remaining 3 tablespoons water, and scrape up any browned bits from the bottom of the pan. Simmer, stirring constantly, until the sauce is reduced by half, about 2 minutes. Serve the chicken with the sauce.

PER SERVING (1 piece chicken with 1 teaspoon sauce): 248 Cal, 4 g Fat, 1 g Sat Fat, 0 g Trans Fat, 74 mg Chol, 224 mg Sod, 21 g Carb, 1 g Fib, 30 g Prot, 25 mg Calc. *POINTS* value: *5.*

MAKES 6 SERVINGS

⅔ cup **reduced-sodium chicken broth**

½ cup **couscous**

3 (¾-pound) **bone-in chicken breast halves,** skinned and cut in half the short way

¼ cup **golden raisins**

1 **scallion,** thinly sliced

1 teaspoon chopped **fresh thyme**

¼ teaspoon **salt**

Freshly ground pepper

6 tablespoons **water**

2 tablespoons **fig jam**

½ teaspoon **ground ginger**

Bacon-Wrapped Chicken Breasts

Here's a very simple way of making plain, boneless chicken breasts truly special. You can use any combination of dried fruits, such as dried cranberries and cherries, instead of apricots and prunes and you could substitute fresh basil or oregano for the rosemary. If you like, have your butcher make pockets in the chicken breasts.

1. Preheat the oven to 400°F. Spray a 9-inch square baking dish with nonstick spray.

2. Mix the apricots, prunes, rosemary, and pepper in a small bowl.

3. Make a pocket in the side of each chicken breast by inserting a sharp paring knife into the thickest part, then gently cutting back and forth until a small chamber has opened in the side. Do not cut through to the back or the sides of the breasts. Enlarge the pockets gently with your fingers.

4. Stuff one-quarter of the dried fruit filling into each breast. Wrap a slice of bacon around each breast, over the opening with the filling. Place the wrapped breasts in the baking dish. Bake until the bacon is brown and crisp and the chicken breasts are cooked through, about 40 minutes. Let the chicken stand about 5 minutes before serving.

PER SERVING (1 stuffed chicken breast): 285 Cal, 9 g Fat, 2 g Sat Fat, 0 g Trans Fat, 84 mg Chol, 451 mg Sod, 22 g Carb, 3 g Fib, 30 g Prot, 34 mg Calc. *POINTS* value: *6*.

MAKES 4 SERVINGS

6 large **dried apricots**, chopped, about ⅔ cup

4 large **pitted prunes**, chopped, about ⅔ cup

4 teaspoons chopped **fresh rosemary**

Freshly ground pepper

4 (¼-pound) **skinless boneless chicken breast halves**

4 slices **turkey bacon**

Mediterranean Chicken Casserole

Tomatoes, olives, and fennel are baked with bone-in breasts for an easy, mid-week supper, or an elegant entrée for your next dinner party. The fennel will stay slightly crunchy, producing a nice texture contrast to the soupy tomatoes and the tender chicken. You can get many colorful, enameled cast iron Dutch ovens and casserole dishes that are suitable for cooking both on top of the stove and in the oven—and they make great serving dishes. Serve with a few leafy greens on the side.

1. Preheat the oven to 350°F.

2. Spray a Dutch oven or large flameproof casserole dish with nonstick spray and set over medium-high heat. Add the chicken breasts and brown about 2 minutes on each side.

3. Add the tomatoes and broth to the Dutch oven; bring to a boil, scraping up any browned bits from the bottom of the pot. Add the fennel, olives, garlic, rosemary, salt, saffron, and pepper. Stir, making sure chicken breasts are partially submerged in liquid.

4. Cover the Dutch oven and bake 45 minutes. Uncover and stir in the cornmeal until it is incorporated into the sauce. Continue baking until an instant-read thermometer inserted in a breast registers 170°F and the sauce is slightly thickened, about 10 minutes longer. Serve the chicken with the vegetables and sauce.

PER SERVING (1 piece chicken with ¾ cup vegetables and sauce): 217 Cal, 5 g Fat, 1 g Sat Fat, 0 g Trans Fat, 74 mg Chol, 429 mg Sod, 12 g Carb, 4 g Fib, 30 g Prot, 79 mg Calc. *POINTS value: 4*.

tip To trim a fennel bulb, remove the feathery fronds and any thick stalks that protrude from the bulb. (These can be saved for stock, if you like.) Cut about ¼ inch off the bottom of the bulb, then cut the bulb into slices.

MAKES 6 SERVINGS 🖝

3 (¾-pound) **bone-in chicken breast halves**, skinned and cut in half the short way

1 (14½-ounce) **can no-salt-added diced tomatoes**

1 cup **reduced-sodium chicken broth**

2 **fennel bulbs**, trimmed and thinly sliced (about 4 cups)

10 **pitted green olives**, rinsed and chopped

1 **garlic clove**, minced

2 teaspoons chopped **fresh rosemary**

¼ teaspoon **salt**

⅛ teaspoon **saffron threads**

Freshly ground pepper

3 tablespoons **yellow cornmeal**

Mediterranean Chicken Casserole

Porcini-Stuffed Chicken Breasts

Porcini mushrooms, also known as cepes, have a pungent, woodsy flavor and are highly prized. Traditionally from Italy, but now cultivated in the United States, they're more affordable dried than fresh. In this easy bake, the dried mushrooms are reconstituted in hot water, then they (and their resulting broth) are used to make a delicious sauce.

1. Place the mushrooms in a small bowl; pour the boiling water over them. Set aside to soak until softened, about 10 minutes. Drain, reserving the soaking liquid.

2. Spray a medium nonstick skillet with nonstick spray and set over medium heat. Add the onion and celery; cook, stirring frequently, until slightly softened, about 2 minutes. Add the softened mushrooms and cook, stirring constantly, about 1 minute. Add the vermouth and scrape up any browned bits from the bottom of the skillet. Transfer the mixture to a medium bowl. Add the cornflakes, sage, thyme, salt, and ¼ cup of the reserved mushroom liquid. Set aside until the cornflakes absorb all the liquid, about 3 minutes.

3. Preheat the oven to 350°F. Spray a 9-inch square baking dish with nonstick spray.

4. Make a pocket in the side of each chicken breast by inserting a sharp paring knife into the thickest part, then gently cutting back and forth until a small chamber has opened in the side. Do not cut through to the back or the sides of the breasts. Enlarge the pockets gently with your fingers.

5. Stuff one-quarter of the stuffing into each breast. Place the breasts in the baking dish. Bake, basting occasionally with the remaining mushroom liquid, until the chicken is browned on the outside and cooked through, about 40 minutes. Let the chicken stand about 5 minutes before serving.

PER SERVING (1 stuffed chicken breast): 192 Cal, 4 g Fat, 1 g Sat Fat, 0 g Trans Fat, 68 mg Chol, 331 mg Sod, 12 g Carb, 1 g Fib, 26 g Prot, 24 mg Calc. *POINTS* value: *4.*

MAKES 4 SERVINGS

½ ounce **dried porcini mushrooms**

1 cup boiling **water**

1 small **onion**, chopped

1 **celery stalk**, chopped

1 tablespoon **dry vermouth**

1½ cups **cornflakes**

1 tablespoon finely chopped **fresh sage**

1 teaspoon finely chopped **fresh thyme**

¼ teaspoon **salt**

4 (¼-pound) **skinless boneless chicken breast halves**

Chicken Rollatini

For this quick but elegant entrée, chicken breasts are layered with peppery arugula, soft goat cheese, and sun-dried tomatoes, then rolled, sealing the stuffing inside. Look for soft goat cheese in the dairy case of your local supermarket, or at the cheese counter of a gourmet market. For best results, let it come to room temperature before using.

MAKES 6 SERVINGS ☞

6 (¼-pound) **skinless boneless chicken breast halves**

18 **arugula leaves**, tough stems removed

1 ounce **low-fat soft goat cheese**

12 **marinated sun-dried tomatoes**, patted dry and halved

¼ cup **apple juice**

1½ teaspoons **salt-free lemon pepper seasoning**

1. Preheat the oven to 350°F. Spray a 9 x 13-inch baking dish with nonstick spray.

2. Place a sheet of plastic wrap on a work surface, place a chicken breast on top of it, then cover with a second sheet of plastic wrap. Pound the breast to ¼-inch thickness with a meat mallet or a heavy saucepan. Remove the top layer of plastic wrap, set the chicken breast aside on its bottom layer of plastic wrap, and repeat with the remaining chicken breasts.

3. Top each breast with 3 arugula leaves. Spread 2 teaspoons goat cheese evenly across the leaves on each breast. Place 4 sun-dried tomato halves on the cheese. Roll the chicken breasts up, pulling off plastic wrap as you go. Place breasts, seam-side down, in the baking dish. Sprinkle the apple juice over the chicken, then sprinkle with the lemon pepper seasoning.

4. Bake, basting occasionally with the pan juices, until the chicken is cooked through, about 45 minutes. Let the chicken stand about 5 minutes before serving.

PER SERVING (1 stuffed chicken breast): 220 Cal, 8 g Fat, 2 g Sat Fat, 0 g Trans Fat, 71 mg Chol, 140 mg Sod, 11 g Carb, 2 g Fib, 28 g Prot, 44 mg Calc. *POINTS* value: *5*.

tip Can't find arugula at your market? Shred a leaf of escarole and use it instead. Or substitute baby spinach leaves for the arugula and grind some fresh pepper on top of the cheese.

Moroccan Chicken
Pockets

Moroccan Chicken Pockets

While these bundles take some time to prepare, they make an elegant choice for a buffet dinner or potluck supper. To save time on serving day, bake the pockets ahead and freeze them in zip-close plastic bags. Don't defrost them—simply reheat in a 350°F oven until hot and crisp, about 15 minutes.

1. Spray a large skillet with nonstick spray and set over medium heat. Add the onion and garlic; cook, stirring frequently, until softened, about 3 minutes. Add the chicken and cook, stirring occasionally, until lightly browned, about 5 minutes.

2. Add the cumin, ginger, turmeric, and salt; cook, stirring constantly, until fragrant, about 30 seconds. Add the broth and bring the mixture to a simmer, scraping up any browned bits from the bottom of the skillet. Transfer the mixture to a large bowl; stir in the parsley, almonds, and currants. Set aside to cool, about 10 minutes, then stir in the egg whites.

3. Preheat the oven to 350°F. Line a rimmed baking sheet with parchment paper or a silicon baking mat. Mix the sugar and cinnamon together in a small bowl.

4. Place 1 sheet of phyllo dough on a work surface with one long side close to you; cut the sheet in half crosswise. Sprinkle both halves with a dash of the cinnamon-sugar. Spread a scant ¼ cup of the filling on each half, placing the filling ½ inch from the edge that is closest to you, spreading it out in a 2-inch-thick line, and leaving a ½-inch border on each side. Fold the short sides of the dough over filling, then roll up the packet, creating a large egg roll. Place seam-side down on baking sheet. Repeat with the remaining 5 sheets of phyllo, the cinnamon-sugar, and the filling, making a total of 12 rolls. Lightly spray each roll with nonstick spray. Bake until golden brown, about 45 minutes.

PER SERVING (2 pockets): 241 Cal, 5 g Fat, 1 g Sat Fat, 0 g Trans Fat, 46 mg Chol, 364 mg Sod, 26 g Carb, 2 g Fib, 21 g Prot, 45 mg Calc. *POINTS* value: *5*.

MAKES 6 SERVINGS

- 1 medium **onion**, finely chopped
- 2 **garlic cloves**, minced
- 1 pound **chicken tenders**, chopped
- 1 teaspoon **ground cumin**
- 1 teaspoon **ground ginger**
- 1 teaspoon **turmeric**
- ½ teaspoon **salt**
- ¼ cup **reduced-sodium chicken broth**
- ¼ cup chopped **fresh parsley**
- ¼ cup sliced **almonds**
- ¼ cup **currants or raisins**
- 2 **egg whites**, lightly beaten
- 1 tablespoon **sugar**
- 1½ teaspoons **cinnamon**
- 6 (12x17-inch) **sheets phyllo dough**, thawed according to package directions

Chicken Eggplant Parmesan

We all know eggplant Parmesan as that fried-then-baked concoction, smothered in cheese—which bears no resemblance to how it's fixed in Italy, a land famous for food prepared simply and beautifully. It was probably elaborated upon in America, where immigrants wanted to been seen living better—i. e., eating richer—than in Europe. Tastes have changed, of course. So we've revisited this classic, returning it to its roots: a fresh, light, and flavorful casserole. A tablespoon of freshly grated Parmesan cheese, sprinkled over each serving at the last minute, will add satisfying flavor and only boost the *POINTS* value to 5 per serving.

1. Preheat the oven to 350°F. Spray a 1½–2-quart baking dish with nonstick spray.

2. Make a pocket in the side of each chicken breast by inserting a sharp paring knife into the thickest part, then gently cutting back and forth until a small chamber has opened in the side. Do not cut through to the back or the sides of the breasts. Place 1 slice of cheese in each pocket. Place chicken in baking dish.

3. Spray a large nonstick skillet with nonstick spray and set over medium heat. Add the onion and cook, stirring frequently, until slightly softened, about 2 minutes. Add the garlic and cook 15 seconds. Add the eggplant and cook, stirring frequently, until it begins to soften, about 4 minutes.

4. Add the tomatoes, wine, oregano, thyme, salt, pepper, and crushed red pepper, if using, to the skillet. Cook, stirring frequently, just until the tomatoes begin to break down, about 2 minutes. Pour mixture over the chicken. Cover and bake 30 minutes. Uncover, baste the chicken with any juices in the pan, and continue baking, uncovered, basting every 5 minutes, until chicken is cooked through, about 15 minutes longer.

PER SERVING (1 piece chicken with ½ cup vegetables and sauce): 202 Cal, 4 g Fat, 1 g Sat Fat, 0 g Trans Fat, 71 mg Chol, 535 mg Sod, 10 g Carb, 2 g Fib, 30 g Prot, 152 mg Calc. *POINTS* value: *4*.

MAKES 4 SERVINGS

- 4 (¼-pound) **skinless boneless chicken breast halves**

- 2 ounces **fat-free mozzarella cheese**, cut into 4 long, thin slices

- 1 small **onion**, chopped

- 1 **garlic clove**, minced

- 1 (8-ounce) **eggplant**, cut into ½-inch chunks

- 3 **plum tomatoes**, chopped

- 1 tablespoon **dry Marsala wine**

- 2 teaspoons chopped **fresh oregano**

- 1 teaspoon chopped **fresh thyme**

- ½ teaspoon **salt**

- **Freshly ground pepper**

- ¼ teaspoon **crushed red pepper** (optional)

Chicken and Mushroom Casserole

Look no further for the classic chicken casserole—satisfying for the whole family, yet elegant enough for guests. The brown rice adds a nutty taste to the dish; the dried cranberries, a sparkly finish. Best of all, the chicken breasts stay tender and moist.

1. Preheat the oven to 350°F.

2. Spray a Dutch oven or large flameproof casserole dish with nonstick spray and set over medium heat. Add the chicken breasts in one layer, working in batches if necessary, and cook until browned on one side, about 2 minutes. Transfer the chicken to a plate.

3. Add the mushrooms and scallions to the Dutch oven; cook, stirring frequently, until the mushrooms give off their liquid and it reduces to a glaze, about 4 minutes. Add the vermouth and simmer for 10 seconds, scraping up any browned bits from the bottom of the pan.

4. Add the thyme, salt, and pepper; cook, stirring constantly, until fragrant, about 10 seconds. Add rice and cranberries, stir once, then stir in broth. Add chicken breasts, browned-side up, and bring to a simmer.

5. Remove the Dutch oven from the heat, cover, and bake until the chicken is cooked through and the rice is tender but still toothsome, about 55 minutes.

PER SERVING (1 piece chicken with ¾ cup rice and vegetables): 292 Cal, 5 g Fat, 1 g Sat Fat, 0 g Trans Fat, 68 mg Chol, 309 mg Sod, 29 g Carb, 3 g Fib, 31 g Prot, 33 mg Calc. *POINTS* value: *6*.

tip Use unsweetened dried cranberries. They'll give the dish a gentle but slightly sour taste, a good foil to the chicken and mushrooms.

MAKES 6 SERVINGS ☞

- 6 (¼-pound) **skinless boneless chicken breast halves**

- ¾ pound **cremini or white button mushrooms**, thinly sliced

- 2 **scallions**, thinly sliced

- 2 tablespoons **dry vermouth**

- 1 teaspoon chopped **fresh thyme**

- ¼ teaspoon **salt**

- **Freshly ground pepper**

- 1 cup **brown rice**

- 2 tablespoons **dried cranberries**

- 1 (14½-ounce) **can reduced-sodium chicken broth**

Drumsticks Roasted with Garlic

Onion and apples give off so much liquid in this weekday dish, it's almost like a stew—hearty and comforting. But talk about quick and easy—the drumsticks are simply roasted on a bed of vegetables laced with unpeeled garlic cloves. The garlic mellows considerably—squeeze out the pulp and eat it with the chicken, or spread it on crisp slices of toasted French baguette. One ounce (3 to 4 thin slices) of baguette for each serving will up the *POINTS* value by 1.

1. Preheat the oven to 350°F. Spray a 9 x 13-inch baking pan with nonstick spray.

2. Combine the celery, onion, apple, tarragon, and thyme in a large bowl; turn into the baking pan and spread out, making a bed for the drumsticks. Tuck the bay leaves into the vegetables, then sprinkle the salt and pepper over the mixture. Lay the drumsticks on top, then tuck in the garlic cloves, pushing them down among the vegetables.

3. Cover the baking pan and bake until the vegetables are soft and an instant-read thermometer inserted in a drumstick registers 180°F, about 1½ hours

4. To serve, discard the bay leaves, place 2 drumsticks in each of 4 bowls, then spoon the vegetables and roasted garlic around them, like a stew.

PER SERVING (2 drumsticks with 1 cup vegetables and sauce): 207 Cal, 4 g Fat, 1 g Sat Fat, 0 g Trans Fat, 98 mg Chol, 402 mg Sod, 16 g Carb, 3 g Fib, 27 g Prot, 67 mg Calc. *POINTS* value: *4*.

tip Garlic's healing powers have been touted for centuries in folk medicine, and today many believe this celebrated member of the lily family has antibiotic properties. Look for garlic heads that are firm and store in a cool, dry place.

MAKES 4 SERVINGS

4 **celery stalks**, cut into ½-inch pieces

1 large **onion**, chopped

1 large **Golden Delicious apple**, cored and chopped

2 teaspoons finely chopped **fresh tarragon**

1 teaspoon finely chopped **fresh thyme**

2 **bay leaves**

½ teaspoon **salt**

Freshly ground pepper

8 (¼-pound) **skinless chicken drumsticks**

1 large head **garlic**, broken into cloves but not peeled

Drumsticks Roasted
with Garlic

Apricot Chicken

This simple, slow-baked chicken is not only delicious—tasting of tart, yet sweet, apricots, sweet honey, and aromatic rosemary and orange zest—it looks beautiful, too, since the apricots create a deep orange glaze over the chicken. You might like to serve this with a packaged blend of leafy greens and a light vinaigrette dressing.

1. Preheat the oven to 350°F. Spray a 9 x 13-inch baking pan with nonstick spray.

2. Place the apricot halves and their juice, the orange juice, honey, rosemary, and orange zest in a food processor. Pulse until smooth, scraping down the sides of the bowl as necessary.

3. Place the chicken legs in the pan, arranging them to fit in one layer. Spoon the apricot puree over the chicken, spreading it smooth. Bake, uncovered, until an instant-read thermometer inserted in a thigh registers 180°F and the glaze is golden, basting occasionally with the pan juices, about 1 hour and 20 minutes. Serve with the couscous.

PER SERVING (1 leg and ⅓ cup couscous): 298 Cal, 7 g Fat, 2 g Sat Fat, 0 g Trans Fat, 81 mg Chol, 214 mg Sod, 28 g Carb, 2 g Fib, 30 g Prot, 43 mg Calc. *POINTS* value: *6*.

tip Omit the couscous and serve the chicken with steamed asparagus or broccoli instead. You'll lower the per-serving *POINTS* value by 1.

MAKES 6 SERVINGS

1 (15-ounce) **can apricot halves** in juice, undrained

2 tablespoons **orange juice**

1½ tablespoons **honey**

2 teaspoons chopped **fresh rosemary**

1 teaspoon grated **orange zest**

6 (½-pound) **whole chicken legs**, skinned

2 cups hot **cooked couscous**

☑ Easy Chicken Cassoulet

This delicious casserole is inspired by the famous French stew which usually takes hours—or even days—to prepare. Cassoulet is often made with a combination of meats; we use chicken thighs and Canadian bacon, which, with fresh vegetables and herbs, give a well-rounded flavor to the dish.

1. Preheat the oven to 350°F.

2. Spray a large Dutch oven or flameproof casserole dish with nonstick spray and set over medium heat. Working in batches if necessary, add the chicken and brown, about 2 minutes on each side. Transfer the chicken to a plate.

3. Add the Canadian bacon to the Dutch oven and cook until lightly browned, about 1 minute. Add the carrots, celery, and leek; cook, stirring frequently, until softened, about 4 minutes. Add the beans, broth, water, thyme, pepper, bay leaves, and cayenne, if using; bring to a simmer.

4. Remove the Dutch oven from the heat; add the chicken and any accumulated juices, nestling the chicken among the vegetables. Cover and bake until the chicken is almost falling off the bone and the sauce is somewhat thickened, about 1 hour and 30 minutes.

5. Discard the bay leaves. Transfer 1 cup of the vegetable and bean mixture to a food processor; pulse until smooth. Stir this puree back into the Dutch oven to thicken the sauce. Stir in the lemon juice.

PER SERVING (1 chicken thigh with ¾ cup vegetables and sauce): 310 Cal, 10 g Fat, 3 g Sat Fat, 0 g Trans Fat, 68 mg Chol, 465 mg Sod, 23 g Carb, 6 g Fib, 32 g Prot, 113 mg Calc. *POINTS* value: *6*.

tip There are often pieces of fat still clinging to chicken after it is skinned. Be sure to trim it away.

MAKES 8 SERVINGS

- 8 (5-ounce) **skinless bone-in chicken thighs**

- 6 ounces **Canadian bacon**, diced

- 2 cups **baby carrots**

- 2 **celery stalks**, chopped

- 1 large **leek**, cleaned and thinly sliced

- 2 (15½-ounce) cans **cannellini (white kidney) beans**, rinsed and drained

- 2 cups **reduced-sodium chicken or vegetable broth**

- ¼ cup **water**

- 1 tablespoon finely chopped **fresh thyme**

Freshly ground pepper

- 2 **bay leaves**

- ⅛ teaspoon **cayenne** (optional)

- ½ teaspoon **fresh lemon juice**

Red-Cooked Chicken and Chestnuts

Red-Cooked Chicken and Chestnuts

Red cooking is a traditional Chinese cooking technique in which ingredients are slowly braised in a wine and soy sauce broth. Surprisingly, soy sauce mellows considerably as it cooks, taking on an earthy taste, in contrast to its usual salty tang. In fact, the term *red cooking* is a reference to the color soy sauce sometimes takes on after it has stewed. In this version, we've used chicken thighs and a thoroughly Western ingredient—chestnuts, which are starchy enough to hold up to the big flavors and long cooking. Serve this dish with brown rice, or the more exotic red rice, available in gourmet markets.

1. Adjust the racks to divide the oven into thirds. Preheat the oven to 350°F.

2. Spray a Dutch oven with nonstick spray and set over medium heat. Add the chicken and cook until lightly browned, about 2 minutes on each side.

3. Add the broth, soy sauce, and sherry, scraping up any browned bits from the bottom of the pan. Stir in the chestnuts, ginger, scallions, garlic, sugar, cinnamon sticks, and anise pods; bring to a simmer.

4. Remove the Dutch oven from the heat. Cover and bake in the lower third of the oven for 1 hour and 20 minutes. Add the watercress, laying it on top of the stew. Cover and bake until the chicken is falling off the bone and the watercress is wilted, about 15 minutes longer. Discard the cinnamon sticks and anise pods. Serve the chicken, vegetables, and sauce in bowls.

PER SERVING (1 chicken thigh with about ⅓ cup vegetables and sauce): 198 Cal, 8 g Fat, 2 g Sat Fat, 0 g Trans Fat, 57 mg Chol, 390 mg Sod, 9 g Carb, 1 g Fib, 21 g Prot, 57 mg Calc. *POINTS* value: *4*.

MAKES 8 SERVINGS ☛

- 8 (5-ounce) **skinless bone-in chicken thighs**
- 1 cup **reduced-sodium chicken broth**
- ¼ cup **reduced-sodium soy sauce**
- ¼ cup **dry sherry or dry vermouth**
- 1 cup **jarred steamed peeled chestnuts**
- ⅓ cup slivered peeled **fresh ginger**
- 4 **scallions**, cut into 3-inch pieces
- 2 **garlic cloves**, minced
- 2 teaspoons **sugar**
- 2 (4-inch) **cinnamon sticks**
- 2 star **anise pods**
- 1 large bunch **watercress**, cleaned and stemmed

Buying and Safe Handling Hints

Like all fresh meats, chicken is perishable and should be stored and handled with care. Proper handling of chicken helps eliminate the risk of bacterial infection. Follow these tips to safeguard your family's health:

- Refrigerate groceries immediately on reaching home. Never leave chicken or other perishables in a hot car.

- Buy uncooked poultry by the "sell-by" date. If you purchase before the sell-by date, make sure you use or freeze within 2 days.

- Buy and use fully cooked poultry by the "use-by" date. If you purchase before the use-by date, make sure you use or freeze within that date.

- Refrigerate raw chicken promptly. Never leave it on countertop at room temperature.

- Packaged fresh chicken may be refrigerated in original wrappings in the coldest part of the refrigerator. Place the package on a plate to prevent juices from dripping onto other foods.

- Freeze uncooked chicken if it is not to be used within 2 days.

- Frozen chicken will maintain top quality in a home freezer for up to 9 months when properly packaged.

- Thaw chicken in the refrigerator—not on the countertop. It takes about 24 hours to thaw a 4-pound chicken in the refrigerator. Cut-up parts, 3 to 9 hours.

- Chicken may be safely thawed in cold water. Place the chicken in its original wrap or zip-close plastic bag in cold water. Change the water often. It takes about 2 hours to thaw a whole chicken.

- For quick thawing of raw or cooked chicken you can use a microwave oven—follow the manufacturer's directions. Thawing time will vary.

- When handling raw chicken, always wash hands, countertops, cutting boards, knives and other utensils with soapy water before they come in contact with other raw or cooked foods.

Curried Chicken and Green Bean Casserole

Standard chicken and green bean casserole—the one so many of us grew up with—is given a new twist here with distinctive and flavorful curry powder. Fat-free evaporated milk replaces the traditional cream or cream soup used in the original recipe, while still adding a creamy richness to the sauce. You might like to serve this hearty entrée with a simple salad of lettuce, tomatoes, and radishes, dressed with a splash of fresh lime juice.

1. Preheat the oven to 375°F. Spray a 1½-quart shallow baking dish or au gratin dish with nonstick spray.

2. Spray a large nonstick skillet with nonstick spray and set over medium heat. Add the chicken and cook, turning occasionally, until lightly browned, about 3 minutes. Transfer the chicken to a bowl.

3. Melt the butter in the same skillet over low heat. Add the onion and cook, stirring frequently, until golden, about 10 minutes. Sprinkle the curry powder over the onion and cook until fragrant, about 15 seconds. Add the broth and bring to a simmer, scraping up any browned bits from the bottom of the skillet.

4. Whisk the evaporated milk and flour in a small bowl, then stir some of the hot broth from the skillet into the flour mixture. Return the mixture to the skillet. Cook, stirring constantly, until the mixture bubbles and thickens. Add the chicken, any accumulated juices, and the green beans to the skillet; mix well.

5. Transfer the chicken mixture to the baking dish, sprinkle with the bread crumbs, and bake until cooked through and bubbling, about 45 minutes.

PER SERVING (generous 1 cup): 250 Cal, 9 g Fat, 3 g Sat Fat, 0 g Trans Fat, 59 mg Chol, 239 mg Sod, 19 g Carb, 3 g Fib, 23 g Prot, 178 mg Calc. *POINTS* value: *5.*

MAKES 4 SERVINGS

- ¾ pound **skinless boneless chicken thighs**, cut into 1½-inch pieces

- 2 teaspoons **unsalted butter**

- 1 large **onion**, thinly sliced

- 2 teaspoons **curry powder**

- 1 (14½-ounce) **can reduced-sodium vegetable broth**

- 1 (5-ounce) **can fat-free evaporated milk**

- 2 tablespoons **all-purpose flour**

- 1 (10-ounce) package **frozen cut green beans**, thawed

- 2 tablespoons plain dry **bread crumbs**

Jerk Chicken and Plantains

Jerk is a spicy, Jamaican farrago of spices, often rubbed onto meat and vegetables before grilling. Here, the mixture is rubbed onto chicken thighs before they're baked over plantains, a more-starch-less-sugar member of the banana family, once a staple crop in eastern Africa and readily translatable to Caribbean climates. Look for ripe but firm plantains, ones that are yellow with a few brown spots, and not green at all.

1. Preheat the oven to 350°F. Spray a 9 x 13-inch baking pan with nonstick spray.

2. Rub the jerk seasoning into the chicken; set aside about 5 minutes.

3. Toss together the onion, bell pepper, plantain, and tomatoes in a large bowl. Spread this mixture into the baking pan. Place the chicken on top. Cover and bake until the plantains are soft and the chicken is falling off the bone, about 1 hour and 15 minutes.

PER SERVING (1 chicken thigh with scant ½ cup vegetables): 217 Cal, 8 g Fat, 2 g Sat Fat, 0 g Trans Fat, 57 mg Chol, 118 mg Sod, 17 g Carb, 2 g Fib, 20 g Prot, 50 mg Calc. **POINTS** value: **5.**

tip If you'd like to make your own jerk seasoning, place the following in a mini food processor, a spice grinder, or a clean coffee grinder: 2 teaspoons chili powder, 2 teaspoons dried thyme, 1 teaspoon cinnamon, ½ teaspoon ground ginger, ½ teaspoon ground allspice, ¼ teaspoon garlic powder, and at least ⅛ teaspoon or up to ½ teaspoon cayenne, depending on how hot you want the mixture. Blend until well mixed. To get the taste and smell out of your spice or coffee grinder, wipe the bowl thoroughly, then grind 1 tablespoon uncooked white rice until powdery. Repeat as necessary, wiping out the bowl of the grinder each time.

MAKES 8 SERVINGS

2 tablespoons **salt-free dry jerk seasoning**

8 (5-ounce) **skinless bone-in chicken thighs**

1 large **onion**, coarsely chopped

1 **green bell pepper**, seeded and chopped

1 large ripe **plantain**, peeled, halved lengthwise, and cut into ½-inch pieces

1 (14½-ounce) **can diced tomatoes**, drained

Jerk Chicken and Plantains

Greek Chicken Thighs

The flavors of the Greek Islands are as bright as the sun on the Adriatic sea. In other words, it's all about lemon, feta, dill, and tomatoes. While this casserole practically screams "summer," it would also be a welcome treat in winter, when dazzling sunlight is hard to find.

1. Adjust the racks to divide the oven into thirds. Preheat the oven to 375°F. Spray a shallow baking dish or au gratin dish with nonstick spray.

2. Mix the spinach, feta, 1 tablespoon of the dill, and the lemon zest in a medium bowl. Make football-shaped balls of this mixture, using about 2 tablespoons for each ball.

3. Lay the chicken thighs on a work surface and butterfly them: Cut them almost in half, horizontally, then press them open. Place a ball of the stuffing mixture on one side of a thigh; roll up the thigh. Place seam-side down in the baking dish. Repeat with the remaining thighs and stuffing balls.

4. Combine the tomatoes, olives, and the remaining 2 tablespoons dill in a small bowl; spoon over the stuffed thighs. Sprinkle lemon juice over the chicken.

5. Cover and bake in the lower third of the oven for 30 minutes. Uncover and bake until the chicken is browned on the outside and cooked through, basting twice with the sauce in the baking dish, about 10 minutes longer.

PER SERVING (1 stuffed thigh): 183 Cal, 10 g Fat, 4 g Sat Fat, 0 g Trans Fat, 61 mg Chol, 345 mg Sod, 3 g Carb, 1 g Fib, 20 g Prot, 117 mg Calc. *POINTS* value: *4*.

tip The best way to buy feta is in a block, submerged in water. This keeps it fresh and moist, not dry and crumbly. What's more, feta sold this way has fewer preservatives than packaged, crumbled varieties.

MAKES 6 SERVINGS

- 1 (10-ounce) package **frozen chopped spinach**, thawed and squeezed dry

- 2 ounces **feta cheese**, crumbled

- 3 tablespoons chopped **fresh dill**

- 1 teaspoon **grated lemon zest**

- 6 (3-ounce) **skinless boneless chicken thighs**

- 6 **cherry tomatoes**, quartered

- 12 **pitted green olives**, rinsed and chopped

- 1 teaspoon **fresh lemon juice**

☑ Chicken and Potato Casserole

Potatoes make great noodles. Just slice them into thin strips with a vegetable peeler, then parboil a few minutes, and voilà—noodles with a great and different taste. Here, they're layered in a creamy casserole, reminiscent of paprikash, thickened with lots of sweet paprika.

1. Fill a large bowl with cool water. Cut the potato in half lengthwise. With a vegetable peeler, make long thin "noodles" from the cut sides of the potato, letting the strips fall into the water.

2. Bring a pot of water to a boil. Drain the potato noodles and add them to the pot. Cook just until they lose their crunchy edge, no more than 2 minutes. Drain and refresh under cool water.

3. Preheat the oven to 350°F. Spray a 1-quart shallow baking dish with nonstick spray.

4. Spray a large nonstick skillet with nonstick spray and set over medium heat. Add the onion and celery; cook, stirring frequently, until slightly softened, about 2 minutes. Add the garlic and cook 15 seconds. Add the chicken and cook, breaking it up with a wooden spoon, until browned, about 2 minutes. Add the paprika, salt, and pepper, then pour in the broth, scraping up any browned bits from the bottom of the skillet. Bring to a boil; reduce the heat and simmer 1 minute. Remove from heat and stir in sour cream.

5. Place one-third of the potato noodles in the baking dish, making one overlapping layer. Add one-third of the chicken mixture; spread over the potatoes. Repeat the layering two more times, using the remaining potatoes and chicken mixture. Bake until lightly browned and bubbling, about 40 minutes. Let stand about 5 minutes before serving.

PER SERVING (scant 1 cup): 215 Cal, 4 g Fat, 1 g Sat Fat, 0 g Trans Fat, 52 mg Chol, 444 mg Sod, 22 g Carb, 3 g Fib, 23 g Prot, 98 mg Calc. *POINTS* value: *4.*

MAKES 4 SERVINGS

- 1 (¾-pound) **baking potato**, preferably a russet potato, peeled
- 1 small **onion**, chopped
- 1 **celery stalk**, chopped
- 1 **garlic clove**, minced
- ¾ pound **ground skinless lean chicken breast**
- 2 tablespoons **sweet paprika**
- ½ teaspoon **salt**
- **Freshly ground pepper**
- ½ cup **reduced-sodium chicken broth**
- ½ cup **fat-free sour cream**

Chicken Meatloaf

Chicken Meatloaf

If you like meatloaf made with ground beef, why not try it with ground chicken? It's a lighter, healthier way to make this family favorite. We add chopped apple, which makes the meatloaf moist and slightly sweet.

1. Spray a medium nonstick skillet with nonstick spray and set over medium heat. Add the onion and celery; cook, stirring frequently, until slightly softened, about 2 minutes. Add the apples, reduce the heat to low, and cook, stirring occasionally, until the apples are quite soft, the onion is golden, and the mixture is very fragrant, about 8 minutes. Transfer to a large bowl and let cool 15 minutes.

2. Preheat the oven to 350°F. Spray a 5 x 9-inch loaf pan with nonstick spray.

3. Add the chicken, egg whites, bread crumbs, dill, lemon zest, salt, nutmeg, and pepper to the onion mixture; mix until well combined. Spoon into the loaf pan and pack down. Spread the mustard over the top.

4. Bake until an instant-read thermometer inserted into the middle of the meatloaf registers 165°F, about 1 hour and 15 minutes. Let stand about 5 minutes, then unmold and cut into slices.

PER SERVING (⅙ of meatloaf): 203 Cal, 4 g Fat, 1 g Sat Fat, 0 g Trans Fat, 68 mg Chol, 351 mg Sod, 13 g Carb, 2 g Fib, 27 g Prot, 33 mg Calc. *POINTS* value: *4*.

tip To make fresh bread crumbs, leave 2 or 3 slices of whole-wheat bread uncovered on your counter overnight. Break the bread into quarters, then grind in a food processor or a mini processor just until crumbs form.

MAKES 6 SERVINGS

1 medium **onion**, chopped

2 **celery stalks**, chopped

2 **Golden Delicious apples**, cored and finely chopped

1½ pounds **ground skinless lean chicken breast**

2 **egg whites**, lightly beaten

1 cup fresh **whole-wheat bread crumbs**

2 tablespoons chopped **fresh dill**

1 teaspoon grated **lemon zest**

½ teaspoon **salt**

¼ teaspoon grated **nutmeg**

Freshly ground pepper

2 teaspoons **honey mustard**

Baked Beans with Chicken Sausage

Buy fresh sausage, if you can, made at a local butcher shop. You can even experiment with varieties like chicken and apple or chicken and sage. In any case, check the sodium content (some are loaded with salt). If you're concerned, use no-salt chicken broth and no-salt-added tomato paste for this recipe. Be sure to buy sausages made from ground skinless lean chicken breasts, not from various "chicken parts."

1. Preheat the oven to 375°F.

2. Heat a large nonstick skillet over medium heat. Add the sausage and cook, turning frequently, until browned, about 2 minutes. Use a slotted spoon to transfer the sausage pieces to a 2-quart baking dish. Drain the fat from the skillet.

3. Return the skillet to medium heat; add the onion and bell pepper. Cook, stirring frequently, until softened, about 3 minutes. Add the garlic and jalapeño pepper; cook, stirring constantly, until fragrant, about 30 seconds. Add the beans, broth, and tomato paste; cook, stirring constantly until they create a smooth sauce. Stir in the vinegar, honey, mustard, paprika, salt, pepper, and liquid smoke, if using. Pour the contents of the skillet into the baking dish with the sausage.

4. Cover and bake until bubbling and somewhat thickened, about 1 hour and 30 minutes, stirring about every 30 minutes. Uncover and let stand about 5 minutes before serving.

PER SERVING (1¼ cups): 313 Cal, 8 g Fat, 2 g Sat Fat, 0 g Trans Fat, 33 mg Chol, 841 mg Sod, 42 g Carb, 10 g Fib, 20 g Prot, 77 mg Calc. *POINTS* value: *6*.

tip Battles rage over liquid smoke—some won't touch it; others swear by it. Truth is, it can give casseroles such as this a pleasant smoky edge. There are many brands on the market. Look for one without preservatives or artificial flavors—one that is simply made from hickory or mesquite smoke distillate and water.

MAKES 6 SERVINGS

¾ pound **chicken sausage**, thinly sliced

1 medium **onion**, chopped

1 **green bell pepper**, seeded and chopped

2 **garlic cloves**, minced

1 **jalapeño pepper**, seeded and finely chopped (wear gloves to prevent irritation)

2 (15½-ounce) **cans pinto beans**, rinsed and drained

1 (14½-ounce) **can reduced-sodium chicken broth**

1 (6-ounce) **can reduced-sodium tomato paste**

2 tablespoons **cider vinegar**

2 tablespoons **honey**

1 tablespoon **Dijon mustard**

1 teaspoon **sweet paprika**

¼ teaspoon **salt**

Freshly ground pepper

½ teaspoon **liquid smoke** (optional)

Roast Turkey with Onion Gravy

Nothing says "Thanksgiving" more than our juicy roast turkey, with gravy made from baked onions and pan drippings. You'll have about 2 cups leftover turkey pieces for another day.

1. Preheat the oven to 350°F.

2. Loosen skin around turkey breast by running fingers between skin and meat. Make a 1-inch slit on each thigh and each drumstick; run fingers between skin and meat to loosen skin. Slip 1 tablespoon sage leaves, 1 parsley sprig, and 1 thyme sprig into each slit; then slip 1 tablespoon sage leaves, 2 parsley sprigs, and 2 thyme sprigs under the skin on each side of breast.

3. Place the turkey in a large roasting pan. Arrange the giblets, neck, and onion slices around the turkey. Drizzle the turkey and onions with 1 cup of the broth.

4. Bake until an instant-read thermometer inserted in a thigh registers 180°F, about 2½ hours , basting with additional broth every 20 minutes. When the broth runs out, use pan juices to baste turkey. Transfer the turkey to a carving board and let stand about 10 minutes before carving.

5. Meanwhile, discard giblets and neck from the pan. Transfer onions to a cutting board using a slotted spoon; roughly chop them. Stir browned bits on the bottom of the pan to dissolve them. Strain pan juices into a measuring cup, skim off any visible fat, and add enough water to equal 1½ cups. Pour into a saucepan, add the chopped onions, and heat until simmering.

6. Stir water and arrowroot in a small bowl until dissolved; stir in some of hot pan juices. Return all to saucepan and cook, stirring constantly, until mixture bubbles and thickens. Stir in the salt and pepper; serve with turkey. Remove skin from the turkey.

Per serving (2 slices white turkey and 1 slice dark turkey, with about 3 tablespoons gravy): 228 Cal, 4 g Fat, 1 g Sat Fat, 0 g Trans Fat, 131 mg Chol, 262 mg Sod, 3 g Carb, 1 g Fib, 42 g Prot, 38 mg Calc. *POINTS* value: *5*.

MAKES 12 SERVINGS

- 1 (9½-pound) **turkey with giblets**
- 6 tablespoons packed **fresh sage leaves**
- 8 sprigs **fresh parsley**
- 8 sprigs **fresh thyme**
- 3 medium **onions**, cut into ½-inch slices
- 3 cups **reduced-sodium chicken broth**
- 1 tablespoon **water**
- 2 teaspoons **arrowroot**
- ¼ teaspoon **salt**
- ¼ teaspoon **freshly ground pepper**

Chicken Noodle Casserole

Here's an old-fashioned, family favorite: chicken, peas, and noodles, all bound together in a creamy sauce. No one will ever think it's something you made for your "diet"—and that's because it's not "diet food." It's good, homey fare, prepared so you can honor the choices you've made. This dish is assembled easily, thanks partly to precooked chicken.

1. Preheat the oven to 350°F. Spray a 2-quart high-sided baking dish with nonstick spray.

2. Cook the noodles according to package directions, omitting the salt. Drain and set aside.

3. Meanwhile, whisk the flour and ½ cup of the broth in a small bowl until the flour dissolves.

4. Heat the oil in a large saucepan over medium heat. Add the onion and cook, stirring frequently, until softened, about 3 minutes. Stir in the milk and the remaining ½ cup broth; bring the mixture to a simmer. Whisk in the flour mixture; cook, stirring constantly, until the sauce bubbles and thickens, about 3 minutes. Stir in the mustard, tarragon, salt, and pepper.

5. Remove the pan from the heat and stir in the noodles, peas, chicken, and cheese. Pour the mixture into the baking dish. Bake until bubbling and golden brown, about 40 minutes. Let stand about 5 minutes before serving.

PER SERVING (1⅓ cups): 343 Cal, 6 g Fat, 1 g Sat Fat, 0 g Trans Fat, 42 mg Chol, 543 mg Sod, 44 g Carb, 4 g Fib, 28 g Prot, 200 mg Calc. *POINTS* value: *7*.

MAKES 6 SERVINGS

½ pound **no-yolk egg noodles**

3 tablespoons **all-purpose flour**

1 cup **reduced-sodium chicken broth**

2 teaspoons **canola oil**

1 small **onion**, finely chopped

2 cups **fat-free milk**

1 tablespoon **Dijon mustard**

1 tablespoon chopped **fresh tarragon**

½ teaspoon **salt**

Freshly ground pepper

1 (10-ounce) package **frozen peas**

2 cups chopped **cooked chicken**

½ cup (2 ounces) **shredded reduced-fat cheddar or Swiss cheese**

Chicken Noodle Casserole

Southwestern Turkey Breast

Whole turkey breasts show up regularly in supermarkets—they make great roasts for an easy supper any night of the week, but are special enough for Sunday dinner. Whatever you do, don't save this easy dish just for the holidays! You'll have about 1 cup leftover turkey pieces for another day.

1. Adjust the racks to divide the oven into thirds. Preheat the oven to 350°F. Spray a large roasting pan with nonstick spray.

2. Mix the chili powder and cumin in a small bowl; stir in the oil and lime juice until the mixture forms a thick paste.

3. Loosen the skin around the turkey breast by running your fingers between the skin and the meat, starting at the tips of the breast halves. Once the skin is loosened, divide the spice mixture between the two halves and spread it liberally onto the meat, patting the skin back into place. Place the turkey breast in the roasting pan.

4. Bake in the lower third of the oven, basting with pan juices every 20 minutes, until an instant-read thermometer inserted in the breast registers 170°F, about 2 hours. If the pan juices dry out before the turkey is cooked through, use the broth to baste the bird occasionally. Transfer the turkey breast to a carving board and let stand about 10 minutes before carving. Remove the skin before eating.

PER SERVING (2 slices): 191 Cal, 3 g Fat, 1 g Sat Fat, 0 g Trans Fat, 107 mg Chol, 93 mg Sod, 1 g Carb, 0 g Fib, 38 g Prot, 24 mg Calc. *POINTS* value: *4*.

tip Pumpkin seed oil is a staple in Mexican cooking and is often used in Tex-Mex dishes. It's sometimes sold under the name "pepitá oil." Just a small amount adds a distinctive, slightly smoky flavor.

1½ tablespoons **chili powder**

1 teaspoon **ground cumin**

1 tablespoon **canola oil or pumpkin seed oil**

2 teaspoons **fresh lime juice**

1 (5-pound) **turkey breast**

¼ cup **reduced-sodium chicken broth**, if necessary

Thai Turkey Stew

The secret to the characteristic taste of Thai stews is twofold. First, don't brown the ingredients before they're stewed, and second, use this foursome of flavorings: coconut milk, brown sugar, soy sauce, and fish sauce. Fish sauce is a Southeast Asian condiment, sweet and aromatic. It's available in the Asian aisle of most supermarkets, sold under the name "nam pla" (the Thai version) or "nuoc mam" (the slightly mellower Vietnamese version). Although pungent, fish sauce mellows beautifully when cooked. Look for a bottle without artificial flavors or sweeteners.

1. Preheat the oven to 400°F.

2. Whisk the coconut milk, sugar, soy sauce, fish sauce, and curry paste in a 3-quart baking dish with a tight-fitting lid or a clay Chinese stew pot.

3. Add the turkey, scallions, cauliflower, bell pepper, okra, and peas; mix well. Cover and bake until the sauce is bubbling and the turkey is cooked through, about 55 minutes.

4. Stir the water and arrowroot in a small bowl until dissolved; stir in some of the juices from the baking dish. Return all to the baking dish and stir. Continue baking, uncovered, until slightly thickened, about 10 minutes longer. Let stand 5 minutes before serving.

PER SERVING (generous 1 cup): 237 Cal, 7 g Fat, 5 g Sat Fat, 0 g Trans Fat, 50 mg Chol, 393 mg Sod, 23 g Carb, 6 g Fib, 24 g Prot, 86 mg Calc. *POINTS* value: *5*.

tip Coconut milk is simply made from coconut flesh steeped in water, then pressed out as milk. Light or reduced-fat coconut milk is simply the second pressing of the same coconut solids, with far less fat in the milk.

MAKES 6 SERVINGS

1 (13½-ounce) can **light (reduced-fat) coconut milk**

2 tablespoons packed **light brown sugar**

2 tablespoons **reduced-sodium soy sauce**

1 tablespoon **Asian fish sauce** (nam pla)

2 teaspoons **Thai curry paste**, hot or mild or 2 teaspoons curry powder

1 pound **skinless boneless turkey breast**, cut into 1-inch pieces

2 **scallions**, cut into 1-inch pieces

1 (1-pound) **cauliflower**, trimmed and cut into florets

1 **green bell pepper**, seeded and chopped

1 (10-ounce) package **frozen okra**, thawed

1 cup **fresh shelled peas**, or frozen peas, thawed

1 tablespoon **water**

2 teaspoons **arrowroot or cornstarch**

Turkey Shepherd's Pie

Turkey Shepherd's Pie

For many of us, shepherd's pie—a hearty casserole topped with mashed potatoes—symbolizes comfort food, especially satisfying on a cold evening. Yukon Gold potatoes, a yellow-fleshed potato that now shows up regularly in our markets, make delicious mashed potatoes. If you prefer a lighter, fluffier mash, choose Idaho or russet potatoes. White Worcestershire sauce is sometimes called Worcestershire for chicken.

1. Bring the potatoes, with enough water to cover, to a boil in a large pot. Reduce the heat and simmer, covered, until the potatoes are tender when pierced with a fork, about 12 minutes. Drain and place in a medium bowl. Add the milk, mustard, and ground pepper. Mash with a potato masher or an electric mixer on medium speed until creamy, about 4 minutes by hand or 2 minutes with a mixer; set aside.

2. Preheat the oven to 350°F.

3. Spray a large nonstick skillet with nonstick spray and set over medium heat. Add the onion and cook, stirring frequently, until softened, about 2 minutes. Add the turkey and cook, breaking it up with a wooden spoon, until browned, about 4 minutes.

4. Sprinkle the flour over the turkey mixture. Stir well and cook, just until the flour is absorbed, about 30 seconds. Stir in the Worcestershire sauce, sage, and peppercorns; cook until fragrant, about 10 seconds. Stir in the broth and bring to a boil. Reduce the heat and simmer until the mixture bubbles and thickens, about 1 minute. Stir in the peas and carrots. Pour the mixture into a 9-inch square baking dish.

5. Spoon or pipe the mashed potatoes over the turkey mixture. Sprinkle with the paprika. Place the baking dish on a rimmed baking sheet and bake until bubbling and heated through, about 40 minutes. Let stand about 5 minutes before serving.

PER SERVING (1 cup): 208 Cal, 1 g Fat, 0 g Sat Fat, 0 g Trans Fat, 38 mg Chol, 249 mg Sod, 31 g Carb, 4 g Fib, 19 g Prot, 77 mg Calc. *POINTS* value: *3*.

MAKES 6 SERVINGS

- 3 large **Yukon Gold potatoes** (about 1½ pounds), peeled and quartered
- ¾ cup **fat-free milk**
- 1 tablespoon **Dijon mustard**
- **Freshly ground pepper**
- 1 medium **onion**, chopped
- ¾ pound **ground skinless lean turkey breast**
- 1½ tablespoons **all-purpose flour**
- 2 tablespoons **white Worcestershire sauce**
- 1 teaspoon finely chopped **fresh sage**
- ½ teaspoon **crushed green peppercorns**
- ¾ cup **reduced-sodium chicken broth**
- 1 (10-ounce) package **frozen peas and carrots**, thawed
- ¼ teaspoon **paprika**

Easy Turkey Lasagna

With jarred marinara sauce and no-cook lasagna noodles, it's a snap to make this tasty casserole any night of the week. We jazz it up by topping it with the most flavorful of Parmesan cheeses, Parmigiano-Reggiano.

1. Preheat the oven to 375°F.

2. Spray a large nonstick skillet with nonstick spray and set over medium heat. Add the turkey and cook, breaking it up with a wooden spoon, until lightly browned, about 1 minute. Add the mushrooms and cook until they give off their liquid and it reduces by half, about 4 minutes. Stir in the marinara sauce and bring the mixture to a simmer. Remove the skillet from the heat and set aside.

3. Combine the ricotta cheese, mozzarella cheese, egg whites, and nutmeg in a medium bowl.

4. Spread the tomato sauce evenly across the bottom of a 9 x 13-inch baking pan. Place 5 of the lasagna noodles over the sauce in one layer. Top with one-third of the turkey mixture, then spread half the cheese mixture over the turkey mixture. Repeat the layering one more time, then top with the remaining 5 noodles and the remaining one-third turkey mixture. Sprinkle the Parmigiano-Reggiano over the top.

5. Cover and bake the lasagna 45 minutes. Uncover and bake until bubbling and lightly browned on top, about 10 minutes longer. Let stand about 5 minutes before serving.

PER SERVING (⅒ of lasagna): 306 Cal, 6 g Fat, 3 g Sat Fat, 0 g Trans Fat, 49 mg Chol, 498 mg Sod, 32 g Carb, 2 g Fib, 30 g Prot, 308 mg Calc. *POINTS* value: *6*.

tip Parmigiano-Reggiano is a long-aged cheese from northern Italy, famed for its rich, savory flavor and unique texture. Look for chunks of the cheese at markets with the rind intact and stamped with the name Parmigiano-Reggiano. Avoid grated Parmesan cheese in jars, which may contain hydrogenated oil and stabilizers.

MAKES 10 SERVINGS

- 1 pound **ground skinless lean turkey breast**

- ½ pound **cremini or white button mushrooms,** thinly sliced

- 1 (26-ounce) **jar fat-free marinara sauce**

- 1 (16-ounce) container **fat-free ricotta cheese**

- 2 cups (8 ounces) **shredded part-skim mozzarella cheese**

- 2 **egg whites,** lightly beaten

- ½ teaspoon grated **nutmeg**

- 1 (8-ounce) **can no-salt-added tomato sauce**

- 1 (9-ounce) package **no-boil lasagna noodles**

- ¼ cup (1 ounce) grated **Parmigiano-Reggiano cheese**

Easy Turkey Lasagna

Turkey Breakfast Casserole

Here's a turkey version of the popular bread and cheese strata, often a favorite for holiday brunches. If you're using turkey sausage still in its casing, slip the casings off the meat and use the meat as you would ground beef.

1. Spray a large nonstick skillet with nonstick spray and set over medium heat. Add the onion and cook, stirring frequently, until softened, about 2 minutes. Add the sausage and cook, breaking it up with a wooden spoon, until golden brown, about 2 minutes. Drain any fat from the skillet.

2. Add the chiles, cumin, paprika, and mustard to the sausage in the skillet; cook, stirring constantly, about 1 minute. Transfer the mixture to a large bowl. Stir in the bread pieces and ½ cup of the cheese.

3. Spray a 9 x 13-inch baking pan with nonstick spray. Spread the sausage and bread mixture evenly in the pan. Sprinkle with the remaining ½ cup cheese.

4. Whisk the egg substitute and milk in a medium bowl until foamy; pour over the bread mixture. Press with the back of a spoon to make sure all turkey and bread mixture is submerged in liquid. Cover with foil and refrigerate at least 6 hours, or preferably overnight.

5. Preheat the oven to 350°F. Let the casserole stand at room temperature while the oven heats.

6. Bake the casserole, covered with the foil, 30 minutes. Uncover and bake until a knife inserted in the center comes out clean, about 10 minutes longer.

PER SERVING (⅛ of casserole): 230 Cal, 7 g Fat, 2 g Sat Fat, 0 g Trans Fat, 28 mg Chol, 765 mg Sod, 18 g Carb, 3 g Fib, 24 g Prot, 192 mg Calc. *POINTS* value: *5*.

MAKES 8 SERVINGS

- 1 medium **onion**, chopped
- ¾ pound **turkey sausage**
- 1 (4½-ounce) can chopped **mild or hot green chiles**
- 1 teaspoon **ground cumin**
- 1 teaspoon **mild paprika**
- ½ teaspoon **dry mustard**
- 9 slices **day-old whole-wheat bread**, crusts removed, bread torn into 1-inch pieces
- 1 cup (4 ounces) **shredded reduced-fat cheddar cheese**
- 3 cups **fat-free egg substitute**
- ¾ cup **fat-free milk**

Duck Tzimmes

Tzimmes is a traditional Jewish dish of prunes, sweet potatoes, and brisket, usually eaten at Rosh Hashanah, or the Jewish New Year. It's fairly sweet, said to symbolize the wish for a sweet new year. We've replaced the brisket with duck confit—a French extravagance of duck legs cooked in duck fat. The legs stay plump with a characteristically smoky flavor. You can find duck legs confit at the poultry counter of some large supermarkets and at the butcher counter of almost all gourmet markets.

1. Adjust the racks to divide the oven into thirds. Preheat the oven to 350°F. Spray a 9 x 13-inch baking pan with nonstick spray.

2. Remove any white fat and all the skin from the duck legs confit. Pull off the meat and shred with your hands or two forks. You should have about 1½ cups of meat. Place the meat in a large bowl and combine with the carrots, sweet potatoes, prunes, and cherries.

3. Whisk the broth, honey, salt, cinnamon, and garlic powder in a small bowl until smooth. Pour over the duck and vegetables; toss to coat. Pour this mixture and any juices into the baking pan.

4. Cover the pan with foil and bake in the lower third of the oven, tossing every 15 minutes, until the vegetables are tender, about 1 hour and 10 minutes. Let stand, uncovered, about 5 minutes before serving.

PER SERVING (1 cup): 228 Cal, 3 g Fat, 1 g Sat Fat, 0 g Trans Fat, 33 mg Chol, 253 mg Sod, 42 g Carb, 5 g Fib, 11 g Prot, 51 mg Calc. *POINTS* value: *4*.

MAKES 8 SERVINGS

2 (4-ounce) **fully-cooked duck legs confit**

5 large **carrots**, cut into 1-inch pieces

1 pound **sweet potatoes**, peeled and cut into 1-inch pieces

1 cup **pitted prunes**, quartered

½ cup **dried cherries**

¼ cup **reduced-sodium chicken broth**

3 tablespoons **honey**

½ teaspoon **salt**

½ teaspoon **cinnamon**

¼ teaspoon **garlic powder**

Cranberry-Braised Cornish Hens

Cranberry-Braised Cornish Hens

Here's an idea for Thanksgiving for just two or four people—Cornish game hens, braised in, and glazed with, an aromatic cranberry sauce. But don't wait until November to make this delicious dish. It'll turn any supper into a celebration.

1. Preheat the oven to 350°F.

2. Tie the legs of each hen together with butcher's twine. Tie twine twice around the whole body of each hen. Spray a Dutch oven or 2½-quart flameproof casserole dish with nonstick spray and set over medium heat. Add the hens and brown on all sides, about 4 minutes. Transfer the hens to a plate.

3. Add onion and garlic to Dutch oven; cook, stirring frequently, until softened, about 2 minutes. Stir in the vermouth, cranberry sauce, and marmalade; cook, stirring occasionally, until marmalade melts. Stir in bay leaf, thyme, salt, and pepper. Reduce heat and simmer, uncovered, stirring occasionally, about 5 minutes.

4. Return the hens, breast-side up, to the Dutch oven. Baste once with some of the mixture in the Dutch oven, then cover and bake until an instant-read thermometer inserted in a thigh registers 180°F, about 1 hour. Transfer the hens to a carving board; let stand about 5 minutes. Remove wine, then cut hens in half along breastbone, so that each half has a leg and thigh.

5. Skim any visible fat from the sauce in the Dutch oven. Discard the bay leaf. Place the Dutch oven over medium heat and bring to a simmer.

6. Stir the water and arrowroot in a small bowl until dissolved; stir in some of the hot juices from the Dutch oven. Return all to the Dutch oven and cook, stirring constantly, until the mixture bubbles and thickens. Serve the sauce with the hens.

PER SERVING (½ hen with 2 tablespoons sauce): 239 Cal, 5 g Fat, 1 g Sat Fat, 0 g Trans Fat, 132 mg Chol, 383 mg Sod, 16 g Carb, 1 g Fib, 29 g Prot, 27 mg Calc. **POINTS** value: **5**.

MAKES 4 SERVINGS ☛

- 2 (1¼-pound) **Cornish game hens**, skinned
- 1 small **onion**, finely chopped
- 1 **garlic clove**, minced
- ¼ cup **dry vermouth**
- ⅓ cup **canned whole-berry cranberry sauce**
- 1 tablespoon **orange marmalade**
- 1 **bay leaf**
- 1 teaspoon chopped **fresh thyme**
- ½ teaspoon **salt**
- **Freshly ground pepper**
- 2 teaspoons **water**
- 1 teaspoon **arrowroot or cornstarch**

Grilled and Broiled Meals

CHAPTER SEVEN

✓ Grilled Whole Herbed Chicken

This grilled whole chicken—moist, browned, and flavorful—
is so good that come winter you may be digging your grill out
of the snow to recreate this dish

1. Spray the grill rack with nonstick spray; prepare the
grill for indirect cooking (see tip below) and maintain
a medium-hot fire.

2. Combine the garlic, oil, lemon zest, rosemary, salt,
and pepper in a small bowl; mix well. With your
fingers loosen the skin over the chicken breasts, legs,
and thighs. Rub the garlic mixture into the meat under
the skin. Place the onion and lemon inside the body
cavity. Tuck the wing tips under the chicken and tie
the legs closed with kitchen string to help hold the
shape of the bird during grilling.

3. Place the chicken on the indirect heat section of the
grill rack (away from the heat source), breast-side up.
Cover the grill and grill, without turning, until an
instant-read thermometer inserted in a thigh registers
180°F, about 2 hours and 10 minutes. Transfer the
chicken to a carving board and let stand about
10 minutes before carving. Remove skin before eating.

PER SERVING (⅙ of chicken): 198 Cal, 9 g Fat, 2 g Sat Fat,
0 g Trans Fat, 81 mg Chol, 473 mg Sod, 1 g Carb, 0 g Fib, 27 g Prot,
20 mg Calc. *POINTS* value: *5*.

tip Several of our grilled chicken and turkey recipes call
for preparing the grill for indirect cooking. Here's how to
set it up: If you have a gas grill, preheat only one side. If
you have a charcoal grill, mound the charcoal on one
side of the grill. For indirect cooking, the food is cooked
on the unheated side of the grill, giving larger or thicker
items longer to cook through without burning.

MAKES 6 SERVINGS

5 **garlic cloves**,
thinly sliced

1 tablespoon **olive oil**

1 tablespoon grated
lemon zest

1 tablespoon chopped
fresh rosemary

1 teaspoon **salt**

¼ teaspoon **freshly
ground pepper**

1 (3½–4-pound) **chicken**,
giblets discarded

½ **onion**, peeled and
cut in half

½ **lemon**, cut in half

Chicken Under a Brick

In order to grill a whole chicken, sometimes we split it open so that it will lie flat on the grill and cook evenly and fairly quickly. The method we use to splay chickens open is called spatchcocking—follow our simple directions in step 1. If you don't happen to have a brick, use a heavy cast-iron skillet. And remember to use sturdy oven mitts when removing either the hot bricks or the skillet from the grill.

1. Spray the grill rack with nonstick spray; prepare the grill for indirect cooking (see tip page 228) and maintain a medium-hot fire. Wrap 2 bricks with heavy-duty foil.

2. To spatchcock the chicken, with a sharp knife or poultry shears, remove the wings from the chicken at the first joint. Then remove the backbone and spread the chicken open, like a book, skin-side down. Use a paring knife and cut along each side of the breastbone. Run your thumbs along both sides of the breastbone and pull the white cartilage out, so that the chicken can lie flat. Remove the skin and prick the chicken all over with the tip of a knife.

3. Combine the vinegar, honey, garlic, oil, and oregano in a large zip-close plastic bag; add the chicken. Squeeze out the air and seal the bag; turn to coat the chicken. Refrigerate, turning the bag occasionally, at least 30 minutes or up to overnight.

4. Lift the chicken from the marinade and sprinkle with the salt and pepper. Discard the marinade. Place the chicken, on the indirect heat section of the grill rack (away from the heat source). Place the bricks on top of the chicken and close the grill. Grill 30 minutes. Remove the bricks and turn the chicken over. Grill until an instant-read thermometer inserted in a thigh registers 180°F, about 30 minutes longer. Transfer the chicken to a carving board and let stand about 10 minutes before carving.

PER SERVING (⅙ of chicken): 210 Cal, 8 g Fat, 2 g Sat Fat, 0 g Trans Fat, 92 mg Chol, 482 mg Sod, 2 g Carb, 0 g Fib, 30 g Prot, 18 mg Calc. **POINTS** value: **5.**

MAKES 6 SERVINGS

- 1 (3½–4-pound) **chicken**, giblets discarded
- 3 tablespoons **balsamic vinegar**
- 3 tablespoons **honey**
- 3 **garlic cloves**, minced
- 1 tablespoon **olive oil**
- 1 teaspoon **dried oregano**
- 1 teaspoon **salt**
- ¼ teaspoon **freshly ground pepper**

✔ Grilled Chicken Breasts with Tomato-Corn Salsa

Fresh sweet corn adds a burst of sweetness to this salsa. We grill the corn but, if you have really sweet corn, you don't even have to cook it—simply cut the corn from the cobs and add it raw to the other salsa ingredients. Serrano and habañero chile peppers are extremely hot; substitute the milder jalapeño pepper if you like.

1. Spray the grill rack with nonstick spray; prepare the grill for a medium-hot fire.

2. To make the salsa, place the corn on the grill rack and grill until well marked, about 8 minutes, turning every 2 minutes. Transfer the corn to a cutting board and let cool about 5 minutes. With a sharp knife, cut the kernels from the cobs and transfer to a large bowl. Add the tomatoes, onion, serrano pepper, lime juice, cilantro, and salt; mix well and set aside.

3. Rub the chicken with the oil and sprinkle with Cajun seasoning. Place the chicken on the grill rack and grill until well marked and an instant-read thermometer inserted in a breast registers 170°F, 10–12 minutes on each side. Serve the chicken with the salsa.

PER SERVING (1 piece chicken with 1 cup salsa): 221 Cal, 7 g Fat, 1 g Sat Fat, 0 g Trans Fat, 42 mg Chol, 474 mg Sod, 24 g Carb, 3 g Fib, 19 g Prot, 17 mg Calc. *POINTS* value: *4*.

tip Hot peppers can irritate skin, so if you are handling serrano or habañero peppers, wear surgical gloves (available in drugstores) and do not touch your eyes or any other tender or moist parts of your body without first washing your hands thoroughly.

MAKES 4 SERVINGS

- 3 **fresh ears of corn**, husks and silks removed

- 1 pint **cherry tomatoes**, quartered

- ½ small **red onion**, chopped, about ⅓ cup

- 1 **serrano or habañero chile pepper**, seeded and finely chopped (wear gloves to prevent irritation)

- 2 tablespoons **fresh lime juice**

- 1 tablespoon chopped **fresh cilantro**

- ¼ teaspoon **salt**

- 2 (¾-pound) **bone-in chicken breast halves**, skinned and cut in half the short way

- 1 tablespoon **olive oil**

- 2 teaspoons **Cajun seasoning**

Grilled Chicken Breasts with Tomato-Corn Salsa

Grilled Chicken Breast Satay with Peanut Sauce

Satay (or saté) is an Indonesian specialty of marinated-then-grilled chunks of meat or poultry, usually accompanied by a spicy peanut sauce. You might like to serve this with steamed basmati rice (½ cup per serving will increase the *POINTS* value by 2) and a crisp thinly sliced cucumber salad.

1. Combine the fish sauce, ginger, and garlic in a zip-close plastic bag; add the chicken. Squeeze out the air and seal the bag; turn to coat the chicken. Refrigerate, turning the bag occasionally, at least 1 hour or up to overnight.

2. Spray the grill rack with nonstick spray; prepare the grill for a medium-hot fire.

3. Meanwhile, to make the peanut sauce, combine the coconut milk, peanut butter, vinegar, sugar, and curry paste in a medium saucepan. Cook over medium heat, stirring constantly, until the mixture is smooth and heated through, about 3 minutes. Remove from the heat and stir in the cilantro. Let the sauce cool to room temperature.

4. Lift the chicken from the marinade and place on the grill rack. Discard the marinade. Grill the chicken until well marked and cooked through, 5–6 minutes on each side. Serve the chicken with the sauce.

PER SERVING (1 piece chicken with 3 tablespoons sauce): 277 Cal, 12 g Fat, 4 g Sat Fat, 0 g Trans Fat, 68 mg Chol, 194 mg Sod, 13 g Carb, 1 g Fib, 29 g Prot, 29 mg Calc. *POINTS* value: *6*.

tip To turn this into an appetizer, simply cut each chicken breast into ½-inch-wide strips before marinating, then thread the chicken onto skewers and grill until cooked through, 3 to 4 minutes on each side.

MAKES 4 SERVINGS

- 1 tablespoon **Asian fish sauce** (nam pla)
- 1 tablespoon grated peeled **fresh ginger**
- 2 **garlic cloves**, minced
- 4 (¼-pound) **skinless boneless chicken breast halves**
- ½ cup **light (reduced-fat) coconut milk**
- ¼ cup **reduced-fat peanut butter**
- 1 tablespoon **rice vinegar**
- 2 teaspoons packed **dark brown sugar**
- ¾ teaspoon **Thai green curry paste**
- 1 tablespoon chopped **fresh cilantro**

Grilled Stuffed Chicken Breasts

Elegant enough for entertaining, these chicken breasts are deliciously stuffed with sun-dried tomatoes, a mixture of cheeses, and fresh basil. You could stuff the chicken breasts and keep them refrigerated for up to 24 hours, ready to grill just as your guests arrive.

1. Spray the grill rack with nonstick spray; prepare the grill for a medium-hot fire.

2. Combine the sun-dried tomatoes with enough boiling water to cover in a small bowl. Let stand until softened, about 15 minutes. Drain the tomatoes then finely chop. Transfer the tomatoes to a medium bowl. Add the mozzarella cheese, Parmesan cheese, basil, and 1 teaspoon of the oil; mix well.

3. Make a pocket in the side of each chicken breast by inserting a sharp paring knife into the thickest part, then gently cutting back and forth until a small chamber has opened in the side. Do not cut through to the back or the sides of the breasts. Enlarge the pockets gently with your fingers. Fill each pocket evenly with the filling (about 3 tablespoons in each). Secure the opening with wooden picks.

4. Brush the chicken with the remaining 2 teaspoons oil, then sprinkle with the salt and pepper. Place on the grill rack and grill until well marked and the chicken is cooked through, 8–10 minutes on each side.

PER SERVING (1 stuffed chicken breast): 232 Cal, 10 g Fat, 3 g Sat Fat, 0 g Trans Fat, 76 mg Chol, 472 mg Sod, 5 g Carb, 1 g Fib, 30 g Prot, 130 mg Calc. *POINTS* value: *5*.

MAKES 4 SERVINGS

- 8 **sun-dried tomatoes** (not oil-packed)

- ⅓ cup **shredded part-skim mozzarella cheese**

- 2 tablespoons grated **Parmesan cheese**

- 8 **fresh basil leaves,** chopped

- 3 teaspoons **extra-virgin olive oil**

- 4 (¼-pound) **skinless boneless chicken breast halves**

- ½ teaspoon **salt**

- ¼ teaspoon **freshly ground pepper**

Broiled Buffalo Chicken Tenders

Broiled Buffalo Chicken Tenders

These spicy hot chicken tenders make great Sunday football fare or just a fun lunch. Serve with grilled or toasted sourdough bread for a more satisfying meal (1 slice of bread will up the *POINTS* value by 2). Or, enjoy this with a light beer and increase the *POINTS* value by 2.

1. Spray the grill rack with nonstick spray; prepare the grill for a medium-hot fire. Or spray the broiler rack with nonstick spray and preheat the broiler.

2. Combine the hot sauce and pepper sauce in a small saucepan over medium heat. Bring to a simmer and cook 1 minute. Remove from the heat and swirl in 1 tablespoon of the butter.

3. Melt the remaining ½ tablespoon butter and toss with chicken tenders in a medium bowl. Place the chicken on the grill or broiler rack and grill or broil 4 inches from the heat until cooked through, 4–5 minutes on each side. Transfer the chicken to a clean bowl and toss with the hot sauce mixture. Serve with the carrots, celery sticks, and blue cheese dressing.

PER SERVING (about 2 chicken tenders, a few vegetable sticks, and 1 tablespoon dressing): 224 Cal, 8 g Fat, 4 g Sat Fat, 0 g Trans Fat, 80 mg Chol, 456 mg Sod, 12 g Carb, 1 g Fib, 26 g Prot, 29 mg Calc. *POINTS* value: *5*.

tip To make ahead, toss the cooled cooked chicken with the hot sauce in a casserole dish; cover and refrigerate overnight to allow the chicken to really absorb the flavors from the sauce. Reheat the chicken in the covered casserole dish in a 350°F oven until heated through, about 10 minutes.

MAKES 8 SERVINGS

- ¼ cup **Louisiana-style hot sauce**
- ½ teaspoon **hot pepper sauce**
- 1½ tablespoons **unsalted butter**
- 1 pound **chicken tenders**
- 8 baby **carrots**
- 2 **celery stalks**, cut into 2 x ¼-inch sticks
- ¼ cup **fat-free blue cheese dressing**

☑ Moroccan Chicken Legs

Orange zest and garlic team deliciously with North African spices to give this chicken an exotic, Moroccan flavor. Try serving it with a shepherd's salad of chopped tomatoes, cucumbers, parsley, red-wine vinegar, and scallions.

1. Combine the garlic, scallion, oil, orange zest, mint, cumin, paprika, ginger, and cinnamon in a zip-close plastic bag; add the chicken. Squeeze out the air and seal the bag; turn to coat the chicken. Refrigerate, turning the bag occasionally, at least 4 hours or up to overnight.

2. Spray the grill rack with nonstick spray; prepare the grill for a medium-hot fire.

3. Lift the chicken from the marinade and sprinkle with the salt. Discard the marinade. Place the chicken on the grill rack. Cover the grill and grill until well marked and an instant-read thermometer inserted in a thigh registers 180°F, 12–15 minutes on each side.

PER SERVING (1 chicken leg): 192 Cal, 8 g Fat, 2 g Sat Fat, 0 g Trans Fat, 83 mg Chol, 520 mg Sod, 0 g Carb, 0 g Fib, 28 g Prot, 35 mg Calc. **POINTS** value: **5**.

MAKES 4 SERVINGS

2 **garlic cloves**, minced

1 **scallion**, finely chopped

1 tablespoon **extra-virgin olive oil**

2 teaspoons grated **orange zest**

1 teaspoon **dried mint**

1 teaspoon **ground cumin**

¾ teaspoon **hot paprika**

¼ teaspoon **ground ginger**

¼ teaspoon **cinnamon**

4 (½-pound) **whole chicken legs**, skinned

¾ teaspoon **salt**

Thai Chicken Legs

Thai roasted red chili paste is a condiment made from crushed roasted red Thai chiles, sugar, tamarind, dried shrimp, and several spices. It lends a delicious smoky, spicy flavor to any dish. You can find it in jars in the Asian aisle of large supermarkets.

1. Combine the garlic, ginger, vinegar, fish sauce, sugar, cilantro, mint, lime zest, chili paste, and salt in a zip-close plastic bag; add the chicken. Squeeze out the air and seal the bag; turn to coat the chicken. Refrigerate, turning the bag occasionally, at least 4 hours or up to overnight.

2. Spray the grill rack with nonstick spray; prepare the grill for a medium-hot fire.

3. Lift the chicken from the marinade and place on the grill rack. Discard the marinade. Cover the grill and grill the chicken until well marked and an instant-read thermometer inserted in a thigh registers 180°F, 12–15 minutes on each side.

PER SERVING (1 chicken leg): 188 Cal, 7 g Fat, 2 g Sat Fat, 0 g Trans Fat, 83 mg Chol, 183 mg Sod, 1 g Carb, 0 g Fib, 28 g Prot, 33 mg Calc. *POINTS* value: *4*.

MAKES 4 SERVINGS

- 1 **garlic clove,** minced
- 1 tablespoon grated peeled **fresh ginger**
- 2 tablespoons **rice vinegar**
- 1 tablespoon **Asian fish sauce** (nam pla)
- 1 tablespoon **sugar**
- 1 tablespoon chopped **fresh cilantro**
- 1 tablespoon chopped **fresh mint**
- 2 teaspoons grated **lime zest**
- 1 teaspoon **Thai roasted red chili paste**
- ½ teaspoon **salt**
- 4 (½-pound) **whole chicken legs,** skinned

Chicken Thighs with Grilled Stone-Fruit Salsa

This recipe takes advantage of early summer's bounty of wonderful stone fruit. From mid June through September you should be able to find freestone fruit (fruit with pits easily removed) at local farm stands and supermarkets. A serving of couscous would complete the meal and increase the *POINTS* value by 3.

1. Spray the grill rack with nonstick spray; prepare the grill for a medium-hot fire.

2. To make the salsa, place the peaches, nectarines, and plums on the grill rack and grill until well marked and slightly softened, 4–5 minutes on each side; transfer to a bowl and let cool. Place the onion slices on the grill rack and grill until well marked and tender, 5–6 minutes on each side; transfer to a cutting board and let cool 5 minutes. Coarsely chop the onion, peaches, nectarines, and plums; transfer to a bowl. Add the cilantro, vinegar, sugar, $\frac{1}{4}$ teaspoon of the salt, and $\frac{1}{8}$ teaspoon of the pepper; mix well and set aside.

3. Sprinkle the chicken with the remaining $\frac{1}{2}$ teaspoon salt and $\frac{1}{8}$ teaspoon pepper; place on the grill rack. Grill until an instant-read thermometer inserted in a thigh registers 180°F, about 10 minutes on each side. Serve the chicken with the salsa.

PER SERVING (1 chicken thigh with $\frac{3}{4}$ cup salsa): 278 Cal, 8 g Fat, 2 g Sat Fat, 0 g Trans Fat, 57 mg Chol, 494 mg Sod, 32 g Carb, 4 g Fib, 22 g Prot, 37 mg Calc. *POINTS* value: *5*.

tip When buying stone fruit for grilling, look for fruit with good color that are firm but give just a little when pressed. Fruit that is too ripe turns to mush when cooked.

MAKES 4 SERVINGS

- 3 medium firm-ripe **peaches**, about $\frac{3}{4}$ pound, halved and pitted

- 3 medium firm-ripe **nectarines**, about $\frac{3}{4}$ pound, halved and pitted

- 3 medium firm-ripe **plums**, about $\frac{1}{2}$ pound, halved and pitted

- 1 small **red onion**, cut into $\frac{1}{4}$-inch-thick slices

- 2 tablespoons chopped **fresh cilantro**

- 1 tablespoon **cider vinegar**

- 1 tablespoon **sugar**

- $\frac{3}{4}$ teaspoon **salt**

- $\frac{1}{4}$ teaspoon **freshly ground pepper**

- 4 (5-ounce) **skinless bone-in chicken thighs**

 # Curried Drumsticks

You might like to serve these tangy, fragrant drumsticks with grilled chapati bread—a flatbread from India made from whole-wheat flour (a 5-inch round will up the **POINTS** value by 2) and store-bought mango chutney (a tablespoon will up the **POINTS** value by 1).

1. Combine the yogurt, lemon juice, curry powder, ginger, garlic, coriander, and cayenne in a zip-close plastic bag; add the drumsticks. Squeeze out the air and seal the bag; turn to coat the chicken. Refrigerate, turning the bag occasionally, at least 30 minutes or up to overnight.

2. Spray the grill rack with nonstick spray; prepare the grill for a medium-hot fire.

3. Lift the chicken from the marinade and sprinkle with the salt. Discard the marinade. Place the chicken on the grill rack and grill, turning occasionally, until well marked and an instant-read thermometer inserted in a drumstick registers 180°F, about 18 minutes.

PER SERVING (2 drumsticks): 158 Cal, 4 g Fat, 1 g Sat Fat, 0 g Trans Fat, 99 mg Chol, 525 mg Sod, 2 g Carb, 0 g Fib, 26 g Prot, 61 mg Calc. **POINTS** value: *3*.

tip To broil the drumsticks, spray the broiler rack with nonstick spray and preheat the broiler. Place the chicken on the broiler rack and broil 4 inches from the heat, turning occasionally, until an instant-read thermometer inserted in a drumstick registers 180°F, about 18 minutes.

MAKES 4 SERVINGS

½ cup **fat-free plain yogurt**

2 tablespoons **fresh lemon juice**

1 tablespoon **madras curry powder**

1 tablespoon grated peeled **fresh ginger**

1 **garlic clove**, minced

1 teaspoon **ground coriander**

⅛ teaspoon **cayenne**

8 (¼-pound) **skinless chicken drumsticks**

¾ teaspoon **salt**

Miso-Marinated Chicken Thighs

Miso is a key element of Japanese cuisine. It is made from fermented soybeans and can be found in Japanese markets, health-food stores, and the gourmet section of large supermarkets. Using it in a marinade allows it to impart a mild but distinctive flavor to the chicken.

1. Combine the miso paste, mirin, orange juice, ginger, and oil in a zip-close plastic bag; add the chicken. Squeeze out the air and seal the bag; turn to coat the chicken. Refrigerate, turning the bag occasionally, at least 30 minutes or up to overnight.

2. Spray the grill rack with nonstick spray; prepare the grill for a medium-hot fire.

3. Lift the chicken from the marinade. Wipe the excess marinade from the chicken and place the chicken on the grill rack. Discard the marinade. Cover the grill and grill the chicken until well marked and an instant-read thermometer inserted in a thigh registers 180°F, about 10 minutes on each side.

PER SERVING (1 chicken thigh): 172 Cal, 8 g Fat, 2 g Sat Fat, 0 g Trans Fat, 57 mg Chol, 261 mg Sod, 3 g Carb, 0 g Fib, 20 g Prot, 26 mg Calc. **POINTS** value: **4**.

tip This recipe works equally well broiled: Spray the broiler rack with nonstick spray and preheat the broiler. Broil the chicken 4 inches from the heat until an instant-read thermometer inserted in a thigh registers 180°F, about 10 minutes on each side.

MAKES 4 SERVINGS

⅓ cup **miso paste**

¼ cup **mirin** (rice wine)

¼ cup **orange juice**

1 tablespoon grated peeled **fresh ginger**

1 teaspoon **Asian (dark) sesame oil**

4 (6-ounce) **skinless bone-in chicken thighs**

Tequila-Citrus Chicken

Tequila-Citrus Chicken

Serve these slightly tangy, sweet thighs with fresh lime wedges and grilled corn tortillas for a south-of-the-border taste. You can grill the tortillas directly on the grill rack for about 1 minute on each side. A 6-inch corn tortilla for each serving will increase the *POINTS* value by 2.

1. Combine the garlic, orange juice, tequila, lime juice, oil, and cumin in a zip-close plastic bag; add the chicken. Squeeze out the air and seal the bag; turn to coat the chicken. Refrigerate, turning the bag occasionally, at least 8 hours or up to overnight.

2. Spray the grill rack with nonstick spray; prepare the grill for a medium-hot fire.

3. Lift the chicken from the marinade, shake off the excess marinade, then sprinkle the chicken with the salt and pepper. Discard the marinade. Place the chicken on the grill rack and grill until well marked and cooked through, 6–7 minutes on each side.

PER SERVING (1 chicken thigh): 202 Cal, 10 g Fat, 3 g Sat Fat, 0 g Trans Fat, 71 mg Chol, 359 mg Sod, 1 g Carb, 0 g Fib, 24 g Prot, 29 mg Calc. *POINTS* value: *5*.

tip To broil, spray the broiler rack with nonstick spray and preheat the broiler. Place the chicken on the broiler pan and broil 4 inches from the heat until cooked through, 6–7 minutes on each side.

MAKES 4 SERVINGS

2 **garlic cloves**, minced

½ cup **orange juice**

3 tablespoons **tequila**

2 tablespoons **fresh lime juice**

1 tablespoon **olive oil**

1 teaspoon **ground cumin**

4 (¼-pound) **skinless boneless chicken thighs**

½ teaspoon **salt**

¼ teaspoon **freshly ground pepper**

☑ Moroccan Chicken Kebabs

Moroccan dishes feature a unique contrast of sweet and spicy flavors. That is certainly the case with these juicy kebabs, where the chicken marinates in a delicious blend of lemon juice, fresh ginger, cumin, coriander, cinnamon, and cayenne. Vary the veggies on the kebabs if you like: chunks of bell pepper and onion work well.

1. Combine the lemon juice, ginger, cumin, coriander, cinnamon, and cayenne in a zip-close plastic bag; add the chicken. Squeeze out the air and seal the bag; turn to coat the chicken. Refrigerate, turning the bag occasionally, at least 1 hour or up to 4 hours.

2. Spray a broiler rack with olive oil nonstick spray; preheat the broiler. Alternately thread the chicken and vegetables onto 4 (8-inch) metal skewers; sprinkle both sides evenly with the salt and spray with olive oil nonstick spray. Broil the kebabs 4 inches from the heat, turning occasionally, until the chicken is cooked through and browned, 10–12 minutes.

PER SERVING (1 kebab): 263 Cal, 13 g Fat, 4 g Sat Fat, 0 g Trans Fat, 112 mg Chol, 399 mg Sod, 4 g Carb, 1 g Fib, 32 g Prot, 28 mg Calc. *POINTS* value: *6*.

tip If you prefer white meat, substitute 1½ pounds skinless boneless chicken breasts for the thighs. Refrigerate any extra, unpeeled ginger, sealed tightly in a plastic bag, in the crisper drawer for up to 3 weeks.

MAKES 4 SERVINGS

1 tablespoon **fresh lemon juice**

2 teaspoons grated peeled **fresh ginger**

1½ teaspoons **ground cumin**

1 teaspoon **ground coriander**

¼ teaspoon **cinnamon**

Pinch **cayenne**

1½ pounds **skinless boneless chicken thighs**, cut into 2-inch pieces

2 small **zucchini**, cut into 12 (1½-inch) pieces

8 **cherry tomatoes**

½ teaspoon **salt**

✓ Bacon-Cheddar Turkey Burgers

If you're tired of the same old burgers, then try these juicy patties, studded with bits of Canadian bacon and cheddar cheese. We broil the burgers so they're ready in a flash, but you can also throw them on the grill—just make sure the grill rack is first sprayed with nonstick spray.

1. Spray a broiler rack with canola nonstick spray; preheat the broiler.

2. Meanwhile, combine the mayonnaise and ketchup in a small bowl; set aside.

3. Spray a large nonstick skillet with canola nonstick spray and set over medium heat. Add the bacon and cook, stirring occasionally, until the bacon browns and starts to become crisp, 3–4 minutes. Transfer to a large bowl and let cool completely.

4. Add the turkey, cheese, Worcestershire sauce, salt, and pepper to the bacon in the large bowl. Form into 4 patties. Place the patties on the broiler rack and broil, 4 inches from the heat, until an instant-read thermometer inserted in the side of each patty registers 165°F, 3–4 minutes on each side. Top each burger with 1 tablespoon of the mayonnaise mixture.

PER SERVING (1 burger): 167 Cal, 2 g Fat, 1 g Sat Fat, 0 g Trans Fat, 82 mg Chol, 636 mg Sod, 4 g Carb, 0 g Fib, 32 g Prot, 53 mg Calc. *POINTS* value: *4*.

tip Serve the burgers on high-fiber rolls and you'll increase the per-serving *POINTS* value by 2.

MAKES 4 SERVINGS

3 tablespoons **fat-free mayonnaise**

1 tablespoon **ketchup**

2 slices **Canadian bacon,** cut into small pieces

1 pound **ground skinless lean turkey breast**

3 slices **fat-free sharp cheddar cheese,** cut into small pieces

1 teaspoon **Worcestershire sauce**

¼ teaspoon **salt**

⅛ teaspoon **freshly ground pepper**

Chile Chicken Patties with Chipotle Sauce on Sourdough

Chipotle chiles add intriguing taste to many Mexican dishes. Just one chipotle adds flavor, heat, and a touch of smokiness to these patties. You can find chipotles en adobo sauce in cans or jars in specialty stores and in the ethnic section of most supermarkets. You might like to serve these tasty patties with a cool crisp green salad.

1. Spray the grill rack with nonstick spray; prepare the grill for a medium-hot fire.

2. To make the chipotle sauce, combine the mayonnaise, pickle relish, capers, dill, and chipotle in a small bowl; mix well and set aside.

3. Combine the chicken, chili powder, oregano, and salt in a medium bowl; mix well. Shape the mixture into 4 patties, about 3½ inches in diameter. Place the patties on the grill rack and grill until an instant-read thermometer inserted in the side of a patty registers 165°F, 5–6 minutes on each side. Transfer the patties to a plate.

4. Place the bread slices on the grill rack and grill until lightly toasted, 1–2 minutes on each side. Place the chicken patties on the bread slices and top each evenly with the sauce.

PER SERVING (1 open-face sandwich with 2 tablespoons sauce): 371 Cal, 8 g Fat, 2 g Sat Fat, 1 g Trans Fat, 68 mg Chol, 1204 mg Sod, 43 g Carb, 3 g Fib, 31 g Prot, 74 mg Calc. *POINTS* value: *7*.

MAKES 4 SERVINGS

- 6 tablespoons **low-fat mayonnaise**
- 2 tablespoons **sweet pickle relish**
- 1 tablespoon drained **capers**, chopped
- 2 teaspoons chopped **fresh dill**
- 1 **chipotle en adobo**, minced
- 1 pound **ground skinless lean chicken breast**
- 1 tablespoon **chili powder**
- 1 teaspoon **dried oregano**
- ½ teaspoon **salt**
- 4 slices (about 3 x 4 inches each) **sourdough bread**

Chile Chicken Patties with Chipotle
Sauce on Sourdough

✓ Thanksgiving Turkey

Turkey is a snap to cook on the grill and the best part is your oven is free for cooking the many Thanksgiving accompaniments. Rubbed with garlic, sage, and paprika, this turkey has a deep golden color and is moist with a smoky, herbed flavor. You'll have enough to serve 12 people with about 2½ cups leftover turkey pieces for another day. Refrigerate leftovers promptly and keep no more than 3 days.

1. Spray the grill rack with nonstick spray; prepare the grill for indirect cooking (see tip page 228) and maintain a medium fire.

2. Combine the garlic, sage, paprika, oil, salt, and pepper in a small bowl; mix well. Loosen the skin around the turkey breast by running your fingers between the skin and the meat. Make a 1-inch slit on each thigh and each drumstick; run your fingers between the skin and meat to loosen the skin. Rub the garlic mixture under the skin on each side of the breast and the legs. Tuck the wing tips underneath the turkey and tie the legs together with kitchen string to help hold the shape of the bird during grilling.

3. Place the turkey on the indirect heat section of the grill rack (away from the heat source), cover the grill, and grill until an instant-read thermometer inserted in a thigh registers 180°F, 3–3½ hours Transfer the turkey to a carving board and let stand about 10 minutes before carving. Remove the skin before eating.

PER SERVING (2 slices white turkey, 1 slice dark turkey): 185 Cal, 5 g Fat, 2 g Sat Fat, 0 g Trans Fat, 97 mg Chol, 265 mg Sod, 0 g Carb, 0 g Fib, 33 g Prot, 27 mg Calc. *POINTS* value: *4*.

MAKES 12 SERVINGS

- 4 **garlic cloves**, minced
- 2 tablespoons chopped **fresh sage**
- 1 tablespoon **paprika**
- 1 tablespoon **olive oil**
- 1½ teaspoons **salt**
- ½ teaspoon **freshly ground pepper**
- 1 (10-pound) **turkey**, giblets discarded

Whole Turkey Breast with Zesty Cranberry Relish

A quarter teaspoon of crushed red pepper may not seem like a lot but it does add quite a zing to the relish. For a less spicy taste, reduce the amount used to ⅛ teaspoon. You can make the relish ahead and store it in the refrigerator for up to 2 weeks.

1. Spray the grill rack with nonstick spray; prepare the grill for indirect cooking (see tip page 228) and maintain a medium fire.

2. Combine the oil, garlic, oregano, salt, and ground pepper in a small bowl; mix well. Loosen the skin around the turkey breast by running your fingers between the skin and the meat, starting at the tips of the breast halves. Once the skin is loosened, divide the spice mixture between the two halves and spread it liberally onto the meat, patting the skin back into place.

3. Place the turkey breast, breast-side up, on the indirect heat section of the grill rack (away from the heat source), cover the grill, and grill until an instant-read thermometer inserted in the breast registers 170°F, 2½–3 hours.

4. Meanwhile, combine the sugar, orange juice, water, onion, and crushed red pepper in a medium saucepan; bring to a boil. Add the cranberries and return to a boil. Reduce the heat and simmer, stirring occasionally, until the mixture thickens slightly and the cranberries pop, about 15 minutes. Remove from the heat and stir in the lime zest. Let the mixture cool about 30 minutes, then chill until ready to serve.

5. Transfer the turkey breast to a carving board and let stand about 10 minutes before carving. Remove the skin before eating. Serve with the relish.

PER SERVING (2 slices turkey with ⅓ cup relish): 348 Cal, 3 g Fat, 1 g Sat Fat, 0 g Trans Fat, 138 mg Chol, 288 mg Sod, 29 g Carb, 2 g Fib, 49 g Prot, 34 mg Calc. *POINTS* value: *7*.

MAKES 12 SERVINGS

- 1 tablespoon **extra-virgin olive oil**
- 4 **garlic cloves**, minced
- 1 tablespoon chopped **fresh oregano**
- 1 teaspoon **salt**
- ½ teaspoon **freshly ground pepper**
- 1 (7-pound) **turkey breast with ribs**
- 1¼ cups **sugar**
- 1 cup **orange juice**
- 1 cup **water**
- ½ cup chopped **sweet onion**, such as Vidalia
- ¼ teaspoon **crushed red pepper**
- 1 (16-ounce) bag **fresh or frozen cranberries**
- 2 teaspoons grated **lime zest**

Grilling and Transporting Tips

We do most of our grilling during hot summer months—often in the backyard, but sometimes at a picnic site. Be sure to follow our simple tips for storing, transporting, and cooking food to keep it safe for you and your family.

• Keep the chicken refrigerated until ready to cook when barbecuing chicken outdoors.

• Store food to be grilled outdoors in a cooler. Place the cooler in a shady spot and avoid opening the lid too often.

• Marinate food in the refrigerator, not on the counter. Marinade in which raw chicken has been soaking should never be used on cooked chicken. When brushing chicken with raw marinade, stop brushing 5 minutes before cooking is finished. Then, either discard the remaining marinade or bring it to a rolling boil and boil for 2 minutes before serving with the dish.

• Do not place cooked chicken on the same plate used to transport raw chicken to the grill.

• Remove all visible fat from poultry and meat before barbecuing. This cuts the fat and prevents charring and flare-ups.

• Bring water for preparation and cleaning when barbecuing away from home. Or pack wet wipes and towels for cleaning hands and surfaces.

• Cook chicken to a safe internal temperature to destroy harmful bacteria. Grilled chicken often browns on the outside before cooking through to the center and needs to be cooked by indirect heat (see tip page 228). Use an instant-read meat thermometer to be sure the chicken has reached a safe internal temperature. The internal temperature should reach 180°F for whole chicken or turkey and bone-in thighs and drumsticks, 170°F for bone-in breasts, and 165°F for boneless parts and burgers made from ground chicken or turkey. For burgers, test the internal temperature by inserting the thermometer into the side of the burger.

• Don't let food sit out for longer than 1 hour if it gets to above 80°F.

• Put cooked chicken in an insulated container, or ice chest, when transporting it to a picnic site. Keep below 40°F or above 140°F. Standard size casserole dishes are available to purchase with insulated carrying bags with a pack that you can either freeze or heat to maintain the food at a safe temperature.

• Be sure to wrap raw chicken well when transporting it, so none of the juices drip on other foods in the ice chest.

North African Turkey Kebabs

You'll love the hot and spicy flavors of these quick-to-fix ground turkey skewers. They are perfect served on a bed of whole-wheat couscous (⅔ cup will increase the **POINTS** value by 2).

1. Spray the grill rack with nonstick spray; prepare the grill for a medium-hot fire.

2. Combine the turkey, garlic, cilantro, lemon juice, ginger, coriander, hot pepper sauce, cumin, salt, and cinnamon in a large bowl; mix well. Divide the mixture into 4 equal portions. Roll each portion into a cylinder 5 inches long and 1½ inches in diameter. Chill 30 minutes. Insert a skewer, lengthwise, into the center of each cylinder.

3. Place the kebabs on the grill rack and grill, turning every 3 minutes, until the turkey is cooked through, 12–15 minutes.

PER SERVING (1 kebab): 132 Cal, 1 g Fat, 0 g Sat Fat, 0 g Trans Fat, 75 mg Chol, 502 mg Sod, 2 g Carb, 0 g Fib, 27 g Prot, 27 mg Calc. **POINTS** value: *3*.

tip To get a head start on this recipe, you can make the cylinders of turkey the day before and refrigerate them, covered, until you're ready to grill them. Added bonus—the flavors will get a chance to blend and develop this way.

MAKES 4 SERVINGS

- 1 pound **ground skinless lean turkey breast**
- 2 **garlic cloves**, minced
- 2 tablespoons chopped **fresh cilantro**
- 1 tablespoon **fresh lemon juice**
- 2 teaspoons grated peeled **fresh ginger**
- 1 teaspoon **ground coriander**
- 1 teaspoon **hot pepper sauce**
- ¾ teaspoon **ground cumin**
- ¾ teaspoon **salt**
- ¼ teaspoon **cinnamon**

Grilled Sausage and Peppers with Parmesan Polenta

Store-bought, prepared polenta (a mush made from cornmeal) is a great time-saver. It comes in tubes and can be found in the dairy section of most supermarkets in a variety of flavors, such as Italian herb and wild mushroom. We recommend using plain polenta for this recipe.

1. Spray the grill rack with nonstick spray; prepare the grill for a medium-hot fire.

2. Place the sausages on the grill rack and grill, turning occasionally, until browned and cooked through, 12–15 minutes. Transfer to a plate and keep warm.

3. Meanwhile, combine 2 teaspoons of the oil with the vinegar in a small bowl; mix well. Brush the onion slices and bell peppers with the oil mixture and sprinkle with the salt and pepper. Grill the onions and peppers until well marked and tender, 6–7 minutes on each side; transfer to a cutting board and roughly chop.

4. Brush both sides of the polenta slices with the remaining 1 teaspoon oil. Place on the grill rack and grill 4 minutes; turn and sprinkle each slice with 1 teaspoon of the cheese. Grill 4 minutes longer. Transfer the polenta slices to 4 plates. Top each slice with one-quarter of the vegetables and 1 sausage.

PER SERVING (1 slice polenta, ½ cup vegetables, and 1 sausage): 260 Cal, 14 g Fat, 4 g Sat Fat, 0 g Trans Fat, 51 mg Chol, 797 mg Sod, 16 g Carb, 2 g Fib, 17 g Prot, 55 mg Calc. *POINTS* value: *6*.

MAKES 4 SERVINGS

¾ pound **sweet Italian turkey sausage** (4 sausages)

3 teaspoons **olive oil**

1 teaspoon **balsamic vinegar**

1 large **red onion,** cut into ¼-inch-thick slices

2 **assorted color bell peppers,** seeded and cut into eighths

¼ teaspoon **salt**

⅛ teaspoon **freshly ground pepper**

1 (8-ounce) tube refrigerated **fat-free plain polenta,** cut into 4 rounds

4 teaspoons grated **Parmesan cheese**

Grilled Sausage and Peppers
with Parmesan Polenta

Peppered Orange Quail

Quail is a game bird related to the partridge and is characterized by light, delicately flavored meat. Most quail sold today is farm-raised. Look for it in the frozen section of your local supermarket or ask your butcher to order it for you.

1. Spray the grill rack with nonstick spray; prepare the grill for a medium-hot fire.

2. Combine the molasses, orange zest, vinegar, and pepper in a zip-close plastic bag; add the quail. Squeeze out the air and seal the bag; turn to coat the quail. Refrigerate, turning the bag occasionally, about 15 minutes.

3. Lift the quail from the marinade and sprinkle with the salt. Discard the marinade. Place the quail on the grill rack and grill until cooked through, about 5 minutes on each side.

PER SERVING (1 quail): 168 Cal, 7 g Fat, 2 g Sat Fat, 0 g Trans Fat, 64 mg Chol, 369 mg Sod, 4 g Carb, 0 g Fib, 23 g Prot, 47 mg Calc. *POINTS* value: *4*.

tip To broil, spray the broiler rack with nonstick spray and preheat the broiler. Place the quail on the broiler rack and broil 4 inches from the heat until cooked through, about 5 minutes on each side.

MAKES 4 SERVINGS

- 2 tablespoons **molasses**

- 1 tablespoon grated **orange zest**

- 1 teaspoon **balsamic vinegar**

- ¾ teaspoon **cracked black pepper**

- 4 (¼-pound) **semi-boneless quail**, thawed, skin removed, and split open down the back

- ½ teaspoon **salt**

Hoisin Duck Tacos with Cucumber Salsa

East meets west in this combination of ingredients where Asian flavors dominate and are pulled together by the Mexican tortilla.

1. Combine the hoisin sauce and sake in a zip-close plastic bag; add the duck. Squeeze out the air and seal the bag; turn to coat the duck. Refrigerate, turning the bag occasionally, at least 1 hour or up to overnight.

2. Spray the grill rack with nonstick spray; prepare the grill for a medium-hot fire.

3. To make the salsa, combine the cucumber, bell pepper, scallion, soy sauce, vinegar, sugar, and salt in a medium bowl; mix well.

4. Wipe the excess marinade from the duck and place the duck on the grill rack. Discard the marinade. Cover the grill and grill the duck until cooked through, 4–5 minutes on each side. Let stand about 5 minutes, then thinly slice the duck across the grain.

5. Warm the tortillas directly on the grill rack, about 30 seconds on each side. Place a tortilla on each of 4 plates; top each tortilla with ¼ cup cabbage and 1 sliced duck breast. Serve with the salsa.

PER SERVING (1 taco with ⅓ cup salsa): 224 Cal, 2 g Fat, 1 g Sat Fat, 0 g Trans Fat, 83 mg Chol, 585 mg Sod, 18 g Carb, 2 g Fib, 32 g Prot, 93 mg Calc. *POINTS* value: *4*.

MAKES 4 SERVINGS

- 3 tablespoons **hoisin sauce**
- 2 tablespoons **sake or white wine**
- 4 (5–6-ounce) **skinless boneless duck breasts**
- 1 **cucumber**, peeled, seeded, and cut into ¼-inch dice
- ½ **red bell pepper**, seeded and cut into ¼-inch dice
- 1 **scallion**, chopped
- 1 tablespoon **reduced-sodium soy sauce**
- 2 teaspoons **rice vinegar**
- 1½ teaspoons **sugar**
- ½ teaspoon **salt**
- 4 (6-inch) **corn tortillas**
- ⅛ small head **napa cabbage**, shredded, about 1 cup

15-Minute Express Entrées

CHAPTER EIGHT

Spiced Chicken with Orange-Chipotle Glaze

For a double dose of flavor, skinless boneless chicken breasts are rubbed with cumin and coriander. Then, while cooking on a grill pan, they're basted with a smoky chile-orange marmalade glaze.

1. Combine the orange juice, marmalade, and chipotle in a small bowl. Combine the cumin, coriander, and salt in a large bowl; add the chicken tossing to coat with the spices.

2. Spray a nonstick ridged grill pan with nonstick spray and set over medium-high heat. Add the chicken and cook, turning and brushing with the glaze every 4 minutes, until browned on the outside and cooked through, about 12 minutes.

PER SERVING (1 piece chicken): 177 Cal, 4 g Fat, 1 g Sat Fat, 0 g Trans Fat, 68 mg Chol, 369 mg Sod, 9 g Carb, 0 g Fib, 25 g Prot, 24 mg Calc. *POINTS* value: *4*.

tip If you're in a time-crunch, you can make the glaze while the chicken cooks.

MAKES 4 SERVINGS

- ¼ cup **orange juice**
- 2 tablespoons **orange marmalade**
- 1 teaspoon chopped **chipotle en adobo**
- 1½ teaspoons **ground cumin**
- ½ teaspoon **ground coriander**
- ½ teaspoon **salt**
- 4 (¼-pound) **skinless boneless chicken breast halves**

✔ Sautéed Chicken with Artichokes, Olives, and Oregano

This skillet dinner features simple sun-drenched flavors of the Mediterranean. You might like to serve it over pasta, (1 cup cooked whole-wheat pasta per serving will up the *POINTS* value by 3), with a fresh salad of thinly sliced fennel, dressed with lemon juice, salt, and pepper.

1. Sprinkle the chicken with the oregano, salt, and pepper. Heat the oil in a large nonstick skillet over medium-high heat. Add the chicken and cook until browned on the outside and cooked through, about 3 minutes on each side. Transfer the chicken to a serving plate; cover and keep warm.

2. Add the broth, artichoke hearts, olives, and lemon juice to the skillet; bring to a boil, scraping any browned bits from the bottom of the pan. Reduce the heat and simmer, uncovered, until the liquid is reduced slightly, about 2 minutes. Stir in the parsley, then spoon the sauce over the chicken.

PER SERVING (1 piece chicken with ¼ cup sauce): 217 Cal, 7 g Fat, 2 g Sat Fat, 0 g Trans Fat, 68 mg Chol, 524 mg Sod, 10 g Carb, 4 g Fib, 28 g Prot, 63 mg Calc. *POINTS* value: *4*.

MAKES 4 SERVINGS ☞

- 4 (4–5-ounce) thin-sliced **chicken breast cutlets**
- 1 teaspoon **dried oregano**
- ⅛ teaspoon **salt**
- ¼ teaspoon **freshly ground pepper**
- 2 teaspoons **olive oil**
- ¾ cup **reduced-sodium chicken broth**
- 1 (14-ounce) **can artichoke hearts**, drained and halved
- ¼ cup **pitted kalamata olives**, halved
- 2 tablespoons **fresh lemon juice**
- 2 tablespoons chopped **flat-leaf parsley**

Chile-Rubbed Chicken with Fresh Pineapple Salsa

Chile-Rubbed Chicken with Fresh Pineapple Salsa

For fiery flavor in a flash, thin-sliced chicken breasts are rubbed with chile powder, then topped with a refreshing fruit salsa to tame the heat. Convenient precut fresh pineapple lets you assemble the salsa in seconds. Add ½ cup cooked rice to each serving (you'll increase your **POINTS** value by 2) and you've got a meal.

1. Rub the chicken with the chile powder and the ¼ teaspoon salt. Heat the oil in a large nonstick skillet over medium-high heat. Add the chicken and cook until browned on the outside and cooked through, about 3 minutes on each side. Transfer the chicken to a serving plate; cover and keep warm.

2. Meanwhile, combine the pineapple, bell pepper, chutney, cilantro, the remaining ⅛ teaspoon salt, and the ground pepper in a small bowl. Serve the chicken with the salsa and the lime wedges.

PER SERVING (1 piece chicken with ½ cup salsa): 214 Cal, 6 g Fat, 1 g Sat Fat, 0 g Trans Fat, 68 mg Chol, 304 mg Sod, 14 g Carb, 2 g Fib, 26 g Prot, 25 mg Calc. **POINTS** value: **4**.

MAKES 4 SERVINGS

- 4 (4–5-ounce) thin-sliced **chicken breast cutlets**

- 2 teaspoons **ancho chile powder**

- ¼ + ⅛ teaspoon **salt**

- 2 teaspoons **canola oil**

- 1 (8-ounce) package peeled and diced **fresh pineapple**

- ½ **red bell pepper**, seeded and diced

- 3 tablespoons **mango chutney**

- 2 tablespoons chopped **cilantro**

- Pinch **freshly ground pepper**

- 4 **lime wedges**

Grilled Chicken with Raspberries and Greens

Chicken and fruit has always been a winning flavor combination and this elegant entrée takes full advantage of summer berries. Raspberry vinegar and a touch of raspberry preserves give the dressing a sweet-tart taste that bursts with delicious berry flavor.

1. Sprinkle the chicken evenly with the thyme, the $\frac{1}{4}$ teaspoon salt, and $\frac{1}{8}$ teaspoon of the pepper. Spray a nonstick ridged grill pan with nonstick spray and set over high heat. Add the chicken and cook until browned on the outside and cooked through, about 3 minutes on each side.

2. Meanwhile, combine the vinegar, shallots, preserves, oil, and the remaining $\frac{1}{8}$ teaspoon salt and $\frac{1}{8}$ teaspoon pepper in a large bowl. Add the greens and toss to coat with the dressing.

3. Arrange a chicken breast on each of 4 serving plates; surround each with one-quarter of the salad and garnish with the raspberries.

PER SERVING (1 piece chicken with about 2 cups salad): 184 Cal, 6 g Fat, 1 g Sat Fat, 0 g Trans Fat, 68 mg Chol, 286 mg Sod, 6 g Carb, 1 g Fib, 25 g Prot, 23 mg Calc. *POINTS* value: *4*.

MAKES 4 SERVINGS

- 4 (4–5-ounce) thin-sliced **chicken breast cutlets**
- $\frac{1}{2}$ teaspoon **dried thyme**
- $\frac{1}{4}$ + $\frac{1}{8}$ teaspoon **salt**
- $\frac{1}{4}$ teaspoon **freshly ground pepper**
- 2 tablespoons **raspberry vinegar**
- 2 tablespoons finely **chopped shallots**
- 1 tablespoon **all-fruit raspberry preserves**
- 2 teaspoons **olive oil**
- 1 (4-ounce) package **mixed salad greens**
- $\frac{1}{2}$ cup **fresh raspberries**

Grilled Chicken with
Raspberries and Greens

Chicken Cheese Steaks

If you are a fan of the Philly cheese steak, but want to skip the beef and trim the fat, check out this healthier interpretation. Poblano chiles stand in for the usual bell peppers to give the sandwich extra flavor and a touch of heat. The poblano is a dark green chile pepper, about 5 inches long and 2½ inches wide. It can range from mild to moderately hot.

1. Heat the oil in a large nonstick skillet over medium heat. Add the onion, poblano chile, and garlic; cook, partially covered, stirring occasionally, until golden and softened, 3–4 minutes.

2. Add the chicken and salt; cook, uncovered, turning occasionally, until the chicken is browned and cooked through, about 4 minutes. Remove the skillet from the heat. Top the chicken with the cheese; cover the skillet and let stand until the cheese melts, about 1 minute.

3. Fill each roll with half of the chicken filling. Cut each sandwich in half.

PER SERVING (½ sandwich): 326 Cal, 10 g Fat, 4 g Sat Fat, 0 g Trans Fat, 78 mg Chol, 593 mg Sod, 25 g Carb, 2 g Fib, 32 g Prot, 157 mg Calc. **POINTS** value: *7*.

tip While you're preparing the filling, toast the hero rolls in a toaster oven or under the broiler.

MAKES 4 SERVINGS ☛

- 1 teaspoon **olive oil**
- ½ medium **onion**, thinly sliced
- ½ small **poblano chile**, seeded and thinly sliced
- 1 **garlic clove**, crushed through a press
- 1 pound **chicken tenders**
- ¼ teaspoon **salt**
- 2 (1-ounce) slices **provolone cheese**
- 2 (3-4-ounce) **hero or hoagie rolls**, split and toasted

Chicken and Edamame Stir-Fry

Edamame, the Japanese name for fresh green soybeans, have become so popular in this country they're now available shelled and frozen—good news for speedy stir-fry dishes like this one.

1. Combine the broth, vinegar, soy sauce, and cornstarch in a small bowl until smooth; set aside.

2. Heat a nonstick wok or a large skillet over high heat until a drop of water sizzles. Add 1 teaspoon of the oil, swirl to coat the pan, then add the edamame. Stir-fry until lightly browned, 2–3 minutes. Transfer the edamame to a plate.

3. Add the remaining 1 teaspoon oil to the wok, swirl to coat the pan, then add the ginger, garlic, and crushed red pepper. Stir-fry until fragrant, about 15 seconds. Add the chicken; stir-fry until lightly browned, 3–4 minutes. Stir in the broth mixture and cook, stirring constantly, until the mixture bubbles and thickens and the chicken is just cooked through, 1–2 minutes. Stir in the edamame and heat through, about 1 minute.

PER SERVING (1 cup): 271 Cal, 11 g Fat, 2 g Sat Fat, 0 g Trans Fat, 68 mg Chol, 222 mg Sod, 10 g Carb, 3 g Fib, 34 g Prot, 118 mg Calc. *POINTS* value: *6*.

tip To thaw edamame quickly, rinse in a colander under warm water.

MAKES 4 SERVINGS

- ½ cup **reduced-sodium chicken broth**

- 2 teaspoons **rice-wine vinegar**

- 2 teaspoons **reduced-sodium soy sauce**

- 1 teaspoon **cornstarch**

- 2 teaspoons **canola oil**

- 1 (10-ounce) package **frozen edamame** (green soybeans), thawed (2 cups)

- 1 teaspoon grated peeled **fresh ginger**

- 1 **garlic clove**, crushed through a press

- ¼ teaspoon **crushed red pepper**

- 1 pound **chicken tenders**, cut into 1-inch chunks

 # Thai Chicken Salad

Sweet, sour, salty—those are but a few of the contrasting flavors that make Thai cuisine exceptionally delicious. We use short-cut ingredients in this salad: precooked chicken, packaged baby greens, and shredded carrots, giving you plenty of time to squeeze fresh lime juice. Don't be tempted to substitute bottled.

Whisk together the lime juice, oil, fish sauce, soy sauce, and sugar in a large bowl. Add the chicken, salad mix, mint, carrots, and onion to the dressing; toss well to coat. Serve at once.

PER SERVING (2 cups): 171 Cal, 6 g Fat, 1 g Sat Fat, 0 g Trans Fat, 57 mg Chol, 229 mg Sod, 7 g Carb, 2 g Fib, 22 g Prot, 57 mg Calc. *POINTS* value: *4*.

tip Feel free to experiment with different assortments of packaged greens in this salad—any variety works well. Or try a combination of 1 large bunch watercress, cleaned and ½ cup fresh cilantro leaves, if you can spare the time.

MAKES 4 SERVINGS

3 tablespoons **fresh lime juice**

2 teaspoons **canola oil**

2 teaspoons **Asian fish sauce** (nam pla)

1½ teaspoons **reduced-sodium soy sauce**

½ teaspoon **sugar**

2 cups shredded **cooked chicken breast**

1 (5-ounce) package **baby Asian salad mix**

1 cup loosely packed **mint leaves**

1 cup shredded **carrots**

1 small **red onion**, thinly sliced

Chicken Picadillo Wraps

Picadillo—usually a mixture of ground pork and beef, onions, and tomatoes—is a favorite in many Spanish-speaking countries. We substitute chicken for the pork and beef, and, as in Mexico, we add raisins to the mix, which may sound a bit unusual, but their sweetness perfectly complements the hot jalapeños.

1. Heat the oil in a large nonstick skillet over medium-high heat. Add the chicken and cook, breaking it up with a wooden spoon, until browned and cooked through, about 5 minutes. Stir in the cumin, oregano, and salt; cook about 1 minute. Stir in the tomatoes, beans, and raisins; bring to a boil. Reduce the heat and simmer, uncovered, about 2 minutes.

2. Meanwhile, stack the tortillas on a microwavable plate. Cover with a damp paper towel and microwave on High, about 30 seconds. Divide the chicken filling evenly onto each warm tortilla. Fold the sides over and roll up to enclose the filling. Cut each wrap in half.

PER SERVING (½ wrap): 399 Cal, 6 g Fat, 1 g Sat Fat, 0 g Trans Fat, 68 mg Chol, 1023 mg Sod, 54 g Carb, 5 g Fib, 33 g Prot, 127 mg Calc. *POINTS* value: *8*.

tip Without increasing your *POINTS* value (and if you have time), you can add ½ cup shredded lettuce and 1 tablespoon each of chopped cilantro and red onion to each serving of filling before folding and rolling the tortillas.

MAKES 4 SERVINGS

- 1 teaspoon **olive oil**
- 1 pound **ground skinless lean chicken breast**
- 2 teaspoons **ground cumin**
- 1 teaspoon **dried oregano**
- ¼ teaspoon **salt**
- 1 (14½-ounce) **can diced tomatoes with jalapeños**
- 1 cup rinsed and drained **canned black beans**
- ⅓ cup **golden raisins**
- 2 (10-inch) **fat-free flour tortillas**

Chicken Stir-Fry with Almonds and Snap Peas

Delightfully sweet sugar snap peas are a quick cook's best friend. They're entirely edible, pod and all, so there's practically no prep involved. Plus, they taste best when only cooked briefly—or not cooked at all—so they retain their crisp texture. Available during the spring and fall, select sugar snaps with plump, bright green pods.

1. Heat a nonstick wok or a large skillet over high heat until a drop of water sizzles. Add 1 teaspoon of the oil, swirl to coat the pan, then add the almonds. Stir-fry until lightly browned, about 2 minutes. Transfer the almonds to a plate.

2. Meanwhile, combine the sherry, soy sauce, water, cornstarch, and five-spice powder in a small bowl until smooth; set aside.

3. Add the remaining 1 teaspoon oil to the wok, swirl to coat the pan, then add the chicken. Stir-fry until lightly browned, 3–4 minutes. Add the snap peas, scallions, and garlic; stir-fry about 1 minute. Stir in the sherry mixture and cook, stirring constantly, until the mixture bubbles and thickens, and the chicken is just cooked through, 1–2 minutes. Stir in the almonds.

PER SERVING (scant 1 cup): 235 Cal, 9 g Fat, 2 g Sat Fat, 0 g Trans Fat, 68 mg Chol, 465 mg Sod, 8 g Carb, 2 g Fib, 28 g Prot, 57 mg Calc. *POINTS* value: *5*.

tip If you can't find sugar snap peas, substitute snow peas. The cooking time will remain the same.

MAKES 4 SERVINGS ☛

- 2 teaspoons **canola oil**
- ¼ cup sliced **almonds**
- 3 tablespoons **dry sherry**
- 3 tablespoons **reduced-sodium soy sauce**
- 2 tablespoons **water**
- 2 teaspoons **cornstarch**
- ½ teaspoon **five-spice powder**
- 1 pound **chicken tenders**, cut into 1-inch chunks
- ¼ pound fresh **sugar snap peas**, trimmed
- 3 **scallions**, cut into 1-inch pieces
- 2 **garlic cloves**, crushed through a press

Chicken Stir-Fry with
Almonds and Snap Peas

Cumin-Spiced Chicken with Pears

Cumin-Spiced Chicken with Pears

Consider serving this fall-inspired dish with the first cold snap. It's wonderful prepared with a variety of seasonal pears, such as Bartlett, Anjou, or Comice. More than any other skinless chicken part, thighs tend to have fat still attached to them, so be sure to trim away as much of the fat as possible. Steamed baby carrots make a great go-along here.

1. Sprinkle the chicken with the cumin, salt, and pepper. Heat the oil in a large nonstick skillet over medium-high heat. Add the chicken and cook until browned on the outside and cooked through, about 4 minutes on each side. Transfer to a serving platter; cover and keep warm.

2. Meanwhile, to cut the pear, set it upright on its base. Cut in ½-inch slices down the length of the pear towards the base; remove any seeds. (You should have eight ½-inch-thick slices.)

3. Add the pear slices to the skillet; reduce the heat to medium and cook until lightly browned, about 1 minute on each side. Transfer the pears to the serving platter.

4. Add the cider and vinegar to the skillet; bring to a boil, scraping any browned bits from the bottom of the pan. Boil 1 minute. Spoon the sauce over the chicken and pears.

PER SERVING (2 chicken thighs, 2 pear slices, and about 1 tablespoon sauce): 297 Cal, 13 g Fat, 4 g Sat Fat, 0 g Trans Fat, 88 mg Chol, 229 mg Sod, 14 g Carb, 1 g Fib, 30 g Prot, 52 mg Calc.
POINTS value: *7.*

tip Pears are best bought while still firm, so they won't get damaged in transit from the market. They will ripen on a counter at room temperature in a day or two. To avoid letting them get overripe, refrigerate them after they have ripened.

MAKES 4 SERVINGS 🐄

8 small **skinless boneless chicken thighs** (about 1¼ pounds)

2 teaspoons **ground cumin**

¼ teaspoon **salt**

¼ teaspoon **freshly ground pepper**

1 teaspoon **olive oil**

1 large ripe **pear**

¾ cup **apple cider**

2 tablespoons **apple-cider vinegar**

 Asian Turkey Lettuce Wraps

Lettuce leaves make an instant, no-**POINTS** value wrapper—perfect for the time-pressed cook. They also offer cool contrast to this spicy turkey filling with crunchy bell peppers and fragrant ginger.

1. Heat the oil in a large nonstick skillet over medium-high heat. Add the scallions, bell pepper, and ginger; cook, stirring constantly, about 1 minute.

2. Add the turkey and chili powder; cook, breaking it up with a wooden spoon, until browned and cooked through, about 5 minutes. Stir in the soy sauce.

3. Divide the turkey mixture evenly among the lettuce leaves; roll up tightly and serve at once.

PER SERVING (2 wraps): 155 Cal, 2 g Fat, 1 g Sat Fat, 0 g Trans Fat, 75 mg Chol, 456 mg Sod, 5 g Carb, 1 g Fib, 28 g Prot, 33 mg Calc. **POINTS** value: **3**.

tip We think ground turkey, with its rich flavor, is best suited to this dish, but you can use ground skinless lean chicken breast, if you prefer. For a heartier meal, try using 2 (10-inch) flour tortillas for the wrappers instead of the 4 lettuce leaves, making half a tortilla per serving and increasing your *POINTS* value by 2.

MAKES 4 SERVINGS

1 teaspoon **canola oil**

3 **scallions**, thinly sliced

1 **yellow or red bell pepper**, seeded and diced

½ teaspoon grated peeled **fresh ginger**

1 pound **ground skinless lean turkey breast**

½ teaspoon **chili powder**

3 tablespoons **reduced-sodium soy sauce**

8 large **iceberg lettuce leaves**

Chicken Caesar Pitas

Here's a great portable way to get all the zest of Caesar salad when you're on the run. We use whole-wheat pitas, but you can substitute 8 thin slices of whole-wheat bread.

1. Combine the yogurt, mayonnaise, cheese, garlic, lemon juice, mustard, anchovy paste, and pepper in a medium bowl. Add the chicken and toss to coat with the dressing.

2. Cut a pocket in each pita. Fill each pita with one-quarter of the chicken mixture and 2 lettuce leaves.

PER SERVING (1 sandwich): 304 Cal, 6 g Fat, 2 g Sat Fat, 0 g Trans Fat, 61 mg Chol, 522 mg Sod, 34 g Carb, 4 g Fib, 29 g Prot, 100 mg Calc. *POINTS* value: *6*.

tip Although this wouldn't be as strict an interpretation of a Caesar salad, peppery watercress is a delightful substitute for the romaine lettuce. You would need 1 small bunch, cleaned.

MAKES 4 SERVINGS

¼ cup **plain low-fat yogurt**

2 tablespoons **low-fat mayonnaise**

2 tablespoons grated **Parmesan cheese**

1 small **garlic clove**, crushed through a press

2 teaspoons **fresh lemon juice**

½ teaspoon **Dijon mustard**

¼ teaspoon **anchovy paste**

¼ teaspoon **freshly ground pepper**

2 cups chopped **cooked chicken breast**

4 (6-inch) **whole-wheat pita breads**

8 small **romaine lettuce** leaves

Chicken with Couscous, Tomatoes, and Mint

Chicken with Couscous, Tomatoes, and Mint

This Aegean-inspired dish makes a lovely lunch or light supper. It's terrific with a number of fresh herbs. You can replace the mint with an equal amount of chopped fresh basil or 1 to 2 tablespoons of chopped fresh dill. If you've got the time, it's equally delicious served at room temperature or chilled.

1. Heat the oil in a medium saucepan over medium heat. Add the garlic and cook, stirring constantly, until fragrant, about 15 seconds. Stir in the broth; cover and bring to a boil. Stir in the couscous; remove from the heat. Cover and let stand 5 minutes.

2. Fluff the couscous with a fork. Add the chicken, tomatoes, onion, mint, feta cheese, vinegar, and pepper; toss lightly until combined. Serve at once while still warm.

PER SERVING (1¼ cups): 357 Cal, 9 g Fat, 3 g Sat Fat, 0 g Trans Fat, 68 mg Chol, 348 mg Sod, 37 g Carb, 3 g Fib, 30 g Prot, 95 mg Calc. *POINTS* value: *7*.

tip You can skip the feta and lower the per-serving *POINTS* value by 1.

MAKES 4 SERVINGS ☛

2 teaspoons **extra-virgin olive oil**

2 large **garlic cloves**, crushed through a press

1¼ cups **reduced-sodium chicken broth**

1 cup **couscous**

2 cups chopped **cooked chicken breast**

2 **plum tomatoes**, diced

¼ cup finely chopped **red onion**

¼ cup **fresh mint leaves**, coarsely chopped

⅓ cup crumbled **feta cheese**

1 tablespoon **sherry vinegar**

¼ teaspoon **freshly ground pepper**

Citrus Chicken and Napa Slaw

Don't mistake napa cabbage for ordinary green cabbage. With its thin, crisp, cream-colored leaves and delicate flavor, napa cabbage makes a wonderful addition to salads, stir-fries, and soups. Also called Chinese cabbage, this vegetable is available in the produce section of the supermarket or in Asian markets.

Whisk together the mirin, lime juice, oil, salt, and pepper in a large bowl. Add the cabbage, chicken, carrots, scallions, and cilantro; toss well to coat. Serve at once, or cover and refrigerate until ready to serve, up to 2 hours.

PER SERVING (1½ cups): 187 Cal, 6 g Fat, 1 g Sat Fat, 0 g Trans Fat, 57 mg Chol, 370 mg Sod, 9 g Carb, 4 g Fib, 22 g Prot, 102 mg Calc. *POINTS* value: *3*.

tip It's easy to buy cooked chicken at the supermarket, but if you have the time, you can cook the chicken yourself. You'll need ³⁄₄ pound skinless boneless chicken breast for this recipe. Place the chicken on a baking sheet lightly sprayed with nonstick spray. Lightly spray the chicken with nonstick spray. Cover the baking sheet tightly with foil and bake the chicken in a 400°F oven until cooked through, 30 to 35 minutes. Let the chicken cool, then tear it into shreds. (This recipe can easily be doubled for additional meals.)

MAKES 4 SERVINGS

- 3 tablespoons **mirin** (rice wine)
- 2 tablespoons **fresh lime juice**
- 2 teaspoons **canola oil**
- ½ teaspoon **salt**
- ¼ teaspoon **freshly ground pepper**
- 5 cups thinly sliced **napa cabbage**
- 2 cups shredded **cooked chicken breast**
- 1 cup shredded **carrots**
- 3 **scallions**, thinly sliced
- ¼ cup chopped **fresh cilantro**

Citrus Chicken and Napa Slaw

5-Ingredient Fixes

CHAPTER NINE

Rosemary Roast Chicken with Potatoes

Rosemary's assertive flavor goes particularly well with chicken and potatoes. To ensure even cooking the chicken is "butterflied," that is, the bird is cut down the backbone and flattened. It's a simple enough procedure, but you can ask the butcher to do it for you.

1. Preheat the oven to 425°F. Spray the bottom of a broiler pan with nonstick spray.

2. To butterfly the chicken, with a large knife or poultry shears, cut the chicken down the backbone. Turn the chicken, breast-side up, and push down on the backbone to flatten slightly.

3. Combine the rosemary, garlic, ¼ teaspoon of the salt, and ¼ teaspoon of the pepper in a small bowl. Gently lift the skin from the chicken breast and legs; spread the herb mixture evenly under the skin. Place the chicken in the pan. Scatter the potatoes around the chicken; sprinkle the potatoes with the remaining ¼ teaspoon salt and ¼ teaspoon pepper.

4. Roast the chicken and potatoes 20 minutes. Add ½ cup of the wine to the pan. Roast 15 minutes longer, then turn the potatoes and add the remaining ½ cup wine. Roast until an instant-read thermometer inserted in a thigh registers 180°F and the potatoes are tender, about 20 minutes longer. Cut the chicken into 8 pieces and serve with the potatoes. Remove the skin from the chicken before eating.

PER SERVING (1 piece chicken with ½ cup potatoes): 236 Cal, 5 g Fat, 1 g Sat Fat, 0 g Trans Fat, 61 mg Chol, 216 mg Sod, 23 g Carb, 2 g Fib, 22 g Prot, 25 mg Calc. *POINTS* value: *5*.

MAKES 8 SERVINGS 🍳

- 1 (3½-pound) **chicken**, butterflied (see step 2)

- 4 teaspoons chopped **fresh rosemary**

- 2 large **garlic cloves**, minced

- ½ teaspoon **salt**

- ½ teaspoon **freshly ground pepper**

- 6 medium **Yukon Gold potatoes** (about 2 pounds), cut into 1-inch chunks

- 1 cup **dry white wine**

Rosemary Roast Chicken
with Potatoes

Lemon-Coriander Chicken

Lemon lovers will thoroughly enjoy this easy dish, where the chicken can either be grilled or broiled to perfection. We use a quartered versus a cut-up chicken in the recipe, so there are fewer pieces to turn while cooking.

1. Combine the lemon juice, scallions, garlic, coriander, lemon zest, salt, and pepper in a small bowl. Measure ½ cup of the juice mixture into another small bowl.

2. Pour the remaining juice mixture into a zip-close plastic bag; add the chicken. Squeeze out the air and seal bag; turn to coat chicken. Refrigerate, turning the bag occasionally, at least 4 hours or overnight.

3. Spray the grill or broiler rack with nonstick spray; prepare the grill or preheat the broiler.

4. Transfer the chicken pieces from the bag to the grill or broiler rack; discard the marinade in the bag. Grill or broil the chicken 5 inches from the heat, turning and basting occasionally with the ½ cup reserved marinade, until an instant-read thermometer inserted in a thigh registers 180°F, 20–25 minutes. Cut each chicken quarter into 2 pieces.

PER SERVING (1 piece chicken): 142 Cal, 5 g Fat, 1 g Sat Fat, 0 g Trans Fat, 64 mg Chol, 176 mg Sod, 2 g Carb, 0 g Fib, 21 g Prot, 18 mg Calc. *POINTS* value: *3*.

tip Coriander has an aromatic flavor, like a blend of citrus, sage, and caraway. You can substitute the same amount of ground cumin, if you like, which will give the dish a slightly nutty and peppery taste.

MAKES 8 SERVINGS

¾ cup **fresh lemon juice**

6 **scallions**, finely chopped

3 large **garlic cloves**, crushed through a press

1 tablespoon **ground coriander**

1 tablespoon grated **lemon zest**

¾ teaspoon **salt**

½ teaspoon coarsely ground **black pepper**

1 (3¼-pound) **chicken**, quartered and skinned

Harissa and Yogurt Chicken

Harissa is a fiery hot sauce from the Middle East made with chiles, garlic, spices, and olive oil. It's the traditional accompaniment for couscous, but it also adds flavor to meat, poultry, and rice or grain dishes. *Harissa* may be purchased at Middle Eastern specialty stores and some large supermarkets. The addition of yogurt and chopped fresh mint helps tame the heat in this dish. You might like to serve this with couscous seasoned with chopped fresh mint and grated lemon zest. Increase the **POINTS** value by 1 for every ⅓ cup cooked couscous.

1. Preheat the oven to 400°F. Line a baking sheet with foil; spray the foil with nonstick spray.

2. With a small, sharp knife, make 3 shallow slashes in each chicken breast, thigh, and drumstick.

3. Combine the yogurt, mint, cumin, harissa sauce, and salt in a large bowl. Add the chicken and toss to coat. Place the chicken on the baking sheet, spooning any excess sauce over the pieces. Roast until an instant-read thermometer inserted in a thigh registers 180°F, about 45 minutes.

PER SERVING (1 chicken quarter): 335 Cal, 12 g Fat, 4 g Sat Fat, 0 g Trans Fat, 141 mg Chol, 486 mg Sod, 5 g Carb, 0 g Fib, 48 g Prot, 142 mg Calc. *POINTS* value: *8*.

tip Make this dish serve eight instead of four and cut the *POINTS* value in half.

MAKES 8 SERVINGS

- 1 (3½-pound) **chicken**, quartered and skinned

- 1 (8-ounce) container **plain low-fat yogurt**

- ⅓ cup chopped **fresh mint**

- 2 teaspoons **ground cumin**

- 1 teaspoon **harissa sauce**

- ½ teaspoon **salt**

Green-Olive Roast Chicken

✓ Green-Olive Roast Chicken

The gutsy flavor of green olives pairs perfectly with our combo of chicken, lemon, tomatoes, and garlic. This is delicious with whole-wheat spaghetti—$\frac{2}{3}$ cup will up the **POINTS** value by 2.

1. Preheat the oven to 400°F. Spray a roasting pan with nonstick spray. Place the chicken in the roasting pan. Sprinkle the chicken with the salt and pepper; spray with nonstick spray (preferably olive-oil spray).

2. Combine the tomatoes, lemon juice, olives, and garlic in a large bowl; pour over the chicken.

3. Roast the chicken 20 minutes, then baste with the tomato mixture. Roast until an instant-read thermometer inserted in a thigh registers 180°F, 20–25 minutes longer. Transfer the chicken to a serving platter. Place the roasting pan directly on top of two burners over medium heat. Add the water and bring to a simmer, stirring up the browned bits from the bottom of the pan. Pour the tomato mixture over the chicken.

PER SERVING (2 pieces chicken with about 3 tablespoons tomato mixture): 293 Cal, 12 g Fat, 3 g Sat Fat, 0 g Trans Fat, 118 mg Chol, 518 mg Sod, 6 g Carb, 1 g Fib, 39 g Prot, 36 mg Calc. **POINTS** value: **7**.

MAKES 4 SERVINGS ☛

- 1 (3-pound) **chicken**, cut into 8 pieces and skinned
- ¼ teaspoon **salt**
- ¼ teaspoon **freshly ground pepper**
- 1 pint **grape or cherry tomatoes**
- ¼ cup **fresh lemon juice**
- 12 **green olives**, pitted and coarsely chopped
- 2 large **garlic cloves**, finely chopped
- ¼ cup **water**

Chicken with 40 Cloves of Garlic

Don't let the amount of garlic scare you—slow roasting brings out its natural sweetness. To serve, squeeze the garlic from the roasted cloves onto slices of crusty baguette and dunk into the sauce. A 1-ounce chunk of French baguette will increase the *POINTS* value by 2.

1. Preheat the oven to 425°F.

2. Place the garlic in a single layer in a small baking dish; spray with nonstick spray (preferably olive-oil spray). Cover tightly with foil and roast 15 minutes. Stir, then cover and roast until the garlic just begins to brown, about 15 minutes. Uncover, then stir and spray with nonstick spray and roast until browned and tender, about 10 minutes longer.

3. Meanwhile, sprinkle the chicken with the salt and pepper. Heat the oil in a large cast-iron or other ovenproof skillet over medium-high heat. Add the chicken and cook until browned, about 5 minutes on each side. Transfer the chicken to a large plate. Add the wine and broth to the skillet; bring to a boil, scraping any browned bits from the bottom of the skillet. Add the garlic to the skillet, then add the chicken, nestling the pieces among the garlic cloves.

4. Place the skillet in the oven and roast the chicken until an instant-read thermometer inserted in a thigh registers 180°F, about 20 minutes. Lift the chicken from the broth mixture in the skillet and transfer to a serving dish; cover with foil and keep warm. Transfer 12 of the garlic cloves to a fine sieve. Arrange the remaining garlic around chicken. With a rubber spatula, press the reserved garlic through the sieve into a bowl; discard the skins. Whisk pressed garlic paste into the broth mixture in the skillet; bring to a simmer. Serve the chicken with the roasted garlic and the sauce.

PER SERVING (1 piece chicken, about 3 cloves roasted garlic, and 2 tablespoons sauce): 194 Cal, 8 g Fat, 2 g Sat Fat, 0 g Trans Fat, 69 mg Chol, 205 mg Sod, 6 g Carb, 0 g Fib, 24 g Prot, 43 mg Calc. *POINTS* value: *5*.

MAKES 8 SERVINGS

- 3 medium **garlic bulbs** (about 40 cloves), separated and unpeeled

- 1 (3½–4-pound) **chicken**, cut into 8 pieces and skinned

- ¼ teaspoon **salt**

- ¼ teaspoon **freshly ground pepper**

- 2 teaspoons **extra-virgin olive oil**

- 1 cup **dry white wine**

- 1 cup **reduced-sodium chicken broth**

Chicken with Banana-Curry Sauce

Bananas lend a subtle sweetness to many Caribbean-style curries. You might like to serve this one with aromatic rice, such as basmati or texmati, and a peppery watercress salad to balance the spicy-sweetness of the dish. Be sure to up the *POINTS* value by 2 for every ½ cup of cooked rice. Finish the watercress salad with a squeeze of fresh lime juice without increasing the *POINTS* value.

1. Preheat the oven to 425°F. Spray a roasting pan with nonstick spray.

2. Puree the bananas, ¼ cup of the water, the yogurt, curry powder, oil, salt, and pepper in a food processor or blender.

3. Place the chicken in the roasting pan. Pour the curry mixture over the chicken. Roast until an instant-read thermometer inserted in a breast registers 170°F, 30–35 minutes.

4. Transfer the chicken to a platter; cover loosely with foil and keep warm. Place the roasting pan directly on top of two burners over medium heat. Whisk in the remaining ½ cup water. Simmer, whisking up the browned bits from the bottom of the pan, until heated through. Strain the sauce through a sieve into a sauce boat; serve with the chicken.

PER SERVING (1 piece chicken with about 3 tablespoons sauce): 293 Cal, 8 g Fat, 2 g Sat Fat, 0 g Trans Fat, 100 mg Chol, 400 mg Sod, 16 g Carb, 2 g Fib, 38 g Prot, 67 mg Calc. *POINTS* value: *6*.

tip If you prefer a thinner sauce, increase the water to ¾ cup in step 4.

MAKES 4 SERVINGS

- 2 ripe **bananas**, cut up
- ¾ cup **water**
- ⅓ cup **plain low-fat yogurt**
- 1 tablespoon **curry powder**
- 2 teaspoons **canola oil**
- ½ teaspoon **salt**
- ¼ teaspoon **freshly ground pepper**
- 4 (½-pound) **bone-in chicken breast halves**, skinned

Porcini Chicken

If you love the taste of mushrooms, dried porcini mushrooms are a must-have ingredient to keep on hand. Soaking the mushrooms brings out their wonderful meaty texture, plus the soaking liquid acquires its own earthy flavor that becomes a critical component of the sauce.

1. Combine the mushrooms and the water in a small bowl; let soak about 20 minutes. With a slotted spoon, lift the mushrooms from the liquid, rinse thoroughly, and coarsely chop. Line a strainer with a paper towel. Pour the mushroom liquid through the strainer; reserve ½ cup of the liquid.

2. Sprinkle the chicken with the salt and pepper. Spray a large nonstick skillet with nonstick spray (preferably olive-oil spray) and set over high heat. Add the chicken and cook until lightly browned, about 1 minute on each side. Reduce the heat to medium. Sprinkle the chicken with the shallots; spray with the nonstick spray. Cook until the chicken is browned on the outside and cooked through, about 3 minutes longer on each side. Transfer the chicken and shallots to a serving platter; cover and keep warm.

3. Add the chopped mushrooms to the skillet and cook, stirring constantly, about 30 seconds. Add the reserved mushroom liquid and bring to a boil, scraping any browned bits from the bottom of the pan, until the liquid is almost evaporated. Add the wine and boil until reduced by half, about 2 minutes. Remove the pan from the heat; stir in the butter until melted. Serve the sauce with the chicken.

PER SERVING (1 piece chicken with 2 tablespoons sauce): 163 Cal, 5 g Fat, 2 g Sat Fat, 0 g Trans Fat, 72 mg Chol, 361 mg Sod, 2 g Carb, 0 g Fib, 25 g Prot, 22 mg Calc. **POINTS** value: **4**.

tip Look for dried porcini mushrooms that come in larger pieces, as opposed to small bits, and be sure they have a pungent woodsy aroma. Porcini can be quite gritty, so rinse them thoroughly after soaking.

MAKES 4 SERVINGS

½ ounce **dried porcini mushrooms**

1 cup hot **water**

4 (4–5-ounce) thin-sliced **chicken breast cutlets**

½ teaspoon **salt**

¼ teaspoon **freshly ground pepper**

3 tablespoons minced **shallots**

½ cup **dry red wine**

½ tablespoon **unsalted butter**

Porcini Chicken

Hoisin Chicken Drumettes

Sweet and spicy hoisin sauce isn't just for dousing Peking duck. It's also great for marinating chicken when you're trying to keep the ingredient list short. Once it's opened, hoisin sauce will keep indefinitely in the refrigerator (so it's ready and waiting for your next batch of drumettes!).

1. Combine the hoisin sauce, wine, garlic, and ginger in a zip-close plastic bag; add the chicken. Squeeze out the air and seal the bag; turn to coat the chicken. Refrigerate, turning the bag occasionally, at least 2 hours or up to overnight.

2. Preheat the oven to 425°F. Line the bottom of a baking sheet with foil; spray the foil with nonstick spray. Place the chicken in a single layer on the baking sheet. Roast until the chicken is browned and cooked through, 20–25 minutes.

PER SERVING (5 chicken-wing drumsticks): 189 Cal, 5 g Fat, 1 g Sat Fat, 0 g Trans Fat, 86 mg Chol, 405 mg Sod, 10 g Carb, 1 g Fib, 25 g Prot, 39 mg Calc. *POINTS* value: *4*.

tip For a little crunch, you can sprinkle the chicken with 2 teaspoons toasted sesame seeds just before serving. To toast the seeds, place them in a small dry skillet over medium-low heat. Cook, shaking the pan and stirring constantly, until fragrant, 1 to 2 minutes. Just watch them carefully, as the seeds can burn quickly. Transfer the toasted seeds to a plate to cool.

MAKES 4 SERVINGS 🐄

⅓ cup **hoisin sauce**

¼ cup **dry white wine**

2 large **garlic cloves**, crushed through a press

2 teaspoons grated peeled **fresh ginger**

2 pounds **chicken-wing drumsticks** (about 20), skinned

Chicken-Prosciutto Bundles

Tucked inside each of these savory chicken breasts is melted mozzarella cheese and fresh basil. And if that doesn't sound delicious enough, each breast is wrapped in prosciutto, which locks in the flavors while keeping the chicken juicy.

1. Preheat the oven to 400°F.

2. Make a pocket in the side of each chicken breast by inserting a sharp paring knife into the thickest part, then gently cutting back and forth until a small chamber has opened in the side. Do not cut through to the back or the sides of the breasts. Enlarge the pockets gently with your fingers. Stuff each pocket with 1 slice cheese and 3 basil leaves. Sprinkle the chicken with the pepper and wrap 2 slices prosciutto around each stuffed chicken breast half.

3. Heat the oil in a large ovenproof skillet over medium-high heat. Add the chicken and cook until lightly browned, about 3 minutes on each side. Transfer the chicken in the skillet to the oven and bake until cooked through, 12–15 minutes.

PER SERVING (1 piece chicken): 267 Cal, 10 g Fat, 4 g Sat Fat, 0 g Trans Fat, 107 mg Chol, 514 mg Sod, 1 g Carb, 0 g Fib, 40 g Prot, 124 mg Calc. *POINTS* value: *6*.

tip Prosciutto adds full, rich flavor to this dish. For best flavor, choose prosciutto imported from Italy such as prosciutto di Parma, also called Parma ham. Have the prosciutto sliced into paper-thin slices in the deli department of the supermarket, if you can.

MAKES 4 SERVINGS ☛

4 (5-ounce) **skinless boneless chicken breast halves**

4 (¼-inch-thick) slices **part-skim mozzarella cheese** (½-ounce each)

12 **fresh basil leaves**

¼ teaspoon **freshly ground pepper**

8 thin slices **prosciutto** (about 4 ounces)

1 teaspoon **extra-virgin olive oil**

Beer-Broiled Chicken Drumsticks

Beer-Broiled Chicken Drumsticks

Beer has traditionally been used to make beef stew and chili, but it's also great with chicken. We use economical drumsticks, but skinless bone-in thighs would work equally well. Simply increase the broiling time by about 5 minutes.

1. Combine 1 cup of the beer, the jalapeño pepper, garlic, five-spice powder, and salt in a zip-close plastic bag; add the chicken. Squeeze out the air and seal the bag; turn to coat the chicken. Refrigerate, turning the bag occasionally, at least 2 hours or up to overnight.

2. Spray the broiler rack with nonstick spray; preheat the broiler.

3. Transfer the chicken from the bag to the broiler rack; discard the marinade. Broil the chicken 5 inches from the heat, turning occasionally and basting with the remaining ½ cup beer, until an instant-read thermometer inserted in a drumstick registers 180°F, about 20 minutes.

PER SERVING (2 chicken drumsticks): 154 Cal, 4 g Fat, 1 g Sat Fat, 0 g Trans Fat, 102 mg Chol, 147 mg Sod, 1 g Carb, 0 g Fib, 26 g Prot, 29 mg Calc. *POINTS* value: *3*.

tip If you want to add smoky flavor to the marinade, substitute 1 teaspoon finely chopped chipotle en adobo for the jalapeño pepper.

MAKES 4 SERVINGS

- 1 (12-ounce) bottle **dark beer**

- 1 tablespoon seeded and minced **jalapeño pepper** (wear gloves to prevent irritation)

- 3 **garlic cloves**, crushed through a press

- 2 teaspoons **five-spice powder**

- ½ teaspoon **salt**

- 8 (¼-pound) **skinless chicken drumsticks**

Thai-Style Grilled Chicken

Grilled chicken is common fare in Thailand, but our version is anything but ordinary. It's the coconut milk in the marinade that does the trick, making this chicken particularly succulent and rich in flavor.

1. Combine the coconut milk, cilantro, fish sauce, garlic, and pepper in a zip-close plastic bag; add the chicken. Squeeze out the air and seal the bag; turn to coat the chicken. Refrigerate, turning the bag occasionally, at least 4 hours or up to overnight.

2. Spray the grill or broiler rack with nonstick spray; prepare the grill or preheat the broiler.

3. Transfer the chicken from the bag to the grill rack; discard all but ¼ cup of the marinade. Grill or broil the chicken 5 inches from the heat, 10 minutes. Baste with the reserved marinade. Turn the chicken and grill or broil until an instant-read thermometer inserted in a thigh registers 180°F, about 10 minutes longer.

PER SERVING (1 leg): 210 Cal, 9 g Fat, 4 g Sat Fat, 0 g Trans Fat, 83 mg Chol, 218 mg Sod, 3 g Carb, 0 g Fib, 29 g Prot, 34 mg Calc. *POINTS* value: *5*.

tip Be sure not to confuse light coconut milk with cream of coconut, which is used primarily for beverages and desserts and has a much higher calorie content.

MAKES 4 SERVINGS

- 1 cup **light (reduced-fat) coconut milk**

- 2 tablespoons chopped **fresh cilantro**

- 2 tablespoons **Asian fish sauce** (nam pla)

- 2 large **garlic cloves**, crushed through a press

- ½ teaspoon **freshly ground pepper**

- 4 (½-pound) **whole chicken legs**, skinned

Caribbean Grilled Drumsticks

For a taste of the tropics, we slather chicken drumsticks with lemon juice, brown sugar, and a good dose of Jamaican jerk seasoning (a blend of thyme, cayenne, and allspice). The result? Chicken with the perfect flavor balance of sweetness and peppery heat.

1. Combine the lemon juice, sugar, garlic, jerk seasoning, and salt in a zip-close plastic bag; add the chicken. Squeeze out the air and seal the bag; turn to coat the chicken. Refrigerate, turning the bag occasionally, at least 4 hours or up to overnight.

2. Spray the grill or broiler rack with nonstick spray; prepare the grill or preheat the broiler.

3. Transfer the chicken from the bag to the grill rack; discard the marinade. Grill or broil the chicken 5 inches from the heat, 10 minutes. Turn the chicken and grill or broil until an instant-read thermometer inserted in a drumstick registers 180°F, about 8 minutes longer.

PER SERVING (2 drumsticks): 159 Cal, 4 g Fat, 1 g Sat Fat, 0 g Trans Fat, 102 mg Chol, 74 mg Sod, 3 g Carb, 0 g Fib, 26 g Prot, 28 mg Calc. *POINTS* value: *4*.

tip Mash 2 cooked sweet potatoes (7 ounces each) with 2 teaspoons butter for a great side to this dish. They will up the per-serving *POINTS* value by 2.

MAKES 4 SERVINGS

¼ cup **fresh lemon juice**

3 tablespoons packed **dark brown sugar**

2 large **garlic cloves**, crushed through a press

1 tablespoon **Jamaican jerk seasoning**

½ teaspoon **salt**

8 (¼-pound) **skinless chicken drumsticks**

Spicy Oven-Fried Chicken

How do we make "fried" chicken from the oven finger lickin' good? First the chicken is dipped in buttermilk to keep it juicy and tender, then it's coated with seasoned bread crumbs and ground almonds for crunch and a delicious nutty flavor.

1. Preheat the oven to 425°F. Line a roasting pan with foil; spray the rack of the roasting pan with nonstick spray and place it in the pan.

2. Combine the buttermilk and hot pepper sauce in a 9 x 13-inch baking dish. Place the chicken in the buttermilk mixture, turning to coat; set aside.

3. Combine the bread crumbs, almonds, salt, and pepper on a shallow plate. Dip the chicken into the crumb mixture, turning to coat all sides. Discard the excess buttermilk mixture and bread crumb mixture. Place the chicken on the rack; lightly spray the chicken with nonstick spray.

4. Bake 20 minutes, then lightly spray the chicken again with nonstick spray. Bake until the chicken is golden and an instant-read thermometer inserted in a thigh registers 180°F, about 25 minutes longer.

PER SERVING (1 chicken thigh): 222 Cal, 11 g Fat, 3 g Sat Fat, 0 g Trans Fat, 58 mg Chol, 207 mg Sod, 7 g Carb, 1 g Fib, 22 g Prot, 69 mg Calc. *POINTS* value: *5*.

tip Substitute an equal amount of cornflake crumbs for the ground almonds. You'll decrease the per-serving *POINTS* value by about 1.

MAKES 8 SERVINGS

½ cup **low-fat buttermilk**

2 teaspoons **hot pepper sauce**

8 (5-ounce) **skinless bone-in chicken thighs**

½ cup **seasoned dry bread crumbs**

½ cup ground **almonds**

¼ teaspoon **salt**

½ teaspoon **freshly ground pepper**

Spicy Oven-Fried Chicken

Turkey Sausage with Polenta and Greens

This robust meal-in-a-bowl is the perfect warming solution for a chilly winter day. Instead of mustard greens, you can substitute whatever chopped greens are available in the freezer case, such as kale or spinach.

1. Thaw the mustard greens in the microwave according to package directions.

2. Meanwhile, spray a large nonstick skillet with nonstick spray and set over medium-high heat. Add the sausages and cook, breaking them up with a wooden spoon, until browned and cooked through, about 4 minutes. Add the mustard greens and cook, stirring frequently, until thoroughly heated through, about 2 minutes.

3. Meanwhile, bring the water to a boil in a medium saucepan. Whisking constantly, gradually add the polenta in a slow, steady stream; reduce the heat and cook, stirring constantly, until thick, but not stiff, 3–4 minutes. Whisk in the salt.

4. Divide the polenta among 4 serving bowls; top with sausage and greens, then sprinkle evenly with the Parmesan cheese.

PER SERVING (⅔ cup polenta, ½ cup sausage and greens, and ½ tablespoon cheese): 204 Cal, 7 g Fat, 2 g Sat Fat, 0 g Trans Fat, 31 mg Chol, 685 mg Sod, 22 g Carb, 4 g Fib, 12 g Prot, 140 mg Calc. *POINTS* value: *4*.

MAKES 4 SERVINGS

1 (10-ounce) package **frozen chopped mustard greens**

2 (3½-ounce) **hot Italian turkey sausages**, casings removed

3 cups **hot water**

⅔ cup **instant polenta**

½ teaspoon **salt**

2 tablespoons grated **Parmesan cheese**

Roasted Orange-Herb Game Hens

Fines herbes—a traditional blend of chervil, parsley, chives, and tarragon—is available as a dried-herb blend in the spice aisle at the supermarket. It goes beautifully with citrus (in this case, orange) and poultry. If you feel like splurging on ingredients, use an assortment of chopped fresh herbs (you'll need about ⅓ cup for this recipe) instead of the fines herbes.

1. Preheat the oven to 450°F. Combine the shallots, fines herbes, orange zest, salt, and pepper in a small bowl. Transfer 1 tablespoon of the herb mixture to another small bowl; set aside.

2. Gently loosen the skin from the breast meat of each hen half. Rub the 1 tablespoon herb mixture into the meat, under the skin, of each of the hen halves.

3. Place the hens in a roasting pan and roast 10 minutes. Add the broth. Roast, basting the hens twice with the broth, until an instant-read thermometer inserted in a thigh registers 180°F, about 30 minutes longer.

4. Transfer the hens to a platter; cover loosely with foil and keep warm. Place the roasting pan directly on top of two burners over high heat. Add the orange juice and the remaining herb mixture; bring to a boil, scraping any browned bits from the bottom of the pan. Reduce the heat and simmer until the sauce is reduced to about 1 cup, about 4 minutes. Serve the hens with the sauce. Remove the skins from the hens before eating.

PER SERVING (½ Cornish game hen with ¼ cup sauce): 237 Cal, 6 g Fat, 2 g Sat Fat, 0 g Trans Fat, 159 mg Chol, 366 mg Sod, 6 g Carb, 1 g Fib, 37 g Prot, 45 mg Calc. *POINTS* value: *5*.

tip If shallots are not available in your market, substitute ⅓ cup minced onion and 1 teaspoon minced garlic.

MAKES 4 SERVINGS

- ⅓ cup minced **shallots**
- 1 tablespoon **dried fines herbes**
- 2 teaspoons grated **orange zest**
- ¼ teaspoon **salt**
- ¼ teaspoon **freshly ground pepper**
- 2 (1½-pound) **Cornish game hens**, halved
- 1 cup **reduced-sodium chicken broth**
- ¾ cup **fresh orange juice**

Chicken-Couscous Bake with
Capers and Tomatoes

☑ Chicken-Couscous Bake with Capers and Tomatoes

This one-dish entrée is easy enough for a weeknight meal or elegant enough for company. If you're looking for additional fiber, check out the whole-wheat couscous at the market. Also, check out the variety of seasoned chicken broths now available in your market. We use broth with lemon and herbs, but you might like to try the roasted vegetable and herb variety.

1. Preheat the oven to 425°F. Spray a 9-inch square baking dish with nonstick spray; set aside.

2. Sprinkle the chicken with the pepper and salt. Spray a large nonstick skillet with nonstick spray and set over medium-high heat. Add the chicken and cook until browned, about 3 minutes on each side. Transfer the chicken to a plate.

3. Add the broth and capers to the skillet, scraping any browned bits from the bottom of the pan. Bring the mixture to a simmer.

4. Spread the couscous over the bottom of the baking dish. Pour the broth mixture over the couscous and stir to combine. Place the chicken on top of the couscous, then add the tomatoes. Cover the dish tightly with foil and bake until the chicken is cooked through and the broth is absorbed, about 20 minutes.

5. Transfer the chicken and tomatoes to serving plates. Fluff the couscous with a fork and serve with chicken.

PER SERVING (1 chicken thigh with about ¾ cup couscous mixture): 418 Cal, 12 g Fat, 4 g Sat Fat, 0 g Trans Fat, 88 mg Chol, 660 mg Sod, 36 g Carb, 3 g Fib, 38 g Prot, 50 mg Calc. *POINTS* value: *9*.

tip Cut the chicken thighs into chunks, divide the dish among six people instead of four, and decrease the per-serving *POINTS* value by 3.

MAKES 4 SERVINGS

- 4 (5-ounce) **skinless boneless chicken thighs**
- ¼ teaspoon **freshly ground pepper**
- ⅛ teaspoon **salt**
- 1½ cups **chicken broth with lemon and herbs**
- 2 tablespoons chopped, drained **capers**
- 1 cup **couscous**
- 1 cup **cherry tomatoes**

Slow-Cooker Suppers

CHAPTER TEN

Chicken Breast in Wine
Sauce with Asparagus

Chicken Breast in Wine Sauce with Asparagus

Browning the vegetables in a saucepan before cooking in the slow cooker adds rich flavor to the finished dish here. To add a spark of bright color and crisp-tender texture, we add fresh asparagus and tarragon to the stew during the last 20 minutes of cooking.

1. Heat the oil in a large nonstick saucepan over medium heat. Add the carrots, fennel, and garlic; cook, stirring occasionally, until softened, about 8 minutes. Add the flour and cook, stirring constantly, about 1 minute. Stir in the broth, wine, potatoes, onions, salt, and pepper; bring to a simmer, stirring constantly.

2. Put the chicken in a 5–6-quart slow cooker; pour the vegetable mixture over the chicken. Cover the slow cooker and cook until the chicken and vegetables are fork-tender, 3–4 hours on high or 6–8 hours on low. Lift the chicken from the slow cooker and set aside until cool enough to handle. Pull the chicken from the bones, then tear or cut the chicken into bite-size pieces.

3. Meanwhile, add the asparagus and tarragon to the slow cooker; cover and cook on high until the asparagus is just tender, about 20 minutes. Return the chicken to the slow cooker; cover and cook on high until heated through, about 10 minutes.

PER SERVING (scant 2 cups): 297 Cal, 7 g Fat, 1 g Sat Fat, 0 g Trans Fat, 62 mg Chol, 577 mg Sod, 30 g Carb, 6 g Fib, 29 g Prot, 79 mg Calc. *POINTS* value: *6*.

tip Asparagus is sold in bunches of 1 or 2 pounds. Be sure you pick up a 1-pound bunch for this recipe.

MAKES 4 SERVINGS

- 2 teaspoons **canola oil**
- 4 **carrots**, diced
- ½ **fennel bulb** or **2 celery stalks**, diced
- 2 **garlic cloves**, minced
- 2 tablespoons **all-purpose flour**
- 1½ cups **reduced-sodium chicken broth**
- ½ cup dry **white wine or chicken broth**
- 2 **all-purpose potatoes** (about ¾ pound), peeled and cut into 1-inch cubes
- 1 cup frozen small **whole onions**
- ½ teaspoon **salt**
- ¼ teaspoon **freshly ground pepper**
- 1 (1¼-pound) **bone-in chicken breast**, skinned
- 1 bunch (about 1 pound) **fresh asparagus**, trimmed and cut into 1-inch pieces
- 1½ tablespoons chopped **fresh tarragon**, or 1½ teaspoons dried

Sage Chicken and Red Potatoes

This comforting and hearty stew is similar to the classic French dish "Chicken Bonne Femme," which literally translates as "Good Wife's Chicken." You can substitute tarragon, rosemary, or thyme for the sage, and ½ cup of wine for ½ cup of the broth if you like.

1. Heat the oil in a large nonstick saucepan over medium heat. Add the onion, celery, and garlic; cook, stirring occasionally, until softened, about 8 minutes. Add the flour and cook, stirring constantly, about 1 minute. Add the broth and bring to a simmer, stirring constantly.

2. Put the chicken, potatoes, carrots, bay leaf, salt, and pepper in a 5–6-quart slow cooker; pour the broth mixture over the chicken and vegetables. Cover the slow cooker and cook until chicken and vegetables are fork-tender, 4–5 hours on high or 8–10 hours on low.

3. Discard the bay leaf. Add the parsley, sage, lemon zest, and lemon juice to the slow cooker; cover and cook on high until the flavors blend, about 10 minutes.

PER SERVING (1 drumstick with 1 cup vegetables and sauce): 212 Cal, 4 g Fat, 1 g Sat Fat, 0 g Trans Fat, 51 mg Chol, 366 mg Sod, 28 g Carb, 5 g Fib, 17 g Prot, 64 mg Calc. *POINTS* value: *4*.

MAKES 6 SERVINGS

2 teaspoons **extra-virgin olive oil**

1 large **onion**, chopped

3 **celery stalks**, diced

2 **garlic cloves**, minced

1 tablespoon **all-purpose flour**

1 cup **reduced-sodium chicken broth**

6 (¼-pound) **skinless chicken drumsticks**

1 pound small **red potatoes**, cut into quarters

1 (1-pound) bag **baby carrots**

1 **bay leaf**

½ teaspoon **salt**

¼ teaspoon **freshly ground pepper**

½ cup chopped **fresh parsley**

1 tablespoon chopped **fresh sage**, or 1 teaspoon dried

1 (2-inch) strip **lemon zest**

2 teaspoons **fresh lemon juice**

Sage Chicken and Red Potatoes

Mexican Chicken Soup

Vegetables, such as carrots, can take longer to cook than meat in a slow cooker, so it's important to slice them quite thin. It's also important to thaw the corn (if using frozen) before adding it to the soup, so as not to slow the cooking process. You can quickly thaw frozen corn by putting it in a colander under cold running water for a minute. A squeeze of fresh lime juice at the table adds a nice zing to this soup.

1. Put the chicken, broth, carrots, jicama, cilantro sprigs, garlic, and jalapeño pepper in a 5–6-quart slow cooker; cover and cook until chicken and vegetables are fork-tender, 4–5 hours on high or 8–10 hours on low.

2. Lift the chicken from the soup and set aside until cool enough to handle. Discard the cilantro sprigs. Pull the chicken from the bones, then tear or cut the chicken into bite-size pieces.

3. Meanwhile, add the corn and tomato to the slow cooker; cover and cook on high until heated through, about 20 minutes. Return the chicken to the slow cooker and add the chopped cilantro; cook on high until heated through, about 10 minutes. Serve each bowl of soup sprinkled with a few scallion slices and a few tortilla chips, with a lime wedge on the side.

PER SERVING (generous 2 cups soup with ¼ cup chips): 253 Cal, 6 g Fat, 2 g Sat Fat, 0 g Trans Fat, 42 mg Chol, 662 mg Sod, 29 g Carb, 5 g Fib, 23 g Prot, 57 mg Calc. *POINTS* value: *5*.

tip We recommend using paper towels to help get a good grip when pulling the skin from raw chicken.

MAKES 6 SERVINGS

3 (8–10-ounce) **whole chicken legs**, skinned

7 cups **reduced-sodium chicken broth**

4 **carrots**, thinly sliced on the diagonal

1 cup diced peeled **jicama**

3 sprigs **fresh cilantro**

2 **garlic cloves**, minced

1 **jalapeño pepper**, seeded and finely chopped (wear gloves to prevent irritation)

3 cups **corn kernels**, thawed if frozen

1 **tomato**, chopped

¼ cup chopped **fresh cilantro**

4 **scallions**, thinly sliced

1½ cups **baked tortilla chips**, broken up

6 **lime wedges**

Lemony Chicken and Lentil Soup

Fresh lemon and dill are simple last-minute additions that produce great flavor returns to this hearty and healthy soup.

1. Put the chicken, broth, lentils, onion, bell pepper, garlic, and coriander in a 5–6-quart slow cooker. Cover the slow cooker and cook until the chicken and lentils are tender, 4–5 hours on high or 8–10 hours on low.

2. Lift the chicken from the soup and set aside until cool enough to handle. Pull the chicken from the bones, then tear or cut the chicken into bite-size pieces.

3. Meanwhile, add the spinach, lemon zest, lemon juice, and dill to the slow cooker. Return the chicken to the pot; cover and cook on high until heated through, about 20 minutes.

PER SERVING (2 cups): 386 Cal, 10 g Fat, 3 g Sat Fat, 0 g Trans Fat, 57 mg Chol, 700 mg Sod, 36 g Carb, 13 g Fib, 40 g Prot, 143 mg Calc. *POINTS* value: *8*.

tip To quickly thaw the spinach before adding it to the soup, remove the spinach from its package, put it in a microwavable bowl, and microwave on High until thawed, about 3 minutes.

MAKES 4 SERVINGS

- 1¼ pounds skinless **bone-in chicken thighs**
- 5 cups **reduced-sodium chicken broth**
- 1 cup **dried lentils**, picked over and rinsed
- 1 **onion**, chopped
- 1 **green bell pepper**, seeded and chopped
- 2 **garlic cloves**, minced
- 1 teaspoon **ground coriander**
- 1 (10-ounce) package **frozen chopped spinach**, thawed and squeezed dry
- 1 teaspoon grated **lemon zest**
- 1 tablespoon **fresh lemon juice**
- 2 tablespoons chopped **fresh dill or parsley**

Chicken and Ham Cassoulet

Chicken and Ham Cassoulet

Slow cooking is wonderful for developing flavors and creating delicious juices to make a rich sauce in dishes like this French favorite. Steamed fresh green beans make a crunchy and colorful accompaniment to round out this meal.

1. Combine the garlic and salt in a small bowl; rub the mixture onto the chicken thighs.

2. Heat the oil in a large nonstick skillet over medium-high heat. Add the chicken and cook until lightly browned, about 3 minutes on each side.

3. Place the onion and carrots in a 5–6-quart slow cooker. Place browned chicken and ham on top of the vegetables. Pour tomatoes and wine around chicken; cover and cook until the chicken and vegetables are fork-tender, 4–5 hours on high or 8–10 hours on low.

4. Stir in the beans and thyme; cover and cook on high until heated through, about 30 minutes.

5. Meanwhile, combine the bread crumbs, parsley, and butter in a small bowl. Spoon cassoulet into 6 shallow bowls and serve sprinkled with the crumb topping.

PER SERVING (1 chicken thigh, 1 cup vegetables and beans, and 3 tablespoons crumb topping): 342 Cal, 8 g Fat, 2 g Sat Fat, 0 g Trans Fat, 47 mg Chol, 395 mg Sod, 39 g Carb, 8 g Fib, 28 g Prot, 159 mg Calc. *POINTS* value: *7*.

tip Foods tend to lose their vibrant colors and flavors in slow-cooked dishes, so we stir fresh chopped thyme into the stew the last half-hour to perk things up.

MAKES 6 SERVINGS

3 **garlic cloves**, minced

¼ teaspoon **salt**

6 (¼-pound) **skinless bone-in chicken thighs**

1 teaspoon **extra-virgin olive oil**

1 large **onion**, chopped

2 **carrots**, chopped

1 (1-ounce) piece **cooked ham steak**, diced

1 (14½-ounce) **can diced tomatoes**

½ cup **dry white wine**

2 (15½-ounce) **cans cannellini** (white kidney) **beans**, rinsed and drained

1 tablespoon chopped **fresh thyme**, or 1 teaspoon dried

3 slices **firm white bread**, made into crumbs

3 tablespoons finely chopped **fresh parsley**

1 teaspoon melted **butter** or **extra-virgin olive oil**

Chicken with Rice and Peas

Similar to the favorite Spanish dish, Arroz con Pollo, this one-pot dinner is ideal for making in a slow cooker. The chicken, rice, and vegetables cook perfectly together, without fuss. To give the rice a fluffy texture, you might like to toss the mixture with a fork just before serving. If you like your food spicy, double the cayenne.

1. Put the chicken, onion, carrots, garlic, tomatoes, broth, rice, turmeric, salt, ground pepper, and cayenne in a 5–6-quart slow cooker; cover and cook until the chicken and rice are tender, 4–5 hours on high or 8–10 hours on low.

2. Stir in the peas and bell pepper. Cover and cook on high until heated through, about 20 minutes. Serve sprinkled with the olives.

Per serving (1¼ cups stew with 1 tablespoon olives): 361 Cal, 6 g Fat, 1 g Sat Fat, 0 g Trans Fat, 68 mg Chol, 736 mg Sod, 44 g Carb, 5 g Fib, 32 g Prot, 90 mg Calc. *POINTS* value: *7*.

MAKES 4 SERVINGS ☛

- 1 pound **skinless boneless chicken breast**, cut into ¾-inch pieces
- 1 large **onion**, finely chopped
- 2 **carrots**, finely chopped
- 2 **garlic cloves**, minced
- 1 (14½-ounce) **can diced tomatoes**
- ¾ cup **reduced-sodium chicken broth**
- ⅔ cup **long-grain white rice**
- ½ teaspoon **turmeric**
- ¼ teaspoon **salt**
- ¼ teaspoon **freshly ground pepper**
- ⅛ teaspoon **cayenne**
- 1 cup **frozen green peas**, thawed
- ½ cup finely diced **green bell pepper**
- ¼ cup sliced **pimiento-stuffed green olives**

Chicken with Rice and Peas

Creamy Garlic, Chicken, and Potato Soup

The combination of potatoes and garlic is a match made in stew and soup heaven. Here we combine the two favorites to make a delicious and fragrant soup, then temper the strong taste of garlic with creamy goat cheese and cooked chicken.

1. Melt the butter in a large nonstick saucepan over medium heat. Add the leek and garlic; cook, stirring frequently, until golden, about 10 minutes. Stir in the broth; bring to a boil.

2. Put the potatoes, bay leaf, salt, and pepper in a 5–6-quart slow cooker; pour the broth mixture over the potatoes. Cover the slow cooker and cook until the potatoes are fork-tender, 3–4 hours on high or 6–8 hours on low.

3. Discard the bay leaf. Transfer the mixture to a blender or food processor in batches and puree. Return the mixture to the slow cooker. Add the chicken, goat cheese, and tarragon; cover and cook on high until the chicken is heated through and the cheese melts, about 30 minutes. Serve the soup sprinkled with the parsley.

Per serving (1⅓ cups): 290 Cal, 7 g Fat, 3 g Sat Fat, 0 g Trans Fat, 48 mg Chol, 615 mg Sod, 34 g Carb, 4 g Fib, 22 g Prot, 66 mg Calc. *POINTS* value: *6*.

MAKES 6 SERVINGS

- 1 tablespoon **butter**
- 1 large **leek**, cleaned and sliced (about 4 cups)
- 10 **garlic cloves**, minced
- 4 cups **reduced-sodium chicken broth**
- 4 large **Yukon Gold potatoes** (about 2 pounds), scrubbed and cut into ½-inch pieces (about 5 cups)
- 1 **bay leaf**
- ½ teaspoon **salt**
- ¼ teaspoon **freshly ground pepper**
- 2 cups shredded **cooked chicken breast**
- 2 ounces **goat cheese**, crumbled
- 1 tablespoon chopped **fresh tarragon**, or 1 teaspoon dried
- 3 tablespoons chopped **fresh parsley**

Barbecue-Glazed Turkey Meatloaf

You may think it odd to cook a meatloaf in a slow cooker, but it's easy—no liquid needed and the results are delicious. We line the slow cooker insert with foil—a little trick to help you lift out the finished meatloaf. And, because foods cooked in a slow cooker tend to look pale, we coat the loaf with a colorful barbecue-sauce glaze.

1. Fold a 24-inch length of foil in half lengthwise. Fit into the bottom and up the sides of a 5–6-quart slow cooker insert.

2. Put the turkey, bread crumbs, cheese, onion, egg, oregano, salt, and pepper in a medium bowl; mix with hands until well combined. Shape the mixture into a loaf and place on the foil in the slow cooker.

3. Cover the slow cooker and cook until the meatloaf juices run clear or an instant read thermometer inserted in the center of the meatloaf registers 165°F, 3–4 hours on high or 6–8 hours on low.

4. Combine the ketchup, sugar, Worcestershire sauce, and mustard in a small bowl. Spoon the mixture over the meatloaf, spreading it smooth. Cover the slow cooker and cook until the glaze is heated through, about 30 minutes longer. With the help of the foil, lift the meatloaf from the slow cooker and transfer to a platter. Discard foil and cut the meatloaf into 6 slices.

PER SERVING (1 slice meatloaf): 162 Cal, 2 g Fat, 1 g Sat Fat, 0 g Trans Fat, 99 mg Chol, 332 mg Sod, 8 g Carb, 0 g Fib, 25 g Prot, 71 mg Calc. *POINTS* value: *3*.

MAKES 6 SERVINGS

1¼ pounds **ground skinless turkey breast**

⅓ cup seasoned dry **bread crumbs**

¼ cup (1 ounce) shredded **reduced-fat cheddar cheese**

¼ cup minced **onion**

1 large **egg**, lightly beaten

1 teaspoon **dried oregano**

¼ teaspoon **salt**

¼ teaspoon **freshly ground pepper**

2 tablespoons **ketchup**

2 teaspoons packed **brown sugar**

2 teaspoons **Worcestershire sauce**

1 teaspoon **spicy brown mustard**

Meatballs in Cinnamon-Tomato Sauce

Meatballs in Cinnamon-Tomato Sauce

A hint of cinnamon adds intriguing flavor and scent to this Greek-like entrée. Instead of the orzo, you can serve this with couscous, spaghetti, or rice if you prefer.

1. Heat the oil in a large nonstick skillet over medium-high heat. Add the onion and garlic; cook, stirring frequently, until golden, about 7 minutes. Transfer half of the onion mixture to a medium bowl; set aside.

2. Transfer the remaining onion mixture to a 5–6-quart slow cooker. Add the tomatoes, cinnamon, oregano, sugar, and pepper; stir well.

3. To the onion mixture in the bowl, add the turkey, bread crumbs, egg, and salt; mix well. Shape into 24 meatballs; place on top of the tomato mixture in the slow cooker. Carefully spoon some of the tomato mixture over the meatballs. Cover the slow cooker and cook until the meatballs are cooked through, 3–4 hours on high or 6–8 hours on low. Discard the cinnamon stick. Serve the meatballs and sauce with the orzo.

PER SERVING (6 meatballs, about ¼ cup sauce, and ½ cup orzo): 335 Cal, 6 g Fat, 1 g Sat Fat, 0 g Trans Fat, 128 mg Chol, 689 mg Sod, 35 g Carb, 3 g Fib, 34 g Prot, 92 mg Calc. *POINTS* value: *7*.

tip Avoid lifting the lid of the slow cooker while the food is cooking. This slows down the cooking process.

MAKES 4 SERVINGS

- 2 teaspoons **extra-virgin olive oil**
- 1 large **onion**, chopped
- 3 **garlic cloves**, minced
- 1 (14½-ounce) **can Italian plum tomatoes**, broken up
- 1 (4-inch) **cinnamon stick**
- 1 teaspoon **dried oregano**
- ¼ teaspoon **sugar**
- ¼ teaspoon **freshly ground pepper**
- 1 pound **ground skinless turkey breast**
- ⅓ cup **seasoned dry bread crumbs**
- 1 large **egg**, lightly beaten
- ½ teaspoon **salt**
- 2 cups hot **cooked orzo**

Sausage, Kale, and Shrimp with Black-Eyed Peas

Kale, a member of the cabbage family and very nutritious, stands up well to long, slow cooking. To prepare kale, trim away the stems and tough center ribs, then rinse the kale well to remove any grit before chopping. A dollop of sour cream with a few slivers of fresh oregano make a lovely garnish for this dish. For each serving, 2 tablespoons of reduced-fat sour cream will up the *POINTS* value by 1.

1. Heat the oil in a large nonstick skillet over medium-high heat. Add the sausage, onion, and garlic; cook, breaking up the sausage with a wooden spoon, until browned, about 10 minutes. Add the tomatoes, paprika, and crushed red pepper; bring to a boil, stirring to scrape up the browned bits from the skillet.

2. Put the sausage mixture in a 5–6-quart slow cooker. Add the kale and black-eyed peas; mix well. Cover and cook until the kale is tender, 3–4 hours on high or 6–8 hours on low.

3. Add the shrimp, roasted red peppers, and oregano; mix well. Cover and cook on high until the shrimp are just opaque in the center, about 30 minutes.

PER SERVING (generous 1 cup): 272 Cal, 7 g Fat, 2 g Sat Fat, 0 g Trans Fat, 93 mg Chol, 660 mg Sod, 31 g Carb, 9 g Fib, 24 g Prot, 146 mg Calc. *POINTS* value: *5*.

MAKES 6 SERVINGS

1 teaspoon **extra-virgin olive oil**

½ pound **Italian turkey sausage**, casings removed

1 **Vidalia onion**, chopped

3 **garlic cloves**, minced

1 (14½-ounce) **can crushed tomatoes**

1 tablespoon **paprika**

¼ teaspoon **crushed red pepper**

1 pound **kale**, trimmed and coarsely chopped

2 (15-ounce) **cans black-eyed peas**, rinsed and drained

1 pound **large shrimp**, peeled and deveined

½ cup sliced drained **roasted red peppers**

1 tablespoon chopped **fresh oregano**, or 1 teaspoon dried

Sausage, Kale, and Shrimp
with Black-Eyed Peas

Tequila-Citrus Chicken, page 243

Dry and Liquid Measurement Equivalents

If you are converting the recipes in this book to metric measurements, use the following chart as a guide.

TEASPOONS	TABLESPOONS	CUPS	FLUID OUNCES
3 teaspoons	1 tablespoon		½ fluid ounce
6 teaspoons	2 tablespoons	⅛ cup	1 fluid ounce
8 teaspoons	2 tablespoons plus 2 teaspoons	⅙ cup	
12 teaspoons	4 tablespoons	¼ cup	2 fluid ounces
15 teaspoons	5 tablespoons	⅓ cup minus 1 teaspoon	
16 teaspoons	5 tablespoons plus 1 teaspoon	⅓ cup	
18 teaspoons	6 tablespoons	¼ cup plus 2 tablespoons	3 fluid ounces
24 teaspoons	8 tablespoons	½ cup	4 fluid ounces
30 teaspoons	10 tablespoons	½ cup plus 2 tablespoons	5 fluid ounces
32 teaspoons	10 tablespoons plus 2 teaspoons	⅔ cup	
36 teaspoons	12 tablespoons	¾ cup	6 fluid ounces
42 teaspoons	14 tablespoons	1 cup minus 2 tablespoons	7 fluid ounces
45 teaspoons	15 tablespoons	1 cup minus 1 tablespoon	
48 teaspoons	16 tablespoons	1 cup	8 fluid ounces

VOLUME	
¼ teaspoon	1 milliliter
½ teaspoon	2 milliliters
1 teaspoon	5 milliliters
1 tablespoon	15 milliliters
2 tablespoons	30 milliliters
3 tablespoons	45 milliliters
¼ cup	60 milliliters
⅓ cup	80 milliliters
½ cup	120 milliliters
⅔ cup	160 milliliters
¾ cup	175 milliliters
1 cup	240 milliliters
1 quart	950 milliliters

OVEN TEMPERATURE

250°F	120°C	400°F	200°C
275°F	140°C	425°F	220°C
300°F	150°C	450°F	230°C
325°F	160°C	475°F	250°C
350°F	180°C	500°F	260°C
375°F	190°C	525°F	270°C

LENGTH	
1 inch	25 millimeters
1 inch	2.5 centimeters

WEIGHT	
1 ounce	30 grams
¼ pound	120 grams
½ pound	240 grams
1 pound	480 grams

NOTE: Measurement of less than ⅛ teaspoon is considered a dash or a pinch. Metric volume measurements are approximate.

Index

Notes